Artificial Intelligence for Sustainable Energy Systems 1

Environmental Sustainability and Artificial Intelligence Set

coordinated by

Abhishek Kumar, Arun Lal Srivastav, Ashutosh Kumar Dubey

Artificial Intelligence for Sustainable Energy Systems 1

Intelligent Technologies for Sustainable Energy Management

Edited by

Inam Ul Haq

Sanna Mehraj Kak

Anand Kumar Gupta

Muhammad Sher Ramzan

iSTE

WILEY

First published 2026 in Great Britain and the United States by ISTE Ltd and John Wiley & Sons, Inc.

ISTE Ltd
27-37 St George's Road
London SW19 4EU
UK

www.iste.co.uk

John Wiley & Sons, Inc.
111 River Street
Hoboken, NJ 07030
USA

www.wiley.com

Library of Congress Control Number: 2026935945

British Library Cataloguing-in-Publication Data
A CIP record for this book is available from the British Library
ISBN 978-1-83669-097-9

The manufacturer's authorized representative according to the EU General Product Safety Regulation is Wiley-VCH GmbH, Boschstr. 12, 69469 Weinheim, Germany, e-mail: Product_Safety@wiley.com.

Contents

Preface

The global transition toward sustainable energy systems has become a critical priority in response to climate change, increasing energy demand and the depletion of conventional resources. Renewable energy technologies such as wind, solar and smart power networks offer promising solutions; however, their large-scale integration introduces complex challenges related to efficiency, reliability, forecasting and system management. In this evolving landscape, Artificial Intelligence (AI) has emerged as a transformative tool capable of optimizing energy production, improving grid stability and enabling intelligent decision-making across energy infrastructures.

This volume, *Artificial Intelligence for Sustainable Energy Systems*, presents a comprehensive overview of how AI, machine learning, deep learning, big data analytics and digital technologies are reshaping the future of energy. It explores intelligent renewable systems, smart grids, digital twins, blockchain-based energy trading and predictive maintenance frameworks. By combining theoretical foundations with practical applications, the book aims to serve as a valuable resource for researchers, engineers, policymakers and students working toward resilient, efficient and sustainable energy ecosystems.

Inam UL HAQ
Sanna Mehraj KAK
Anand Kumar GUPTA
Muhammad Sher RAMZAN

April 2026

1

Introduction to Sustainable Energy Systems

The shift toward sustainable energy systems worldwide requires new ways of overcoming the barriers of renewable intermittency and electrical grid complications together with the optimization of the resources. The potential transformation that could be brought about by artificial intelligence (AI) is that predictive analytics, real-time optimization and decision-making can be applied in the entire generation, storage and distribution networks. This chapter gives an introductory description of AI applications in the field of sustainable energy where an individual can listen to machine learning, deep learning, reinforcement learning (RL) and graph-based methods. It sheds light on the way AI can be used to improve energy efficiency, promote the use of renewable energy and help maintain the process of equitable and resilient energy management with the help of case studies and concept models. The combination of smart technologies and sustainable approaches will turn AI into one of the main factors leading to the realization of the net-zero goals and the creation of a stable, low-carbon energy future.

1.1. Introduction

The global energy landscape is undergoing tremendous change due to the efforts of individual countries to realize sustainable development and fight climate change. The shift to sustainable energy systems has become an urgent goal, which was predetermined by the necessity to decrease the emission of greenhouse gas, eliminate climate change consequences and secure energy security in the long term. Traditional energy systems, which are mostly dependent on fossil fuels like coal, oil and natural gas, have been known to offer stable and consistent energy that could be scaled. Nevertheless, their effects on the environment – such as excessive carbon

Chapter written by Inam UL HAQ.

emissions, air pollution and interference with the ecosystem – have compelled the rest of the world to consider cleaner and more renewable alternatives. Sustainable energy systems are sought to promote the combination of various sources of renewable energy, including solar, wind, hydropower, geothermal and biomass, in order to develop a balanced, resilient, environmentally responsible energy infrastructure (Catalão et al. 2011; Colak et al. 2012; Foley et al. 2012; Tascikaraoglu and Uzunoglu 2014; Du et al. 2019).

The creation of a reliable sustainable energy system is complex because renewable energy sources are generally variable and intermittent. Unlike the production of fossil-fuel-based energy that can be brought online to meet demand, the production of solar and wind energy depends on the weather conditions and diurnal cycles. Such variations pose big challenges to energy management, in terms of the stability of the grids, achieving equilibrium between supply and demand, and anticipating consumption patterns. Distributed energy resources (DERs), including rooftop solar panels and microgrids, make the management of energy flows even more complex and require real-time monitoring, adaptive control and predictive planning. The conventional energy management practices that are typically rule based, and grounded on historical trends, cannot adequately deal with these dynamic complexities. AI is a promising technology with the power to revolutionize the problem of sustainable energy systems. AI is able to predict future analytics and real-time optimization, as well as adaptive decision-making, by using advanced computational models. Machine learning models have the potential to predict demand in energy, predict the variability of renewable generation and optimize storage and distribution resource scheduling. Deep learning models are capable of identifying intricate trends in massive power data, such as intake patterns, climatic effects and generation distortions. The RL methods will be able to create adaptive control methods that constantly learn and improve based on the feedback of the system, increasing the effectiveness and stability of smart grids (Wu et al. 2013; Ouyang et al. 2019; Jahangir and Babbar 2020; Sankar et al. 2021). Furthermore, AI enables the composite activation of diverse sources of data such as IoT sensor networks, satellite images and market signals to enable a complete management of the energy system.

Operational efficiency is not the only aspect that AI will apply to sustainable energy systems. It can also assist in strategic planning and policy development, as well as decision-making on many levels, between buildings and national energy systems. Tools based on AI can be used to maximize investment in renewable infrastructure, forecast the effects of regulatory modifications and model the energy situation in different environmental and economic factors. With the ability to make decisions based on the data, AI can help the stakeholders to cut out uncertainty, enhance the use of available resources and speed up the process of transition toward a low-carbon energy future. The advantages of implementing AI in the energy system of sustainability are further upscaled, in association with other complementary technologies like energy storage and smart grid networks. Surplus renewable energy can be captured and used when there is low generation by use of energy storage such as batteries, pumped hydro and thermal storage, which overcome the problem of intermittency. Smart grids have the ability to balance loads in real-time and achieve two-way energy flows. They also allow automatic fault detection and have digital monitoring and communication capabilities. These systems can be optimized with AI algorithms to increase resilience, energy loss and operational costs, which will eventually make energy delivery more reliable and sustainable. Table 1.1 demonstrates the fundamental elements of sustainable power systems and AI contribution to make the system more efficient (Landberg 1999; Lei et al. 2009; Azad et al. 2014; Colak et al. 2015; Feng et al. 2017; Borunda et al. 2020).

Component	Description	Role of AI in enhancement
Renewable energy sources	Solar, wind, hydropower, geothermal, biomass	Forecasting generation, predicting variability, resource planning
Energy storage	Batteries, pumped hydro, thermal storage	Optimal charge/discharge scheduling, loss minimization
Smart grids	Digitized networks enabling two-way energy flow	Real-time optimization, fault detection, load balancing
Energy efficiency	Reducing consumption in buildings, industry and transport	Predictive control, consumption pattern analysis, anomaly detection
IoT and sensors	Field sensors, smart meters, satellite monitoring	Data collection, real-time monitoring, predictive analytics
Predictive and prescriptive AI	Machine learning, deep learning, reinforcement learning	Forecasting demand/supply, adaptive decision-making, optimization

Table 1.1. *The core components of sustainable energy systems and the role AI plays in enhancing their performance*

The combination of AI with these parts converts the sustainable energy systems into intelligent and adaptable infrastructures that should react to the dynamic demands of the modern management of energy. With predictive services, optimization methods and autonomous decisions, AI allows systems to perform effectively in the case of uncertainty, increase the reliability of the grid and minimize the environmental footprint. Moreover, AI-based insights are helpful in policy-making, risk management and planning as they offer stakeholders practical knowledge to promote sustainable energy projects.

1.2. Components of sustainable energy systems

Sustainable energy systems are complicated infrastructures that are created to produce, store, deliver and use energy in a manner that will result in minimum environmental damage without compromising reliability and efficiency. They are based on a number of interdependent elements, each of which is significant to achieve sustainability and resilience. The main elements are renewable energy, energy storage, smart grids and energy conservation.

1.2.1. *Renewable energy sources*

Renewable energy sources form the backbone of sustainable energy systems. Figure 1.1 shows the different types of renewable energy systems. These include the following:

– Solar photovoltaics (PV): solar power transforms sunshine into electricity and is commonly implemented both at home, and at the commercial and utility level. Solar energy is free, clean and very affordable because of technological advancements.

– Wind turbines: these utilize wind as a source of kinetic energy to produce electricity. Wind farms may be onshore or offshore and offer scalable energy solutions in various geographical locations.

– Hydropower: this is a source of electricity that uses flowing or falling water. Hydropower has the potential for energy generation as well as storage using pumped storage plants.

– Geothermal: this uses the heat that is available at the center of the earth to generate electricity or give direct heating. Geothermal energy is very dependable and available 24 hours a day, thus it is good as a baseload power.

– Biomass: this includes organic substances such as crop residues, wood and waste, which may be converted into energy by burning, gasification or biochemical conversion. Biomass reduces waste and generates renewable energy.

– Intermittency and spatial variability are some of the challenges associated with renewable energy integration. High-level forecasting models, which can be based on AI, assist in predicting the patterns of generation, as well as the usage of these resources.

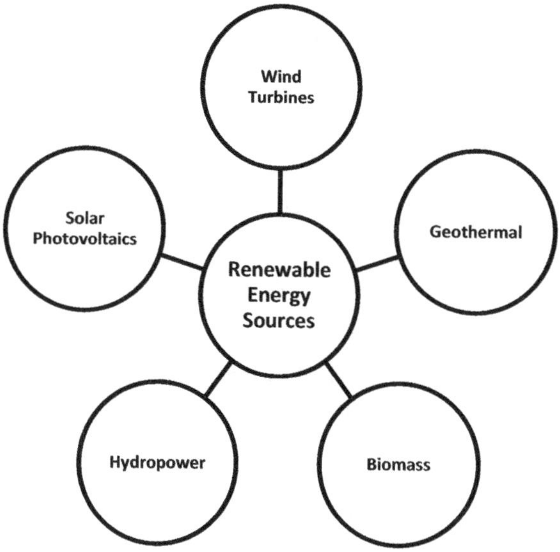

Figure 1.1. *Types of renewable energy sources*

1.2.2. *Energy storage*

Energy storage systems are essential for balancing the supply–demand fluctuations inherent in renewable energy generation. Storage technologies include the following:

– *Batteries*: lithium-ion and flow batteries are widely used for short-term storage, providing rapid response to demand peaks.

– *Pumped hydro storage*: excess electricity pumps water to elevated reservoirs, which is later released to generate power when needed.

– *Thermal storage*: it stores energy in the form of heat or cold for later use in heating, cooling or power generation applications.

– *Emerging technologies*: they include compressed air energy storage (CAES), supercapacitors and hydrogen-based storage.

Efficient storage systems ensure grid stability, allow better utilization of intermittent renewables and reduce dependency on fossil-fuel backup power.

1.2.3. *Smart grids*

Smart grids are digitally integrated electricity networks that monitor, control and optimize energy flow in real-time. They enable:

– *Two-way communication*: between utilities and consumers, facilitating demand response and dynamic pricing.

– *Grid reliability*: rapid fault detection, isolation and restoration during disturbances.

– *Integration of DERs*: seamlessly connects rooftop solar, microgrids and electric vehicles to the main grid.

– *Data analytics*: advanced AI algorithms analyze real-time sensor data for predictive maintenance, load balancing and efficient dispatch of energy resources.

Smart grids transform conventional grids into intelligent, adaptive networks capable of managing complex and decentralized energy systems.

1.2.4. *Energy efficiency*

Energy efficiency reduces energy waste and optimizes consumption across residential, industrial and transportation sectors. Key measures include the following:

– *Building energy management*: AI-based systems optimize heating, cooling, lighting and appliance usage.

– *Industrial process optimization*: it reduces energy use in manufacturing, mining and chemical processes through predictive analytics and automation.

– *Transportation efficiency*: electric vehicles, route optimization and smart charging reduce energy demand and emissions.

By lowering overall energy demand, efficiency measures complement renewable generation and storage solutions, enabling more sustainable and cost-effective energy systems.

1.3. Sustainability issues in energy

Despite impressive technological advancements, the systems of sustainable energy are being faced with diverse challenges that should be resolved to ensure that they offer reliable, efficient and low-carbon energy supply. This is all as a result of the nature renewable energy sources, infrastructures and difficulties in the areas of regulation and data management.

1.3.1. *Unpredictability of renewables*

Renewable energy sources, namely, solar and wind energy, are naturally variable as they are reliant on the weather and environmental conditions. The amount of solar energy that can be generated depends on the cloud cover and day-night cycles, while in comparison, the speed and direction of wind determines the amount of wind power generated. This intermittency poses a challenge of formation of the supply and demand real-time balance. The variability can lead to grid instability, energy shortage or overgeneration without the proper forecasting and adaptive management (Andrade and Bessa 2017). The solutions required to mitigate these fluctuations and ensure stable power supply are energy storage, demand response and predictive analytics powered by AI.

1.3.2. *Investment and infrastructure*

Transforming existing infrastructure into a sustainable energy system is a huge investment. This includes renewable generation facilities, energy storage facilities, smart grids and transmission systems that would support decentralized energy outflows. The high capital costs may be an obstacle to both developed and developing countries. Moreover, retrofitting the existing grids to enable two-way communication, automation and new monitoring should also be properly planned, approved by policy and financed in the long-run (Ramirez-Rosado et al. 2009).

1.3.3. *Policy and regulation*

The implementation of the technologies of sustainable energy is frequently hindered by disjointed policies and differentiated regulations. The differences in incentives, subsidies and technical standards in different regions may impede investment and the adoption of advanced technologies. There should be clear policy directives, supportive regulatory frameworks and international cooperation in order to hasten the integration of renewable energy and obtain the participation of the private sectors. Environmental, social and economic concerns should further be taken care of in policies to make the development of energy sustainable and fair.

1.3.4. *Data and forecasting*

The key to ensuring proper management of sustainable energy systems is the capacity to process and analyze bulk data of a heterogeneous nature from multiple sources, such as weather forecasts, energy consumption patterns and real-time grid monitoring. The proper time series prediction of renewable generation and demand is essential for operational planning, dispatching the energy and reducing the risks. Nonetheless, complex, multi-source data are difficult to manage during data collection, assurance, integration and computation. Predictive analytics, real-time monitoring and decision support can be done with the help of AI and machine learning, although their applications require specific skills and strong digital infrastructure (Hill et al. 2011).

1.4. AI in sustainable energy systems

AI technology has emerged as a disruptive technology in the field of sustainable energy, enabling the control of complex energy systems in an intelligent and data-driven manner. AI can help optimize the design, operation and control of renewable energy networks in the areas of production, storage and distribution, with the assistance of advanced algorithms. It is capable of predictive analytics, optimization, automation and integration with the Internet of Things (IoT) and edge computing, which comes in handy when it comes to dealing with the variability and complexity of sustainable energy systems.

Predictive analytics

The AI-driven predictive analytics can be utilized to predict the demand of energy, renewable generation and storage with specific accuracy. It is possible that the machine learning models can be used to predict short-term and long-term variations by using the past trends in energy consumption, weather and grid data. Such predictions help the utilities and operators to predict their energy dispatch early in advance to minimize shortages and waste.

Optimization

AI algorithms can be used to improve the performance of an energy system, making the system more stable, optimize its loads and coordinate the dispatch of distributed resources. RL and evolutionary algorithms are the search techniques with the potential of finding the most effective operational strategies for microgrids, energy storage and renewable generation plants, to make them as efficient and cost-effective as possible.

Automation

AI-driven automation facilitates the use of smart meters, demand-response and automated control of DERs. Automated systems are capable of dynamically regulating energy consumption based on the real-time conditions, lowering the peak demand and optimizing the use of energy in residential, commercial and industrial sectors.

IoT and edge computing

The synergies between AI, the IoT and edge computing enables collection, analysis and decision-making in real-time with the distributed sensors and smart devices. The edge-based AI systems handle data at the edges, eliminating latency and reliance on centralized servers, which is especially critical to remote or large-scale renewable systems. This integration will guarantee fast adaptive decisions, enhancing the reliability and resilience of the energy network. Table 1.2 demonstrates the main AI applications in sustainable energy systems.

AI capability	Description	Examples/applications
Predictive analytics	Forecast energy demand, renewable generation and storage requirements	Short-term load forecasting, solar/wind generation prediction
Optimization	Enhance grid performance, balance load and coordinate energy dispatch	Microgrid management, storage scheduling, cost optimization
Automation	Enable smart meters, demand response and autonomous control of distributed resources	Dynamic energy pricing, automated HVAC control, EV charging
Integration of IoT and edge computing	Collect and analyze real-time data from distributed sensors for rapid adaptive decision-making	

Table 1.2. *Key roles of AI in sustainable energy systems*

1.4.1. *AI techniques*

The field of AI deals with a wide range of approaches to enhance the operation, management and oversight of the sustainable energy system. Such approaches are applicable and can be used to make accurate predictions, optimize, offer adaptive control and make improved decisions in the renewable generation, energy storage and smart grid networks. Machine learning, deep learning, reinforced learning and graph neural networks (GNNs) are the key AI techniques that are applied in the domain of sustainable energy.

– Machine learning: machine learning is also common in predicting the needs of energy demand, generation and storage. ML models, including regression, classification and ensemble models, can be trained on historical data and make predictions about future trends. To give an example, electricity load and renewable energy output forecasts can be made with random forests and gradient boosting models, and anomalies in grid processes can be identified with classification models. Ensemble models can use several algorithms to enhance accuracy and strength.

– Deep learning: deep learning methods and especially neural networks are good at identifying intricate patterns in energy consumption and production data. CNNs can be used to handle the spatial data of a solar or wind farm, whereas RNNs and long short-term memory (LSTM) networks should be utilized to make time-based predictions of load and generation.

Deep learning models are able to process large amounts of heterogenous data, sensor readings, satellite images and weather predictions to make the predictions accurate and real-time.

– Reinforcement learning: maximization of dynamic energy management tasks involving energy storage dispatch, microgrid operation and balancing grid loads is optimized using RL. RL algorithms gain the best strategies by means of trial-and-error experiences within the environment and they continuously optimize their performance. As an illustration, RL can be used to select the optimal charge–discharge cycle of batteries or to organize energy transfer between distributed generation units to minimize expenses and achieve maximum efficiency.

– Graph neural networks: the model of GNNs has complex interactions in energy networks that capture the relationships between nodes, including the power plants, substations and consumption points. GNNs are specifically useful in predictive maintenance, fault detection and adaptive control of smart grids. By representing the energy system as a graph, GNNs can analyze the flow of electricity, predict potential bottlenecks and support decision-making for load distribution and renewable integration. Table 1.3 shows the applications and AI techniques used in energy systems.

AI technique	Description	Example applications
Machine learning	Regression, classification and ensemble models for prediction	Load forecasting, renewable generation prediction, anomaly detection
Deep learning	Neural networks for pattern recognition in complex data	Solar/wind output forecasting, energy consumption prediction, satellite image analysis
Reinforcement learning	Learning optimal strategies through trial-and-error interaction	Battery dispatch optimization, microgrid energy management, dynamic grid control
Graph neural networks	Modeling networked energy systems and their interactions	Smart grid monitoring, fault prediction, adaptive load balancing

Table 1.3. *AI techniques and applications in sustainable energy*

1.5. Case studies and applications

There are numerous ways in which AI can be applied to sustainable energy systems, for example, when making operational and strategic decisions. Using big, multi-source data, AI will improve energy production, delivery and use efficiency, reliability and sustainability. The subsequent paragraphs point out the most successful spheres of AI application.

1.5.1. *Smart grid optimization*

Smart grids are networks that are digitally incorporated with the monitoring and control of electricity flows in real-time. AI is of great importance in optimizing these grids since it allows us to predict loads, faults and dynamic control of energy. As an example, machine learning models can forecast peak energy demand so that grid operators can dispatch generation or storage upstream. Deep learning algorithms will be able to notice anomalies or possible failures in the distributed networks, reducing maintenance expenses and mini-outages. RL is becoming a popular means of optimizing the flow of energy in real-time in microgrids and DERs (Dowell and Pinson 2015).

1.5.2. *Renewable integration*

The unpredictability of renewable energy sources like solar and wind is problematic for predictable energy supply. The predictive models based on AI can accurately predict the renewable generation and help grid operators to balance the demand and supply. An example is LSTM networks, which are able to predict short-term solar power production when they receive weather data, whereas ensemble models can predict wind energy production over a number of hours or days. The combination of AI and storage and demand–response will guarantee that renewable energy is used effectively and avoid curtailment, as well as the necessity to rely on fossil-fuel backup power (Flores et al. 2012).

1.5.3. *Energy efficiency management*

AI helps in energy efficiency by optimizing energy consumption for the energy, which is used in homes, businesses and industries. The energy management systems that are constructed on the basis of AI are used to observe the heating, ventilation, air conditioning (HVAC), usage of lights and usage of appliances in order to reduce energy waste. In the industrial setting, AI can determine when equipment requires maintenance, run operations during off-peak periods and detect areas of inefficiency on production lines. This optimization helps to save energy money and contributes to sustainability, but does not decrease the performance.

1.5.4. *Decision support systems*

AI is also helping policymakers and energy planners make informed decisions in the transition to sustainable energy. Decision support systems use historical, environmental, economic and technological information to compare various energy scenarios. These systems assist in determining the best places of deployment of renewable, determining policy impacts, efficient allocation of resources and simulating long-term effects of strategic interventions. AI also improves the accuracy of planning by giving practical information, and speeds up the process of implementing strategies of sustainable energy (Yuan et al. 2016).

1.6. Future directions

The extent to which AI can be implemented into sustainable energies remains to be developed, and a lot of opportunities to increase efficiency, resilience and sustainability await exploration. The future is directed toward enhancing transparency, simulating, optimizing resources and providing equitable access to energy. Such innovations would solve the current constraints and introduce smarter and adaptive energy systems.

1.6.1. *Explainable AI (XAI)*

Transparency and interpretability are of great importance as AI-driven systems gain increasing power in energy operations and policy decisions. Explainable AI (XAI) offers information about how models make predictions and recommendations, and enables stakeholders to interpret, trust and justify AI decisions. XAI can be used to explain the basis behind load forecasts, renewable generation predictions or energy dispatch recommendations in energy systems, and hold people accountable and comply with regulations.

1.6.2. *Digital energy systems twins*

Digital twins refer to virtual models of real-life energy systems that replicate, analyze and optimize real-time operations. With the combination of AI and digital twins, operators are able to test the situation and predict failures, as well as assess operational strategies, without endangering real equipment or interrupting energy delivery. An example is a digital twin of a solar farm or smart grid that can simulate the effect of weather variations, demand variability or equipment failures on operation and then perform proactive maintenance and operational efficiency.

1.6.3. *Circular economy integration*

Circular economy principles can be applied to sustainable energy systems and include the efficiency of the resources, the recycling process and the reduction of waste. AI can be used to optimize the use of materials in energy production and storage technology, handle end-of-life technology and achieve energy-efficient production. As an example, AI will be able to predict battery degradation in storage systems; therefore, it is capable of timely recycling or reusing it to increase asset life and minimize environmental impact.

1.6.4. *AI for energy equity*

Equitable access to sustainable energy can also be encouraged by AI so that disadvantaged populations will be served by the deployment and efficiency of renewable energy. Algorithms have the ability to detect areas with limited access, distribute energy and reduce social and environmental risks. AI enables efficient, sustainable and equitable policies and strategies by relying on social, environmental and operational data.

1.7. Conclusion

The future of sustainable energy systems is AI, which allows smarter approaches to generation, distribution and consumption based on data. Thanks to predictive analytics, optimization and autonomous decision-making, AI enables the shift toward resilient, low-carbon and equitable energy systems. The coming together of AI and sustainable energy is one pathway of critical importance toward reaching net-zero goals and creating an energy ecosystem for the future, one that is environmentally friendly and sustainable.

1.8. References

Andrade, J.R. and Bessa, R.J. (2017). Improving renewable energy forecasting with a grid of numerical weather predictions. *IEEE Transactions on Sustainable Energy*, 8(4), 1571–1580.

Azad, H.B., Mekhilef, S., Ganapathy, V.G. (2014). Long-term wind speed forecasting and general pattern recognition using neural networks. *IEEE Transactions on Sustainable Energy*, 5(2), 546–553.

Borunda, M., Rodríguez-Vázquez, K., Garduno-Ramirez, R., de la Cruz-Soto, J., Antunez-Estrada, J., Jaramillo, O.A. (2020). Long-term estimation of wind power by probabilistic forecast using genetic programming. *Energies*, 13(8), 1885.

Catalão, J.P.S., Pousinho, H.M.I., Mendes, V.M.F. (2011). Short-term wind power forecasting in Portugal by neural networks and wavelet transform. *Renew Energy*, 36(4), 1245–1251.

Colak, I., Sagiroglu, S., Yesilbudak, M. (2012). Data mining and wind power prediction: A literature review. *Renewable Energy*, 46, 241–247.

Colak, I., Sagiroglu, S., Yesilbudak, M., Kabalci, E., Bulbul, H.I. (2015). Multi-time series and-time scale modeling for wind speed and wind power forecasting part II: Medium-term and long-term applications. In *2015 International Conference on Renewable Energy Research and Applications (ICRERA)*. IEEE.

Dowell, J. and Pinson, P. (2015). Very-short-term probabilistic wind power forecasts by sparse vector autoregression. *IEEE Trans Smart Grid*, 7(2), 763–770.

Du, P., Wang, J., Yang, W., Niu, T. (2019). A novel hybrid model for short-term wind power forecasting. *Appl Soft Comput.*, 80, 93–106.

Flores, J.J., Graff, M., Rodriguez, H. (2012). Evolutive design of ARMA and ANN models for time series forecasting. *Renew Energy*, 44, 225–230.

Foley, A.M., Leahy, P.G., Marvuglia, A., McKeogh, E.J. (2012). Current methods and advances in forecasting of wind power generation. *Renewable Energy*, 37(1), 1–8.

Hill, D.C., McMillan, D., Bell, K.R., Infield, D. (2011). Application of auto-regressive models to UK wind speed data for power system impact studies. *IEEE Trans Sustain Energy*, 3(1), 134–141.

Jahangir, L. and Babbar, S. (2020). Medium term wind speed using random forest algorithm. *Int Res J Comput Sci Technol*, 47–53.

Landberg, L. (1999). Short-term prediction of the power production from wind farms. *J Wind Eng Ind Aerodyn*, 80(1–2), 207–220.

Lei, M., Shiyan, L., Chuanwen, J., Hongling, L., Yan, Z. (2009). A review on the forecasting of wind speed and generated power. *Renew Sustain Energy Rev*, 13(4), 915–920.

Ouyang, T., Huang, H., He, Y. (2019). Ramp events forecasting based on long-term wind power prediction and correction. *IET Renew Power Gener*, 13(15), 2793–2801.

Ramirez-Rosado, I.J., Fernandez-Jimenez, L.A., Monteiro, C., Sousa, J., Bessa, R. (2009). Comparison of two new short-term wind power forecasting systems. *Renew Energy*, 34(7), 1848–1854.

Sankar, S., Amudha, S., Madhavan, P., Lamba, D.K. (2021). Energy efficient medium-term wind speed prediction system using machine learning models. *IOP Conference Series: Materials Science and Engineering*, 1130(1), 012085.

Tascikaraoglu, A. and Uzunoglu, M. (2014). A review of combined approaches for prediction of short-term wind speed and power. *Renew Sustain Energy Rev.*, 34, 243–254.

Wu, G.Z., Zhang, Y.B., Su, C., Liu, Y.J. (2013). Study on medium-term and short-term wind power forecasting methods. *Applied Mechanics and Materials*, 361, 318–322.

Yuan, C., Liu, S., Fang, Z. (2016). Comparison of China's primary energy consumption forecasting by using ARIMA (the autoregressive integrated moving average) model and GM (1, 1) model. *Energy*, 100, 384–390.

2

Overview of AI, ML and DL Applications in Energy and Sustainability

The adoption of artificial intelligence (AI), machine learning (ML) and deep learning (DL) for energy efficiency, as well as sustainability projects, has grown due to a world that is increasingly focusing on renewable energy and sustainable advancement. These strategies are crucial for enhancing energy allocation, distribution and consumption, while decreasing its effect on the environment. This chapter provides a comprehensive overview of the use of AI, ML and DL for implementing energy efficiency and sustainable techniques. It focuses on how AI provides ongoing evaluation, proactive maintenance and autonomous decision-making in energy systems. Supervised, unsupervised and reinforcement learning are the AI algorithms that allow for accurate energy prediction, load balancing, anomaly detection and defect identification across smart grids. DL techniques, including convolutional neural networks (CNNs) and recurrent neural networks (RNNs), increase the estimation of renewable energy outputs, identify system anomalies, and improve storage and battery adjustment. AI-based methodologies also include elimination of carbon emissions, seamless utilization of renewable resources and adaptive planning for cities. This chapter discusses significant challenges, including the lack of data availability, computational specifications, model understanding and moral implications of applying AI-based energy strategies. It highlights the requirement for transparent, explainable and human-centered techniques, which align with sustainable development goals (SDGs). AI, ML and DL innovation, data-driven insights and ethical management are needed to develop efficient tools to promote flexible, efficient and secure energy systems that can address all future requirements.

2.1. Introduction

As governments address the simultaneous problems of increasing energy demand and climate change, sustainability and energy have been recognized as a global priority in the 21st century (Abualigah et al. 2022).

Chapter written by Priya PANDEY, Ashish PANDEY and Hema MAHAWAR.

The requirement for sustainable and renewable energy sources has grown due to rapid economic development and urban growth, as well as innovations in new technology (Ul Haq et al. 2025b). According to the International Energy Agency (2024), economic growth in developing and emerging economies is expected to drive nearly 25% of the increase in global energy demand by 2050. Despite the increasing deployment of renewable energy resources, a significant share of global energy production still relies on fossil fuels, resulting in substantial emissions that negatively impact human health and environmental sustainability (Alghieth 2025).

Investigators and authorities have made energy savings, system resilience and the combination of renewable resources their major objective due to the rapidly growing global demand for energy and the urgent demand to decrease greenhouse emissions (Ali et al. 2021). The complexity of novel energy systems is growing due to the need for diverse renewables, combinations of electric vehicles, distributed power resources and bidirectional flows in intelligent networks (Ul Haq et al. 2024). These factors highlight the difficulties with operations that are beyond common rule-based and simple control methods. To overcome these challenges, we require data-driven techniques that can learn patterns from heterogeneous, large-scale datasets and promote real-time monitoring (Anastasiadou et al. 2025).

Effective energy management and sustainability are crucial priorities in the modern world due to the growing demand for energy and the environmental difficulties aligned with traditional energy resources. Recent communities are facing growing pressure to minimize greenhouse gas emissions, improve energy functionality and then combine renewable energy solutions to moderate weather change impacts. The introduction of AI, ML and DL technologies is upgrading the energy domains by allowing forecast analytics, alongside real-time tracking of energy systems.

Moreover, the combination of AI-powered structures into renewable energy systems and smart architectures upgrades efficiency, minimizes the impact on the environment and promotes the AI-driven framework; it also contributes to achieving the SDGs. The integration of AI, ML, DL and hybrid represents all of the different ways with regard to energy sustainability management systems (see Figure 2.1), whereas this chapter discusses the overview of AI, ML and DL applications across energy system management in sustainability and its future scope (Anastasiadou et al. 2025).

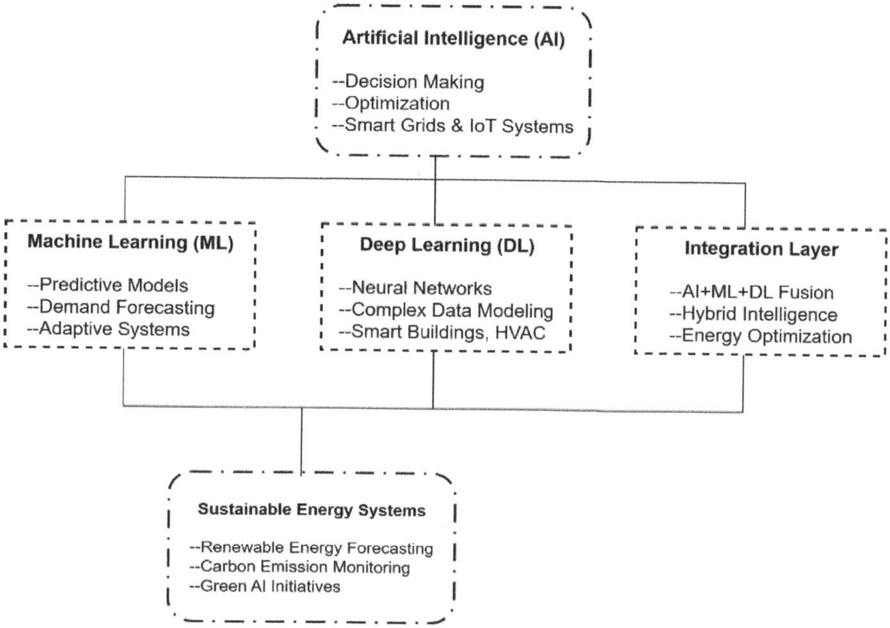

Figure 2.1. *Combination of artificial intelligence, machine learning and deep learning in energy sustainability*

Figure 2.1 illustrates the hierarchical relationship between Artificial Intelligence (AI), Machine Learning (ML), and Deep Learning (DL). AI represents the broader framework for intelligent decision-making systems. ML is a subset of AI that focuses on predictive and adaptive modeling using data-driven approaches. DL, a subset of ML, enables advanced feature extraction and detailed data representation through multi-layer neural networks. Together, these technologies support sustainable energy systems by enabling renewable energy forecasting, carbon emission tracking and intelligent energy management, which is explained in section 2.1.1.

2.1.1. *Brief overview of AI, ML and DL technologies*

The rising demand for sustainable and energy-efficient solutions has highlighted the need for AI, ML and DL with regard to technological transformation in recent industries. These intelligent systems allow automation, AI-driven decision-making and optimization across energy management, environmental monitoring and sustainability applications (Ul

Haq et al. 2022). The merging of AI-driven models into energy systems is no longer an emerging trend, but a fundamental shift toward digital sustainability and efficiency.

2.1.2. *AI and its role in energy sustainability*

AI integrates a broad domain of computational systems that have been designed to replicate human reasoning, problem-solving and learning proficiencies (Arun et al. 2025). AI algorithms are applied for predictive maintenance, performance improvement, smart grid control and renewable resource optimization with reference to energy and sustainability (Aslam et al. 2025). These systems support decision-makers and engineers in formulating adaptive energy strategies, reducing losses and improving energy efficiency across distinct sectors (Bhansali et al. 2023). AI has also been applied to monitor carbon emissions, support sustainable smart city development and optimize distribution and generation.

Furthermore, AI facilitates sustainable urban development through intelligent systems that manage energy distribution and optimize building performance. Several researchers have shown that data-driven models can identify the limitations in public infrastructure and enhance energy management through real-time analytics. AI increases the level of accuracy and precision of these structures when integrated with Internet of Things (IoT) and big data that are connected along with long-term sustainability goals.

2.1.3. *ML and the fundamentals for proactive and adaptive networks*

ML is an area of AI that allows systems to learn and predict from the data without having the specific programming (Ul Haq et al. 2025d). The algorithm of ML applies a procedure including decision trees (DT), support vector machines (SVM), regression and an ensemble approach to examining previous datasets and evaluating hidden patterns (Budennyy et al. 2022). These strategies are commonly used to handle forecasting energy demand, manage smart grids and minimize the usage of renewable energy sources. Further, ML improves error detection tools, energy consumption evaluation and load estimation. Machine learning models can be integrated with IoT devices to improve energy efficiency in smart buildings by analyzing real-time sensor data and optimizing HVAC operations. By continuously adapting to changing consumer demands and environmental conditions, predictive ML algorithms can also enhance power generation efficiency and overall energy management.

The latest improvements in adaptive forecasting and dynamic energy storage systems have shown the possibilities of ML to help sustainable infrastructure. The development of ML systems that promote renewable energy sources with (or without) energy storage represents how these techniques optimize reliability and reduce dependency on fossil fuels.

2.1.4. *DL and its advanced energy efficiency with complex data modeling*

DL illustrates an advanced branch of ML that uses multi-layered neural networks to manage and explore complex data structures (Chauhan et al. 2024). These models are basically effective in context involving large-scale, non-linear datasets such as energy demand prediction and ecosystem forecasting. Their capability to systematically extract features from data allows them to perform like traditional models with regard to adaptability and accuracy. Deep learning models are increasingly used in smart buildings with distributed energy generation systems to improve energy modeling, forecasting and operational efficiency. To design intelligent multi-zone HVAC control strategies, enhancing energy efficiency and user comfort have been illustrated as deep learning reinforcement.

Developing transparent and understandable DL models that integrate with the United Nations SDGs is highly important. Further, the latest research has analyzed the concept of “Green AI”, which highlights the need to reduce the carbon footprint of large AI and DL architecture through energy efficient computing (Ul Haq et al. 2025a). These new prototypes of sustainable AI ensure that the merits of intelligent systems do not come at the expense of environmental health (Entezari et al. 2023).

2.1.5. *Integrating AI, ML and DL for sustainable development*

The integration of AI, ML and DL mechanisms creates a powerful architecture for achieving sustainable energy and environmental procedures that allows a system to not only analyze data, but to self-learn, optimize and predict in real-life (Fan et al. 2023). This combination reinforces the operations ranging from renewable energy forecasting and smart grid balancing to climate modeling and pollution control. Data-driven prediction systems are increasingly deployed to optimize renewable energy architectures and observe carbon emissions.

In addition, a hybrid method that merges DL systems with RL has illustrated functionality in obtaining dynamic energy management in industrial and urban settings. The integration application of these approaches is transforming the universal energy by improving efficiency and allowing AI-powerful sustainability initiatives.

2.1.6. *Motivation for AI, ML and DL adoption in energy and sustainability domains*

The increasing complexity of the global energy sector, driven by renewable energy integration and sustainability challenges, has made conventional management techniques less effective. These mechanisms support the most sustainable, optimized and flexible energy structures.

The core motivations for combining AI, ML and DL in energy and sustainability domains are as follows:

– AI-driven mechanisms facilitate carbon emission tracking, promote clean energy adoption and adjust energy operations with sustainability aims.

– Models such as ML and DL allow energy systems to dynamically address faults, improving reliability and flexibility to ensure stable energy systems.

– AL and ML efficiently help the workflow and examine thorough energy data from consumption, distribution, generation and data-powered decisions, which optimize the complex energy systems.

– Intelligent designs promote real-time optimization of power flow, resource provision, reducing energy costs and task distribution, which enhances the entire energy capability (Farooq and Khan 2025).

– Modern algorithms develop forecasting of renewable energy generation and its demand, which minimizes dependence on conventional estimation structures.

2.1.7. *Scope and objectives*

This chapter highlights an intelligent control technique for multi-zone residential HVAC systems with DL reinforcement, which covers simulation-based addresses to improve energy proficiency and maintain it across various areas, without increasing to full-scale integration with smart grid systems. The chapter explains the areas of AI, ML and DL with regard to growing energy sustainability, which covers the framework to optimize energy systems, etc. It also involves prescriptive and predictive assessments, real-time decision-making, smart grid systems, etc. The major objectives with regard to AI, ML and DL in sustainable energy management systems across different areas as per the recent investigations are listed as follows (Georgiou et al. 2022):

– a deep reinforcement learning–based control strategy to manage multi-zone HVAC systems efficiently;

– to develop an approach against traditional HVAC control systems for increasing energy efficiency;

– to address the various methods to merge renewable energy resources into an existing energy capacity by using intelligent processes (Ikbal 2025).

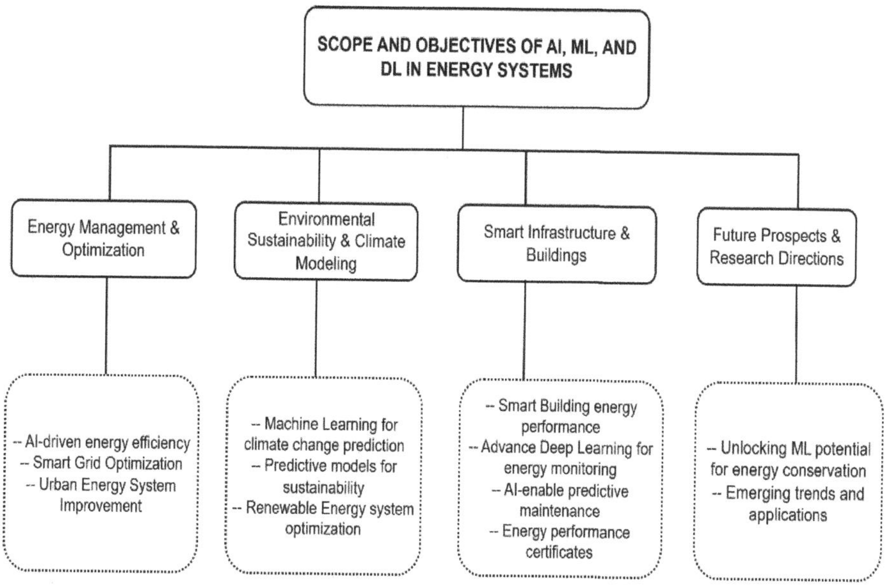

Figure 2.2. *Systematic overview of AI, ML and DL techniques to achieve the core objectives (Ul Haq et al. 2024)*

Figure 2.2 shows the comprehensive overview of the AI, ML and DL approach for achieving the key objectives and scope with energy sustainability in various domains such as (1) energy management and optimization, (2) environmental sustainability and climate modeling, (3) smart infrastructure and buildings, and (4) future prospects and research directions, which were covered in section 2.1.5.

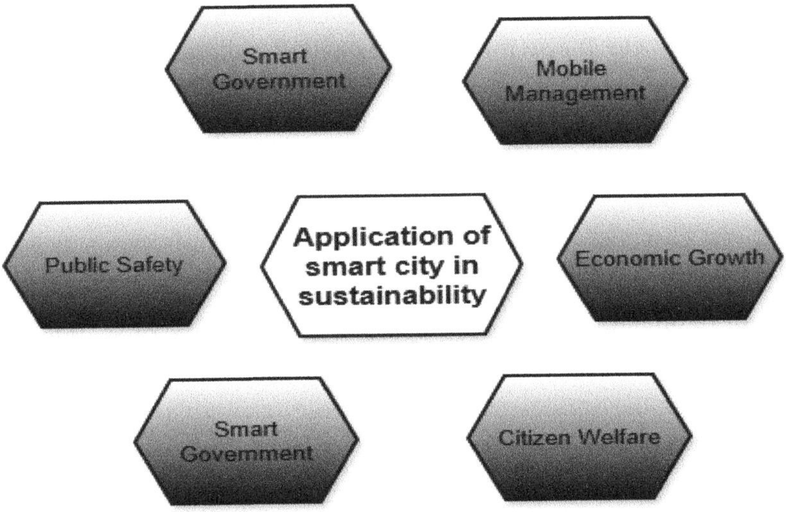

Figure 2.3. *Applications in energy sustainability systems*

Figure 2.3 shows the various applications of the smart city in sustainability processes, such as citizen welfare, mobile management, smart government, public safety, etc., which we will discuss below:

a) *Energy Performance Certificate (EPC) evaluation:* the methods for DL identification and use for EPC system efficiency that include handling the flow of energy and increasing building energy efficiency through the usage of ML and DL techniques (Kamyab et al. 2023; Li and Du 2023; Majnoon and Saifoddin 2025; Manimegalai et al. 2025).

b) *Renewable energy system:* this is categorized in two ways: renewable energy referred to as sustainable energy, which defines zero emissions of carbon and produces power in a biological method such as wind, hydro and solar, and, on the other hand, non-renewable energy, which means that once power sources are consumed, they cannot be recovered in a person's lifetime

(Mhlanga 2022). These are the systems that basically provide energy from renewable self-sustainable resources such as wind, hydro and solar (this has been further explained in section 2.1). Biomass has become increasingly popular as a renewable energy source and is currently used to partially meet thermal energy demand. This is very suitable for efficient functioning and scalability (Nabavi et al. 2021).

2.2. Literature review

In this section, current instances of AI, ML and DL methods have been assessed for their benefits in various sustainable energy management systems (Olawade et al. 2024).

The increasing global demand for energy, coupled with environmental challenges and the need for effective renewable energy integration, has significantly transformed energy management strategies. In recent years, advanced analytical methods have been increasingly utilized to improve the performance, efficiency and sustainability of energy systems. We analyzed ML which permits Quality of Experience (QoE) on buffer and energy. We highlighted the challenges of IoT devices for smart structures and its components, which have been explained across various approaches of ML with IoT to make them energy effective. According to the authors, the study analyzes how artificial intelligence (AI) and machine learning (ML) technologies contributed to mitigating the impacts of the Covid-19 pandemic, while also supporting advancements related to the Fourth Industrial Revolution and the Sustainable Development Goals (SDGs). The research identifies emerging investigation themes and explores future directions for Environmental, Social, and Governance (ESG) scoring using AI- and ML-based models. Furthermore, it highlights the lack of practical educational research and comprehensive evaluation of algorithms based on advanced financial technologies. The current research illustrated the issues that traditional water resource management techniques face with real-world data acquisition and adaptive decision-making. We demonstrated the application of big data analytics and AI to examine the gaps and showed that ML and DL methods improve the quality of water tracking, demand forecasting and so on. They also examined how big data generated from IoT devices and remote sensing technologies can be applied to water management systems. The study suggested a comprehensive structure integrating IoT data collection, AI evaluates, big-data processing and blockchain to enhance VI applications such as automated workflows, which provides benefits and handles timely decisions in a data-intensive environment.

Author(s)/Ref	Year	Domain	Criteria	Scalability	Limitations
Bhansali et al. (2023)	2025	Sustainable energy management	ML models to predict and refine energy losses	Large-scale energy systems	Address data availability for real-time deployment
Chauhan et al. (2024)	2024	Integration of AI and ML ethics	Ethical on AI, ML in sustainability	Broad thematic review	Limited empirical data
Ul Haq et al. (2025a)	2025	Renewable energy management system	Emerging trends in AI	Large-scale energy systems	Lack of empirical data for real-time deployment examinations
Fan et al. (2023)	2023	Renewable energy	AI and DL applications among SDGs	High-dimensional data	Explainability and transparency
Farooq and Khan (2025)	2024	Environmental tracking	AI-driven algorithm	High	Data access
Majnoon and Saifoddin (2025)	2025	Urban energy system	Hybrid machine learning models for load forecasting	Approx. 2000-2022 electricity data for large urban-scale	Require high-quality data, regional data specificity
Manimegalai et al. (2025)	2025	Machine Learning and Deep Learning	Energy management system	High	Data scarcity
Ullah et al. (2024)	2024	IoT and ML, smart cities	Data centric smart environment	Large-scale urban deployment	Data privacy and security
Vijay Kumar and Shahin (2025)	2025	Environmental sustainability	Machine learning approach for environmental systems	Environmental datasets for large-scale climate	Address privacy concerns and data bias

Table 2.1. *Comparative analysis of existing research in different domains*

Table 2.1 illustrates the comparative analysis of previous studies in various domains, criteria, scalability and their limitations. We discussed a DLR, that is, a deep reinforcement learning method for handling HVAC systems in multi-zone residential buildings such as hospitals and public residential, which aims to minimize the energy losses during the maintenance of occupant comfort (Olawumi and Oladapo 2025). They have used a model-free actor-critic algorithm, which interacts with a simulated building environment, where the results showed the DRL method exceeds the conventional rule-based approach and deep Q-network (DQN) to reduce the energy costs. Different techniques have been analyzed which are based on energy conversion systems in self-renewing energy sources, including wind, hydro power and recurrent energy, using the methods of ML and DL. The challenges were evaluated across multiple energy resources using ML and DL approaches. The study introduced a framework that integrates advanced ML models with dual-objective refinement to examine the Carbon Stability Index (CSI) and Return on Energy Investment (REI). The results showed better advancement in REI and CSI, compared to conventional. We demonstrated the requirement of governments to execute a proactive data governance framework to safeguard critical information. The study highlighted the survey of ML and DL in energy management systems that illustrates related drawbacks, benefits and alternative methods in sustainable energy systems. The recent study introduced the feasibility of multi-modal AI structures, combining CNNs for detecting identification, RNNs with energy consumption prediction and reinforcement for innovative refinement that is integrated with IoT-based real-world tracking and supply chain management systems. The outcome represents reductions in energy losses, CO_2 emissions and waste heat recovery. These frameworks are basically scalable and reliable for Industry 4.0, which offers a way among sustainable and carbon-neutral industrial functionality. The previous study was focused on ML applications in the area of RES among various domains of energy systems, such as sustainability and energy policy. The study also discussed the vulnerabilities with regard to ambiguous limitations, such as infrastructure modernization and the need for energy storage. As per the investigation, the study suggested the accuracy of enhancing models through integrated approaches that present substantial opportunities, especially for UN SDGs 7 and 13, so that the impact of environmental and economic growth can become better.

2.3. Methodology

In this chapter, we show the procedures used in renewable energy utilization for sustainability and energy based on learning, which we will discuss in Figure 2.4.

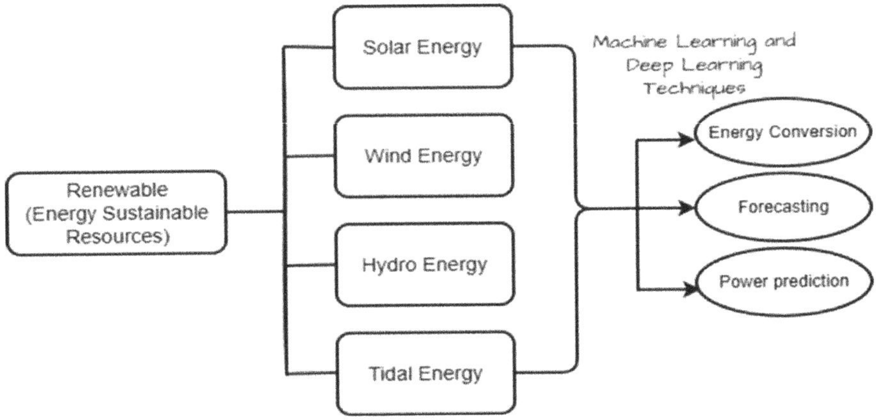

Figure 2.4. *Classification of ML approaches in sustainable energy resources (Bhansali et al. 2023)*

Figure 2.4 represents the classification of ML techniques in sustainable energy resources such as solar energy, wind energy, hydro energy and tidal energy with an ML and DL approach. The utility of DL and ML methods in energy conversion, forecasting and consumption prediction of sustainable energy resources, such as wind energy, solar energy, tidal energy and hydro energy, has been presented. Renewable energy sources are widely considered essential for achieving a sustainable environment, as they significantly reduce greenhouse gas emissions and minimize environmental impacts. Energy planning and power forecasting can help with the application of ML and DL methods, as well as effectively estimating the daily changes of water flow. However, the model needs large volumes of data to train and more time is required for small-scale predictions. To address power prediction challenges, machine learning (ML) and deep learning (DL) techniques have been employed to improve the precision and accuracy of power forecasting (Fan et al. 2023).

We have proposed a novel structure for advance ML methods and deep neural networks, such as random forests and eXtreme gradient boosting through dual optimization, indicating the improvement from 4.83 to 14.43 in REI, which has been increased from 47.4 to 57.98 in CSI from traditional HTC solutions. We have also conducted a comparative analysis from HTC and pyrolysis for SDG7 and SDG15 (Farooq and Khan 2025).

The study achieved the aim for VOSviewer software, which is used to execute the comparative analysis and find out the integration between various research domains. This software was proposed by N.J.V. Ech and L. Waltman with the support of Leiden University. They have been worked in terms of AI and ML, as well as energy, data mining, security, reliability, scalability, sustainability, renewable energy and so on.

Based on these keywords, they evaluated the various studies in these domains and all of the outcomes were imported into the tool as VOSviewer (Farooq and Khan 2025). The authors utilized the Scopus database to identify approximately 2,000 peer-reviewed articles published since 2000 based on relevant keywords. Their analysis highlighted various applications in the energy domain, including fuzzy logic–based air conditioning systems (Ul Haq and Khanday 2025) and others, as shown in Table 2.2.

Objective	Segment and system	Architectures and methods
Prediction	Wind power	Analysis of time series
Sustainable Development	Stochastic systems	Uncertainty analysis
Environmental effect	Smart power grid	Genetic algorithm
Effect evaluation (social, technical and economical)	Renewable resources, buildings, power utilization, power transmission connection	Random forest, artificial neural networks, ant colony optimization and multi-objective optimization
Decision-making	Solar energy	Numerical model

Table 2.2. *Key applications of artificial intelligence and machine learning in the energy domain (Farooq and Khan 2025)*

Table 2.2 shows the key applications of AI and ML in the domain of energy sustainability (Farooq and Khan 2025). We highlighted the importance of integrating policies using the sustainable concepts in order to help the sustainability of the environment and financial security, and identified central scientific clusters for the development of sustainable goals (Saadati and Barutcu 2025). We used CNN-IoT-based energy resource structures in smart buildings, which discussed important developments from previous studies, where outcomes achieved 88% accuracy; this represents the measurements for efficiency and shows a substantial enhancement in forecasting compared to previous techniques, including ELM, LSTM and SVM (Shah et al. 2022). The level of feature development and dataset collection is important with regard to how effectively AL models perform in renewable energy sources. Big data and IoT also play a very important role in sustainable energy management or renewable energy sources, which require a huge number of datasets to examine understanding and patterns (Ul Haq et al. 2025c).

2.4. Challenges

Based on the proposed methodology, the study introduces a novel framework that combines machine learning with process optimization to analyze operating conditions such as temperature and residence time. A comparative evaluation of solid products derived from pyrolysis was conducted, aligning the outcomes with Sustainable Development Goals (SDG 7 and SDG 15). The key challenges have been discussed as per the various research investigations:

– Recent renewable sources may constrain future use, which includes emerging technologies (Ullah et al. 2024).

– Dependency on historical data that may not express further changes, particularly under unpredictable situations (Vijay Kumar and Shahin 2025).

– Challenges in terms of high-density datasets, which restrict model training and its learning (Vinuesa and Sirmacek 2021).

– Obstacles to applying ML and IoT for energy proficiency in smart buildings, such as educational and hospital campuses with IoT (Zekić-Sušać et al. 2021).

– The success of AI and ML depends on the availability of comprehensive, high-quality datasets, which are often fragmented, along with ensuring reliability and scalability (Zhong et al. 2022).

– There is a significant lack of empirical studies and comprehensive evaluations of algorithm-driven financial platforms. Most existing research remains theoretical and has not been validated in real-world scenarios (Ul Haq 2024).

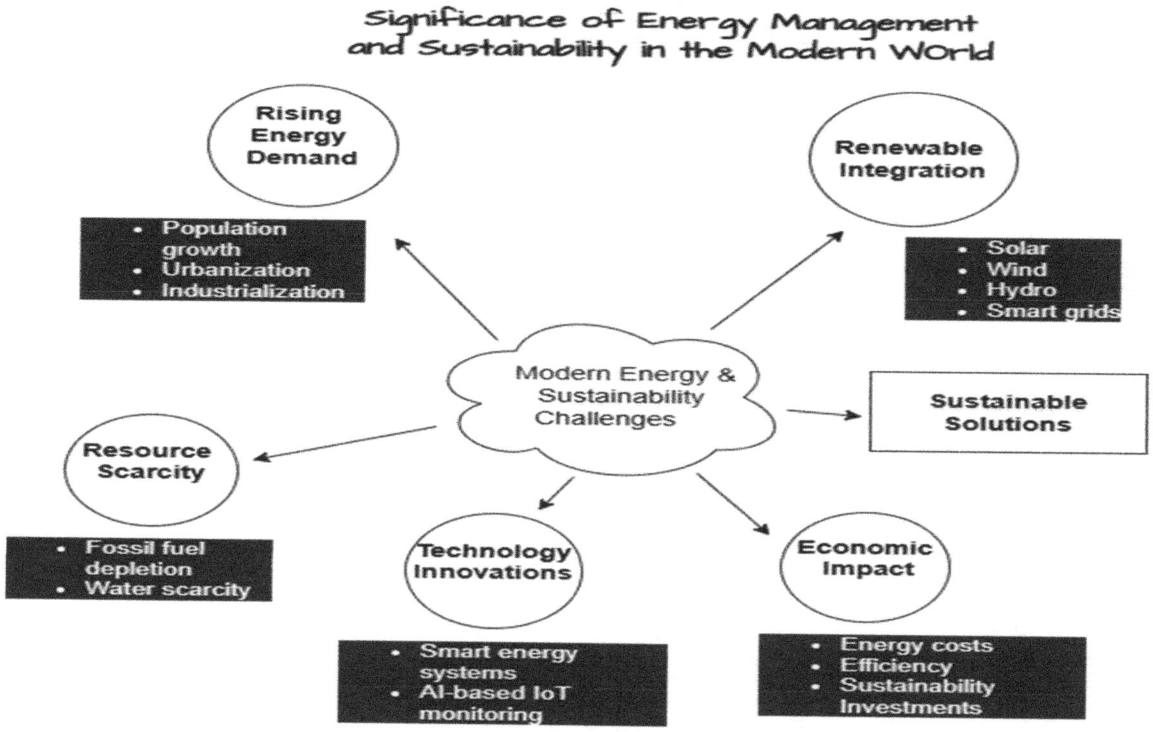

Figure 2.5. *Key challenges in sustainable energy management systems (Ul Haq 2024)*

There are several remaining challenges (that have been presented in Figure 2.5) in sustainability energy systems, such as (1) rising energy demands including population growth, urbanization and industrialization; (2) technology innovations that include smart energy system, and AI-based IoT monitoring; (3) economic impact that covers energy costs, efficiency and sustainability investments; (4) resource scarcity such as fossil fuel depletion and water scarcity; and (5) renewable integration, which focuses on solar, wind, hydro, smart grids, etc., and incorporates the significance of energy management and sustainability in the modern world (Ul Haq 2024).

2.5. Conclusion and future scope

Currently, AI-driven learning models have obtained their capacity to manage real-scenario challenges in the domain of sustainable atmospheres. A framework of AI, ML and DL for sustainability has significantly enhanced the capabilities of modern energy systems. Investigations highlight that data-driven methods improve energy efficiency, proactive maintenance and operational optimization across various domains such as smart buildings, renewable energy systems and public facilities. The execution of ML and DL algorithms leads to enhanced efficiency and decreased carbon emissions, as systems can gather the information from large datasets to improve the addition of unpredictable energy resources. Recent investigations illustrate the purpose of essential and sustainable AI that ensure that real-time frameworks are not only fixed, but also clear and sustainably conscious. The incorporation of AI into smart city initiatives, integrated energy management systems and hybrid renewable energy systems directly contributes to the Sustainable Development Goals (SDGs) by enhancing system efficiency and reducing environmental impacts. Moreover, many challenges such as scalability, reliability, model generalization and energy costs, which have been involved with AI evaluation, maintain critical attention for practical execution.

The combination of AI, ML and DL for energy and sustainability highlights hybrid models that merge physics-informed techniques with AI-driven approaches to develop reliability and accuracy. The improvement of sustainably efficient and understandable AI algorithms will focus on analytical energy costs and transparency, whereas reinforcement learning and dynamic control strategies can refine real-time optimization in smart grids, HVAC systems and renewable energy networks. Combining IoT sensor data, historical energy usage and weather predictions enables energy management, whereas flexible AI allows regional and systematic generalization. Future work may improve decision-making and transparency with the integration of blockchain.

2.6. References

Abualigah, L., Zitar, R.A., Almotairi, K.H., Hussein, A.M., Abd Elaziz, M., Nikoo, M.R., Gandomi, A.H. (2022). Wind, solar, and photovoltaic renewable energy systems with and without energy storage optimization: A survey of advanced machine learning and deep learning techniques. *Energies*, 15, 578.

Alghieth, M. (2025). Sustain AI: A multi-modal deep learning framework for carbon footprint reduction in industrial manufacturing. *Sustainability*, 17, 4134.

Ali, E.S., Hasan, M.K., Hassan, R., Saeed, R.A., Hassan, M.B., Islam, S., Nafi, N.S., Bevinakoppa, S. (2021). Machine learning technologies for secure vehicular communication in Internet of Vehicles: Recent advances and applications. *Security and Communication Networks*, 2021(1), 1–23.

Anastasiadou, M., Duarte dos Santos, V., Sales Dias, M. (2025). Deep learning classification approaches and applications for Energy Performance Certificates (EPCs). *Energy*, 339, 139148.

Arun, M., Barik, D., Othman, N.A., Praveenkumar, S. Tudu, K. (2025). Investigating the performance of AI-driven smart building systems through advanced deep learning model analysis. *Energy Reports*, 13, 5885–5899.

Aslam, S., Aung, P.P., Rafsanjani, A.S. Majeed, A.P.P.A. (2025). Machine learning applications in energy systems: Current trends, challenges, and research directions. *Energy Informatics*, 8(1), 62.

Bhansali, A., Narasimhulu, N., Pérez de Prado, R., Divakarachari, P.B., Narayan, D.L. (2023). A review on sustainable energy sources using machine learning and deep learning models. *Energies*, 16(17), 6236.

Budennyy, S.A., Lazarev, V.D., Zakharenko, N.N., Korovin, A.N., Plosskaya, O.A., Dimitrov, D.V., Akhripkin, V.S., Pavlov, I.V., Oseledets, I.V., Barsola, I.S. et al. (2022). ECO_2AI: Carbon emissions tracking of machine learning models as the first step towards sustainable AI. *Doklady Mathematics*, 106(S1), S118–S128.

Chauhan, V.S., Sharma, R., Shah, H. (2024). Exploring sustainability through clean energy, artificial intelligence, and machine learning: Ethical perspectives. In *AI Applications for Clean Energy and Sustainability*, Riswandi, B.A., Singh, B., Kaunert, C., Vig, K. (eds). IGI Global, Hershey, PA, 119–138.

Entezari, A., Aslani, A., Zahedi, R., Noorollahi, Y. (2023). Artificial intelligence and machine learning in energy systems: A bibliographic perspective. *Energy Strategy Reviews*, 45, 101017.

Fan, Z., Yan, Z., Wen, S. (2023). Deep learning and artificial intelligence in sustainability: A review of SDGs, renewable energy, and environmental health. *Sustainability*, 15(18), 13493.

Farooq, O. and Khan, A. (2025). The impact of machine learning on climate change modeling and environmental sustainability. *Artificial Intelligence and Machine Learning Review*, 6(1), 8–16.

Georgiou, S., Kechagia, M., Sharma, T., Sarro, F., Zou, Y. (2022). Green AI: Do deep learning frameworks have different costs? In *Proceedings of the 44th International Conference Software Engineering*. ACM.

Ikbal, T. (2025) Empowering a sustainable future: Unleashing the potential of machine learning for energy efficiency and conservation. In *Green Machine Learning and Big Data for Smart Grids*, Indragandhi, V., Elakkiya, R., Subramaniyaswamy, V. (eds). Elsevier, Amsterdam.

Javed, H., Eid, F., El-Sappagh, S., Abuhmed, T. (2025). Sustainable energy management in the AI era: A comprehensive analysis of ML and DL approaches. *Computing*, 107(6), 132.

Kamyab, H., Khademi, T., Chelliapan, S., SaberiKamarposhti, M., Rezania, S., Yusuf, M., Farajnezhad, M., Abbas, M., Hun Jeon, B., Ahn, Y. (2023). The latest innovative avenues for the utilization of artificial intelligence and big data analytics in water resource management. *Results in Engineering*, 20, 101566.

Li, F. and Du, Y. (eds) (2023). Intelligent multi-zone residential HVAC control strategy based on deep reinforcement learning. In *Deep Learning for Power System Applications*. Springer, Cham.

Majnoon, A. and Saifoddin, A. (2025). AI-driven energy optimization enhancing efficiency in urban environments with hybrid machine learning models. *Cleaner Engineering and Technology*, 28, 101072.

Manimegalai, V., Raaghav, P.R., Mohanapriya, V., Vashishsdh, T.R., Palaniappan, S. (2025). Machine learning and deep learning methods for energy management systems. In *Artificial Intelligence for Energy Management*, Kumar, R.S., Indragandhi, V., Selvamathi, R., Balakumar, P. (eds). John Wiley & Sons, Hoboken, NJ.

Mhlanga, D. (2022). The role of artificial intelligence and machine learning amid the COVID-19 pandemic: What lessons are we learning on 4IR and the sustainable development goals. *International Journal of Environmental Research and Public Health*, 19(3), 1879.

Nabavi, S.A., Motlagh, N.H., Zaidan, M.A., Aslani, A., Zakeri, B. (2021). Deep learning in energy modeling: Application in smart buildings with distributed energy generation. *IEEE Access*, 9, 125439–125461.

Olawade, D.B., Wada, O.Z., Ige, A.O., Egbewole, B.I., Olojo, A., Oladapo, B.I. (2024). Artificial intelligence in environmental monitoring: Advancements, challenges, and future directions. *Hygiene and Environmental Health Advances*, 12, 100114.

Olawumi, M.A. and Oladapo, B.I. (2025). AI-driven predictive models for sustainability. *Journal of Environmental Management*, 373, 123472.

Saadati, T. and Barutcu, B. (2025). Forecasting solar energy: Leveraging artificial intelligence and machine learning for sustainable energy solutions. *Journal of Economic Surveys*, 39, 1929–1946.

Shah, S.F.A., Iqbal, M., Aziz, Z., Rana, T., Khalid, A., Cheah, Y.N., Arif, M. (2022). The role of machine learning and the Internet of Things in smart buildings for energy efficiency. *Applied Sciences*, 12(15), 7882.

Ul Haq, I. (2024). Diagnosis of neurological disease using bioinspired algorithms. In *Bio-Inspired Optimization for Medical Data Mining*, Srivastava, S., Anand, A., Kumar, A. et al. (eds). John Wiley & Sons, Hoboken, NJ.

Ul Haq, I. and Khanday, A.M.U.D. (2025). Exploring the role of explainable AI in women's health: Challenges and solutions. In *Explainable Artificial Intelligence in the Healthcare Industry*, Kumar, A., Kumar, T.A., Das, P. et al. (eds). John Wiley & Sons, Hoboken, NJ.

Ul Haq, I., Kumar, N., Koul, N., Verma, C., Eneacu, F.M. Raboaca, M.S. (2022). Machine learning techniques for result prediction of one day international (ODI) cricket match. In *The International Conference on Recent Innovations in Computing*. Springer, Singapore.

Ul Haq, I., Kaur, G., Rather, A.H. (2024). Fruit leaf classification using transfer learning for automation and industrial applications. In *Deep Learning Techniques for Automation and Industrial Applications*, Rathore, P.S., Ahuja, S., Burri, S.R. et al. (eds). John Wiley & Sons, Hoboken, NJ.

Ul Haq, I., Khanday, A.M.D., Shah, H.A., Rufai, S.Z. (2025a). Enhancing water security through automation: Case studies and technical advancements in water quality management. In *Computational Automation for Water Security*, Dubey, A.K., Srivastav, A.L., Kumar, A. et al. (eds). Elsevier, Amsterdam.

Ul Haq, I., Kumar, A., Rathore, P.S. (2025b). Machine learning approaches for wind power forecasting: A comprehensive review. *Discover Applied Sciences*, 7(10), 1139.

Ul Haq, I., Malhotra, J., Rawat, V., Kumari, J., Kaur, G. (2025c). Machine learning approaches for early detection of cervical cancer: A comparative study of classification models. In *Targeted Chemotherapy with Personalized Immunotherapy: An AI Approach*, Kumar, A., Das, P., Rathore, P.S. et al. (eds). John Wiley & Sons, Hoboken, NJ.

Ul Haq, I., Nandal, V., Uppal, H. (2025d). Blockchain applications in aviation securing transactions, streamlining operations, and improving passenger experience. In *Blockchain in the Tourism Industry: A New Era of Secure and Transparent Travel Solutions*, Kumar, A., Abreu, A., Batta, P. et al. (eds). Springer, Cham.

Ullah, A., Anwar, S.M., Li, J., Nadeem, L., Mahmood, T., Rehman, A., Saba, T. (2024). Smart cities: The role of Internet of Things and machine learning in realizing a data-centric smart environment. *Complex and Intelligent Systems*, 10(1), 1607–1637.

Vijay Kumar, V.V. and Shahin, K. (2025). Artificial intelligence and machine learning for sustainable manufacturing: Current trends and future prospects. *Intelligent and Sustainable Manufacturing*, 2(1), 10002.

Vinuesa, R. and Sirmacek, B. (2021). Interpretable deep-learning models to help achieve the sustainable development goals. *Nature Machine Intelligence*, 3(11), 926.

Zekić-Sušać, M., Mitrović, S., Has, A. (2021). Machine learning–based system for managing energy efficiency of public sector as an approach towards smart cities. *International Journal of Information Management*, 58, 102074.

Zhong, R., Liu, Y., Mu, X., Chen, Y., Song, L. (2022) AI empowered RIS-assisted NOMA networks: Deep learning or reinforcement learning? *IEEE Journal on Selected Areas in Communications*, 40(1), 182–196.

3

Overview of AI, ML and DL Applications in Energy and Sustainability

In today's technological era, energy use is a major concern because it relies heavily on non-renewable resources. Conserving energy and identifying high-consumption areas are essential to guide effective savings. Emerging technologies such as artificial intelligence (AI), machine learning (ML) and deep learning (DL) support this effort by forecasting energy use, enabling shifts to renewable sources and promoting sustainability across industries. This chapter provides a comprehensive overview of AI, ML and DL techniques for energy management and their applications, followed by a case study that uses ML to analyze and predict abnormal energy consumption in HVAC systems of commercial buildings. The research aligns with the SDGs, particularly clean energy (SDG-7), responsible production and consumption (SDG-12), climate action (SDG-13) through carbon footprint reduction, and sustainable cities and communities (SDG-11).

3.1. Introduction

The United Nations (UN) established 17 Sustainable Development Goals (SDGs) to achieve sustainability by 2030, organized under three pillars: environmental, social and economic development (Figure 3.1). Energy and sustainability are closely interconnected, as energy relates to all three pillars – for example, affordable and clean energy (SDG-7) supports economic development, while SDG-11 promotes social inclusion and environmental protection. According to UN estimates, emerging technologies such as artificial intelligence (AI), machine learning (ML) and deep learning (DL) could contribute to achieving about 79% of the SDGs. This chapter examines the role of AI, ML and DL in the energy sector, with section 3.3 providing an overview of these techniques and their applications in energy and sustainability, and section 3.5 presenting a case study on energy prediction of HVAC plants in commercial buildings.

Chapter written by Mrinal PANDEY and Monika GOYAL.

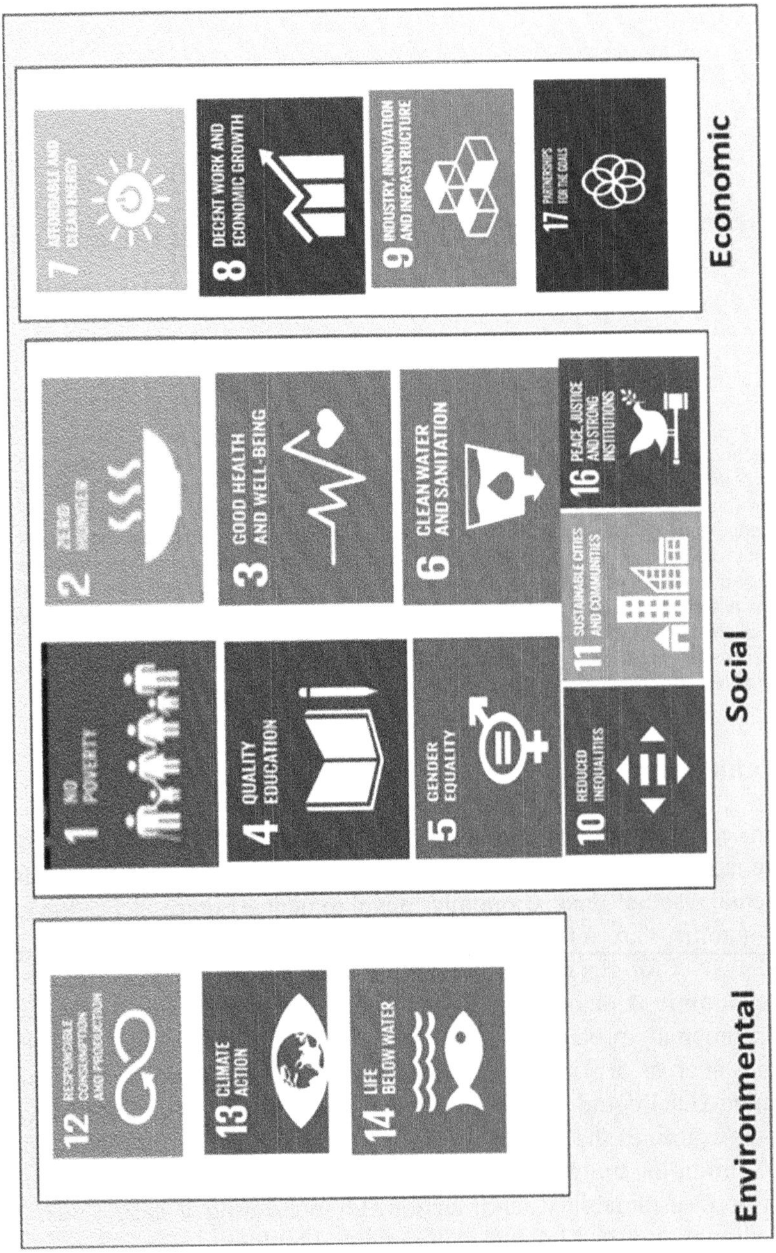

Figure 3.1. *Three pillars of sustainability. For a color version of this figure, see www.iste.co.uk/ulhaq/artificial1.zip*

3.2. Literature survey

The work done by other authors in the energy sector using hybrid techniques has been presented in Table 3.1.

Authors	ML model used	Work done	Results
Bui et al. (2020)	A combination of artificial neural network and electromagnetism-based optimization algorithm using firefly	The model proposed in the article can be helpful for civil engineers in designing buildings that are energy efficient	In the first dataset used, improved RMSE is achieved, which is 93.28%–98.50% better compared to other methods, and the computational performance is five and seven times quicker than ELM and GP. In the second dataset, RMSE, MAE and MAPE were minimum and R-value was maximum along with fast computing time
	Clustering classification (BBN, SVM, ANN)	Energy consumed by smart home appliances and resident behavior	Accuracy = 90%
Ul Haq et al. (2025a)	Ensemble model (autoencoder, SVR, RF)	Anomaly detection in energy consumption, false alarm rate	AUC = 0.97
Araya et al. (2017)	Clustering and prediction algorithms	Predicting energy consumption for the next day, as well as peak power demand	2.32% MAPE for the subsequent-day energy usage and 2.85% MAPE for the highest power demand employing ensemble models
Fan et al. (2014)	Classification, regression and ensemble model	The research work compares several techniques for predicting heating load and cooling load of a building	1.132% MAPE for heating load using SVR and 3.455% MAPE for cooling load using an ensemble model
Ul Haq et al. (2024)	Ensemble model combining feed-forward back propagation ANN and RF	Outdoor air temperature, dew point temperature, RH	RMSE = 4.97 using ANN
Ahmad et al. (2017)	K means clustering	A system for preventing energy losses during transportation has been developed	Loss reduction approximately 20%
Ul Haq et al. (2022)	Clustering (K-means) Classification (KNN)	The research work presents a strategy for cooling control based on the presence of occupants	7%–52% energy savings

Table 3.1. *Literature survey using hybrid models*

3.3. Brief description of AI, ML and DL

AI can be referred to as the potentiality of the machines to impersonate human-like behavior and characteristics, such as solving problems, reasoning, experiential learning, natural language understanding and decision-making. AI is defined formally by McCarthy as "The science and engineering of making intelligent machines, especially intelligent computer programs". The field encompasses the similar job of using machines for understanding human intelligence (Peng et al. 2018).

AI is an umbrella term that encompasses ML, a subfield consisting of several systematic methods that facilitate the machine to learn from the previous data such that the performance gets better with time without any kind of explicit programming (Alpaydin 2020; Ul Haq et al. 2025c, 2025d).

Similarly, DL is seen as a part of ML, which is based on ANNs and is used to learn from large and complex datasets, and automatically extract features from them (Goodfellow et al. 2016; Ul Haq and Khanday 2025; Ul Haq et al. 2025b).

3.3.1. *Relationship between AI, ML and DL*

AI, ML and DL are closely related, and this relationship is shown in Figure 3.2. It is clear from the figure that artificial intelligence comprises a range of techniques, including ML, Robotics, NLP and Computer Vision, among others. ML is further comprised of two categories: supervised learning and unsupervised learning.

Supervised ML has a predictive nature that requires historical data and expected output (class labels). This historical data and expected output feed into the algorithms to learn, and a comparison of the actual (predicted) output is performed with the expected results to verify the correctness in the results. The most common algorithms in supervised learning are naïve Bayes, support vector machines, decision trees, K-nearest neighbors and artificial neural network.

The notion of ANN is similar to the biological neural network that forms the human brain. The neurons in ANN are connected by edges, which mimic the synapses of the brain.

ANN comprises three layers: an input layer, an output layer and a hidden layer. Each input is associated with some weight, and the summation of (input × weight) is passed to the next layer of the nodes. The output of the previous layer is fed into the input of the next layer. Finally, the result of the output layer is compared with the expected output to find the error (Ul Haq 2024).

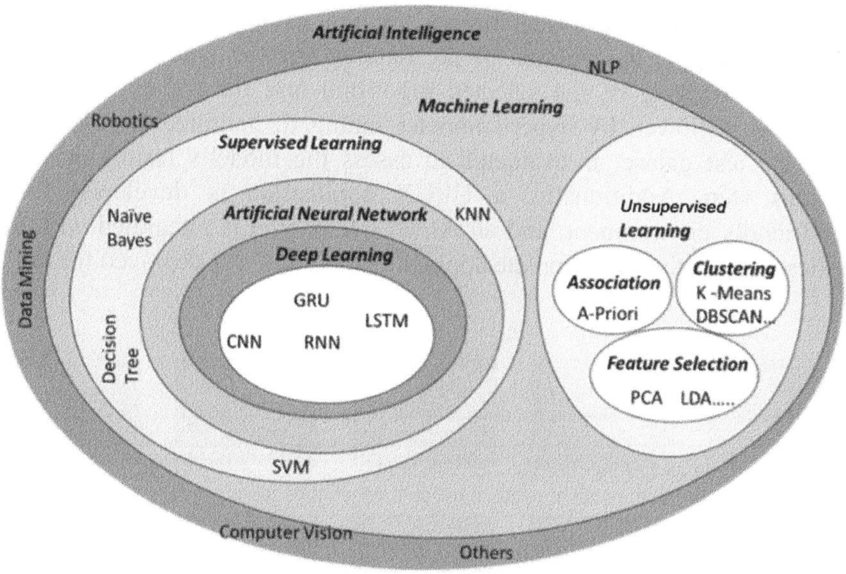

Figure 3.2. *AI–ML–DL relationship and respective techniques*

One of these is ANN and a special case of it is DL. There is more than one hidden layer in a DL architecture, apart from the input and output layers. Different DL architectures include CNN, RNN, LSTM, GRU, etc.

Unsupervised machine learning is based on descriptive analysis and is used to identify hidden patterns in unlabeled data. It includes techniques such as clustering, association rule mining and feature selection.

Clustering methods group data points according to their similarities and differences, with commonly used algorithms including K-means, DBSCAN and hierarchical clustering. Association rule mining, on the other hand, identifies relationships and dependencies among variables within a dataset.

3.3.2. *Steps in AI application development*

Figure 3.3 shows the typical steps followed for any AI application development. The first step starts with problem identification followed by data preparation, which includes data cleaning, as well as data wrangling to prepare accurate data that can be supplied to the ML/DL algorithm in the next step. The next step requires an appropriate algorithm from a vast array of ML/DL algorithms, as determined by the complexity of the problem defined in step 1, the volume of the dataset and the type of the dataset. Thereafter, training of the selected algorithm and the training dataset is performed, followed by hyperparameter tuning to optimize the algorithm. Next, the test dataset is evaluated to assess the model's results from the previous step. Additionally, a UI/UX application is developed for a user-friendly environment, and an AI/ML/DL model is integrated with this application. Lastly, the complete application is tested and deployed for use.

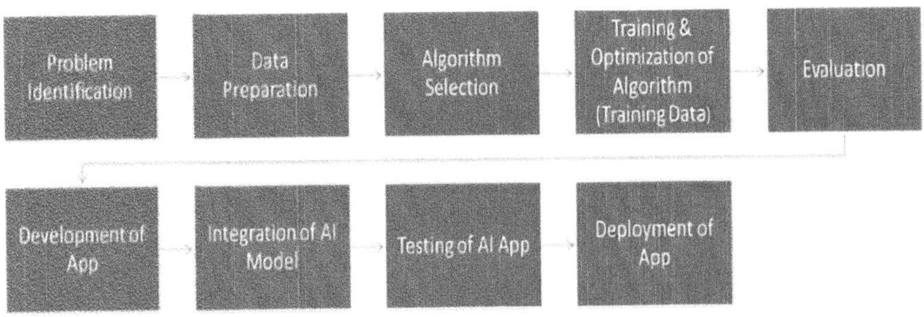

Figure 3.3. *Steps of AI development*

3.4. Applications of AI in energy sectors and sustainability

The models based on AI, ML and DL are being widely employed in the energy sector to leverage the power of predictive techniques for energy forecasting and optimization. In contrast, descriptive techniques are used for anomaly detection and intelligent building management. Additionally, AI-driven models may be utilized to forecast the energy usage by HVAC in buildings and also to facilitate active load balancing in power and systems. AI applications in the energy domain are as follows:

- AI for optimizing energy production and consumption;
- smart grids and EMS (energy management systems);
- renewable energy optimization and energy forecasting;
- monitoring and reducing carbon footprint;
- climate analysis and forecasting;
- contribute to reducing greenhouse gas emissions;
- demand forecasting and load balancing;
- predictive maintenance in energy infrastructure;
- circular energy systems and waste reduction;
- behavioral energy analytics;
- AI in policy and planning.

AI can be employed broadly in four domains in the energy sector: prediction, automation, optimization, as well as decision-making in the energy and sustainability context. Prediction includes predicting the energy consumed in buildings, energy price prediction, climate forecasting and its impact on energy systems, prediction of renewable energy integration, etc.

AI-based automation encompasses the automation of smart cities, smart homes, buildings and industrial plants, leveraging the power of AI-enabled HVAC systems and other appliances.

Similarly, optimization includes traffic optimization, energy optimization in batteries, optimization of solar and wind energy and power grids, optimization for renewable energies and electric vehicle infrastructure optimization.

Decision-making can be applied in various domains of energy and sustainability, for example, in data-driven decisions for the transition to renewable energy in smart cities and infrastructure, as well as in decision-making for policymakers.

3.4.1. *Applications of ML (supervised learning) in the energy sector*

As aforementioned, supervised learning is predictive in nature. It can be used in the following applications:

– energy price prediction;

– fault detection;

– demand and load prediction;

– prediction of energy consumption;

– climate analysis and forecasting.

3.4.2. *Applications of ML (unsupervised learning) in the energy sector*

A few applications of unsupervised ML are listed as follows:

– grouping of energy consumption pattern;

– energy management systems;

– anomaly detection.

3.4.3. *Applications of DL in the energy sector*

A few applications of DL are listed as follows:

– investigate and analyze the thermal image data;

– sensor image data;

– fault detection in renewable energy plants;

– time-series analysis for energy consumption prediction;

– forecasting of renewable electricity generation;

– smart grid optimization.

3.5. Case study

The research article presents a case study, titled "Energy prediction of HVAC plants in commercial buildings using machine learning techniques". The case study was conducted on the dataset for an entire year, which was from a hotel building in New Delhi, India. The data was from the Cooling Tower, an integral component of HVAC (Heating, Ventilation and Air Conditioning unit) (Ul Haq 2024). The data had been recorded using sensors, hence it was raw and unprocessed. Therefore, it was pre-processed to prepare it for experimental work.

3.5.1. *Methodology*

The methodology adopted in the research work can be seen in Figure 3.4.

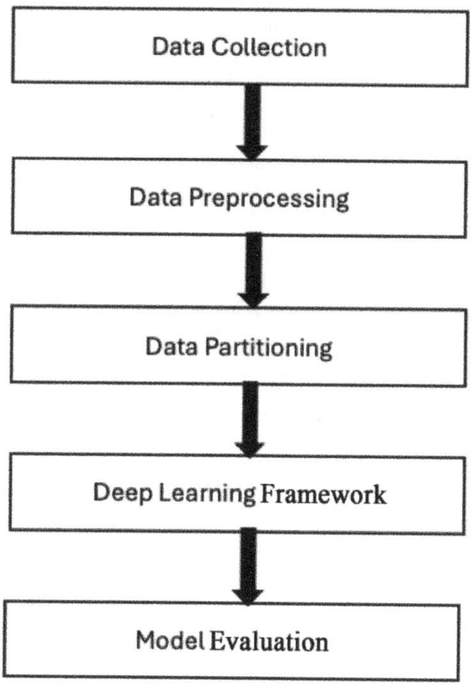

Figure 3.4. *Methodology*

The workflow adopted in this research work begins with collecting data from an HVAC unit in a commercial building, followed by pre-processing, data partitioning and development of a DL framework including the tuning of hyper parameters. Finally, the evaluation of the models developed was performed using standard performance metrics, namely, RMSE, MSE, MAE and R squared for GRU.

There are five input variables (I1, I2, I3, I4 and I5) and an output variable (O1) in the dataset. Table 3.2 shows the description of the attributes used in the dataset, as well as the measurement units of each attribute.

Symbol	Attribute name	Attribute description	Measuring unit
I1	Dry bulb temperature, abbreviated as DBT (Ul Haq 2024)	Ambient temperature (Ul Haq 2024)	°C
I2	Relative humidity abbreviated as RH (Ul Haq 2024)	Water vapor in the air relative to temperature (Ul Haq 2024)	%
I3	Wet bulb temperature abbreviated as WBT (Ul Haq 2024)	The brought down temperature by water evaporation (Ul Haq 2024)	°C
I4	Cooling tower inlet temperature abbreviated as CT-INLET (Goyal and Pandey 2020)	Temperature of the water entering into the cooling tower (Goyal and Pandey 2020)	°C (Goyal and Pandey 2020)
I5	Cooling tower outlet temperature abbreviated as CT_OUTLET (Goyal and Pandey 2020)	Temperature of the water exiting from the cooling tower (Goyal and Pandey 2020)	°C (Goyal and Pandey 2020)
O1	Cooling tower power consumed abbreviated as CT_POWER (Goyal and Pandey 2020)	The power consumed by the cooling tower (Goyal and Pandey 2020)	KW (Goyal and Pandey 2020)

Table 3.2. *Dataset attribute description (Goyal and Pandey 2020)*

The 12 month dataset is divided into two categories, namely, humid months and non-humid months. May to November fall in the category of humid months, and December to April belong to the category of non-humid months. In this research, two months, namely, August and April, have been selected for the analysis from each of the categories.

For data cleaning, several operations have been performed on the dataset, including removal of extra records, integration of files and replacement of missing values with suitable values as per the patterns of the neighboring data points value (as the data is time series). Also, a new parameter, "Wet Bulb Temperature" has been derived. This parameter helps in accurate prediction of energy consumption. Additionally, data scaling has also been performed.

Statistical analysis was also performed, as a part of data preprocessing. Further, data partitioning was done, where the dataset was split into two parts, namely, a training dataset and a testing dataset. The ratio of the partitioned dataset into training and testing data subsets was 70%–30%, respectively.

A DL model created using GRUs has been applied on the commercial building dataset. Five models total were constructed by changing the count of hidden layers and changing the count of neurons present in each hidden layer.

3.5.2. *Comparison of GRU with ensemble models*

The comparative results of GRU with ensemble models, namely, GBM, XGBOOST and Bagging are represented in Table 3.3. The results show that among all the three ensemble models, XGBOOST is performing better compared to GBM and Bagging, with appreciable amounts.

The error values (RMSE, MSE and MAE) obtained are quite low for XGBOOST in comparison to GBM and Bagging models. However, for the DL model, GRU is far better than XGBOOST.

Algorithm family	Name of the algorithm	Root mean squared error (RMSE)		Mean squared error (MSE)		Mean absolute error (MAE)		R squared (coefficient of determination)	
	Month	April	August	April	August	April	August	April	August
Ensemble	Gradient boosting machines	4.12	3.31	28.3	13.83	2.6	0.84	0.8	0.77
	XGBOOST	0.437	2.81	0.19	7.89	0.22	0.6	0.99	0.5
	Bagging	4.63	3.87	21.43	14.97	2.88	0.78	0.61	0.23
ANN (proposed)	GRU	0.0776	0.0699	0.006	0.0049	0.0521	0.0193	0.6012	0.1211

Table 3.3. *Comparison of GRU with ensemble models (Ul Haq 2024)*

3.6. Conclusion

This research proposed a DL framework using gated recurrent units for accurately forecasting the consumption of energy with respect to HVAC plants for a commercial building dataset. The research work concludes that ANN architecture is one of the better choices for energy forecasting, particularly for energy consumption prediction for HVAC plants. GRUs are sufficient enough to handle time series datasets and those with lowest error function values. GRU results are significantly better than state-of-the-art ensemble learning methods, namely, GBM, XGBOOST and Bagging. Since the results of the GRU model outperformed in this research, the model can also be considered useful for energy prediction in similar buildings in the future.

3.7. References

Ahmad, M.W., Mourshed, M., Rezgui, Y. (2017). Trees vs neurons: Comparison between random forest and ANN for high-resolution prediction of building energy consumption. *Energy and Buildings*, 147, 77–89.

Alpaydin, E. (2020). *Introduction to Machine Learning*, 4th edition. MIT Press, Cambridge, MA.

Araya, D.B., Grolinger, K., ElYamany, H.F., Capretz, M.A., Bitsuamlak, G. (2017). An ensemble learning framework for anomaly detection in building energy consumption. *Energy and Buildings*, 144, 191–206.

Bui, D.K., Nguyen, T.N., Ngo, T.D., Nguyen-Xuan, H. (2020). An artificial neural network (ANN) expert system enhanced with the electromagnetism-based firefly algorithm (EFA) for predicting the energy consumption in buildings. *Energy*, 190, 116370.

Fan, C., Xiao, F., Wang, S. (2014). Development of prediction models for next-day building energy consumption and peak power demand using data mining techniques. *Applied Energy*, 127, 1–10.

Goodfellow, Y., Bengio, Courville, A. (2016). *Deep Learning*. MIT Press, Cambridge, MA.

Goyal, M. and Pandey, M. (2020). Towards prediction of energy consumption of HVAC plants using machine learning. In *Data Science and Analytics. REDSET 2019. Communications in Computer and Information Science*, Batra, U., Roy, N., Panda, B. (eds). Springer, Singapore.

Peng, Y., Rysanek, A., Nagy, Z., Schlüter, A. (2018). Using machine learning techniques for occupancy-prediction-based cooling control in office buildings. *Applied Energy*, 211, 1343–1358.

Ul Haq, I. (2024). Diagnosis of neurological disease using bioinspired algorithms. In *Bio-Inspired Optimization for Medical Data Mining*, Srivastava, S., Anand, A., Kumar, A. et al. (eds). John Wiley & Sons, Hoboken, NJ.

Ul Haq, I. and Khanday, A.M.U.D. (2025). Exploring the role of explainable AI in women's health: Challenges and solutions. In *Explainable Artificial Intelligence in the Healthcare Industry*, Kumar, A., Kumar, T.A., Das, P. et al. (eds). John Wiley & Sons, Hoboken, NJ.

Ul Haq, I., Kumar, N., Koul, N., Verma, C., Eneacu, F.M., Raboaca, M.S. (2022). Machine learning techniques for result prediction of one day international (ODI) cricket match. In *The International Conference on Recent Innovations in Computing*. Springer, Singapore.

Ul Haq, I., Kaur, G., Rather, A.H. (2024). Fruit leaf classification using transfer learning for automation and industrial applications. In *Deep Learning Techniques for Automation and Industrial Applications*, Rathore, P.S., Ahuja, S., Burri, S.R. et al. (eds). John Wiley & Sons, Hoboken, NJ, 151–178.

Ul Haq, I., Kumar, A., Rathore, P.S. (2025a). Machine learning approaches for wind power forecasting: A comprehensive review. *Discover Applied Sciences*, 7(10), 1139.

Ul Haq, I., Malhotra, J., Rawat, V., Kumari, J., Kaur, G. (2025b). Machine learning approaches for early detection of cervical cancer: A comparative study of classification models. In *Targeted Chemotherapy with Personalized Immunotherapy: An AI Approach*, Kumar, A., Das, P., Rathore, P.S. et al. (eds). John Wiley & Sons, Hoboken, NJ.

Ul Haq, I., Nandal, V., Uppal, H. (2025c). Blockchain applications in aviation securing transactions, streamlining operations, and improving passenger experience. In *Blockchain in the Tourism Industry: A New Era of Secure and Transparent Travel Solutions*, Kumar, A., Abreu, A., Batta, P. et al. (eds). Springer, Cham.

Ul Haq, I., Shah, H.A., Rufai, S.Z. (2025d). Enhancing water security through automation: Case studies and technical advancements in water quality management. *Computational Automation for Water Security*, Dubey, A.K., Srivastav, A.L., Kumar, A. et al. (eds). Elsevier, Amsterdam.

4

Conceptual and Methodological Insights into AI, ML and DL for Energy and Environmental Challenges

The growing rate of environmental and energy demands in the world has increased the need to have intelligent, anthropomorphic solutions that will aid in the resolution of multifaceted, interrelated issues. Artificial intelligence (AI), machine learning (ML) and deep learning (DL) are new technologies that have allowed perfect prediction, flexibility in decision-making and resource optimization in environmental and energy systems. This chapter has critically presented the theoretical basics and methodological progression of AI-driven tools that can be used in environmental surveillance, climate change management, renewable energy management and sustainable design of infrastructure. The chapter begins with the introduction of the key principles of AI, ML and DL, and how they can be applicable to the current challenges of sustainability. It then proceeds to talk about the various sources of data acquisition such as the Internet of Things (IoT), satellite pictures, sensor networks and remote sensing systems, and how they can be useful in building smart environmental models. In addition, the chapter provides details on how AI-based methods can be used to create a predictive model of climate forecasting, air and water quality evaluation and extreme event detection, which is why adaptive and self-learning systems via reinforcement learning and deep neural networks are discussed in the case of smart grids, precision agriculture and ecosystem management. Other vital issues covered in the chapter include bias in data, model transparency, ethical issues and regulatory barriers. Last but not least, new trends, such as combining blockchain, digital twins and green AI are mentioned as the direction for resilience and sustainability of environmental and energy applications in the future. The article offers scholars, policymakers and practitioners useful information on how to design and implement intelligent systems to promote the objectives of global sustainability.

Chapter written by Inderdeep KAUR.

4.1. Introduction

The high rates of industrialization and urbanization that have been experienced in the last century have led to a great improvement in the living standards of humans, but on the opposite side, there has been extreme destruction of the environment and an unsustainable pressure on natural resources (Kaur and Ali 2024a). Rising global energy requirements, greenhouse gas emission, climate change, air/water pollution, deforestation and loss of biodiversity are some of the most urgent issues afflicting humans today (Saini et al. 2024).

This chapter is devoted to providing a conceptual and methodological understanding of how AI-based methods could be utilized to increase the efficiency of energy, promote renewable energy structures and address the control of environmental risks. AI, ML and DL, through the analysis of trends, can help to create smarter, resilient and sustainable ecosystems of energy and environmental management.

4.1.1. *Background and motivation*

People, economic growth and technology are increasing energy demand, which has resulted in a never before strain on traditional sources of energy such as coal, oil and natural gas. Fossil fuels do not only play a part in depleting resources, but they are also the main source of carbon dioxide and other greenhouse gases that are increasing the pace of global warming.

With the pressure to achieve a transition between traditional energy systems and renewable ones like solar, wind, hydro and geothermal energy, there has been a rush to switch to cleaner sources of energy.

The nature of renewable sources is variable and unpredictable, and remains largely dependent on weather conditions and geographical consideration (Ul Haq et al. 2025a). The control of supply and demand, optimization of storage systems, forecasting of energy generation and incorporation of renewable energy in existing grids are extremely complicated issues.

The nature of energy systems presents high levels of data intensity, dynamism and non-linearity, which are usually difficult to manage using traditional analytical tools. Here, AI, ML and DL can be a great motivation.

These technologies provide the opportunity to process a great amount of structured and unstructured data, find hidden trends, learn from past trends and make correct predictions in the moment (Ul Haq et al. 2024).

AI solutions with good performance have been observed in the last few years in areas such as weather forecasting, optimization of smart grids, energy consumption prediction and monitoring pollution.

This chapter is driven by the growing need to study how these new advanced methods of computation can be exploited as part of a strategic way of eliminating any existing constraints in the managerial treatment of energy and the environment.

Moreover, the combination of AI with IoT, remote sensing systems and big data analytics has provided new opportunities to monitor energy and environmental systems in real-time and control them intelligently. Researchers, policymakers and engineers who aim to find sustainable solutions need to understand the conceptual foundation and methodological approaches of these technologies.

4.1.2. *Energy and environmental challenges in the modern era*

The contemporary world can be defined as one of unprecedented rates of energy usage and influences on the environment. Global energy reports have indicated that the world is projected to experience a high energy demand in the coming decades, especially in third world countries. Performing this requirement using current fossil fuel-powered systems would further aggravate climate change, elevate pollution rates and add to the destruction of the ecosystem.

Climate change is one of the biggest challenges that is due to the carbon emissions of industrial work, transport, power generation and deforestation. The increase in the world temperature leads to melting glaciers, rising sea levels, adverse weather patterns and agricultural cycle disturbances. This, in its turn, poses a threat to food security, availability of water and the health of people globally.

Energy wastage is another major problem. The infrastructure and systems are outdated, which contributes to the wastage of large amounts of energy in production, transmission and consumption. The problems that power grids experience include voltage instability, power losses, load imbalance and outages. At the same time, the storage capacity to contain excess energy produced by renewable energy is minimal, and thus it goes to waste.

Air, water and soil pollution have also increased through urbanization and industrialization. Smog, polluted water and solid waste management are issues in cities. Deforestation, mining and industrial wastes are creating permanent destruction to the ecosystem and biodiversity. Conventional surveillance systems are usually not accurate in terms of real-time and predictability, and as such, it can be difficult to take precautionary measures.

All of these challenges are multi-dimensional, interconnected and complex. They need adaptable and smart solutions that would dynamically respond to the changing circumstances. This has prompted the need to hasten research on AI-driven methodologies that can provide scalable and efficient solutions.

4.1.3. *Role of AI, ML and DL in sustainable development*

ML, AI and DL have a transformative effect on sustainable development and can offer intelligent systems to analyze, predict and optimize complex systems (Shahverdi et al. 2025). The role of AI, ML and DL in sustainable development is depicted in Figure 4.1.

AI algorithms have the capacity to analyze large volumes of data involving satellite imagery, weather sensors, smart meters and environmental monitoring equipment to give precise predictions and intelligent action. ML models in renewable energy systems are also applied to predict solar irradiance and speed of wind, which allows better prediction of energy generation. This helps grid operators to plan energy distribution more effectively and minimize the use of a backup fossil fuel system.

Convolutional neural networks (CNNs) and recurrent neural networks (RNNs) are DL methods that are currently utilized in weather prediction, power load prediction and anomaly detection on smart grids.

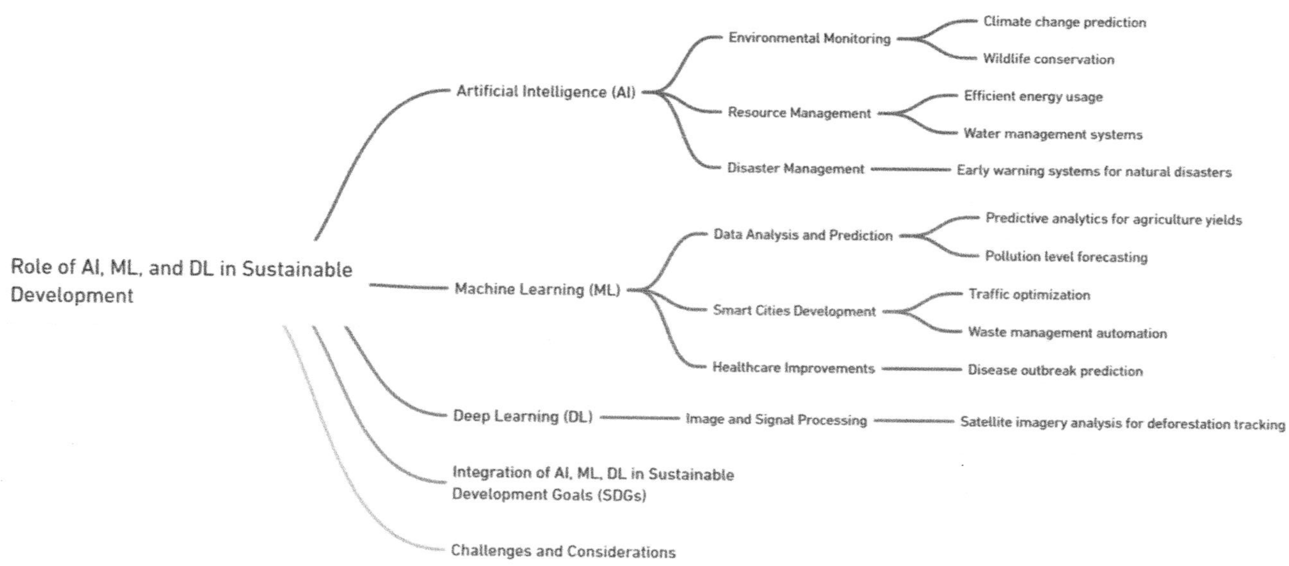

Figure 4.1. *Role of AI, ML and DL in sustainable development. For a color version of this figure, see www.iste.co.uk/ulhaq/artificial1.zip*

AI is also used to achieve better energy use in constructions and factories through optimization of heating, air conditioning (HVAC), ventilation, lighting and production. Energy management systems (Smart) apply reinforcement learning and regulate the amount of energy consumed according to demand patterns, cost indicators and occupancy behavior. The environmental sphere is another area where AI is used to track deforestation, monitor wildlife species, predict floods and drought, and identify pollution rates. AI-enhanced remote sensing and image recognition will enable early identification of environmental degradation, allowing timely responses and implementation of effective conservation strategies. Predictive models help the policy maker to assess the impact of different decisions on the environment over extended periods (Kaur and Ali 2025). Besides that, AI plays a critical role in a circular economy, such as in sorting out waste, recycling optimization and sustainable resources. The given contributions are associated with the sustainability objectives on a worldwide level, and AI can be regarded as one of the most important contributions to implementation of green technologies and environmental sustainability.

4.1.4. *Objectives and scope of the chapter*

The main goal of this chapter is to offer a full picture of how AI, ML and DL may be applied to deal with the urgent energy and environmental issues. It is supposed to link the gap between theoretical knowledge and its practical application by offering both theoretical principles and applications.

In particular, the chapter will aim to:

1) research the key concepts and principles of AI, ML and DL related to the sustainability issue;

2) discuss the ways in which these technologies will be able to maximize the generation of renewable energy, storage and distribution;

3) talk about methodology to use in forecasting energy demands, load balancing and smart grid management;

4) current uses of AI in environmental surveillance, climate prediction and environmental pollution;

5) identify major challenges, limitations and ethical issues related to AI-driven solutions;

6) offer an understanding of future trends and research directions of AI to develop sustainably.

The area of focus in this chapter is broad and covers a large field of topics such as the renewable energy systems, smart cities, environmental, climate change mitigation and sustainable resource management. This chapter aims to provide an invaluable resource to students, researchers, engineers and policymakers who find it necessary to utilize advanced technologies to help them build a more sustainable and resilient future.

4.2. Conceptual foundations of AI, ML and DL

AI, ML and DL are closely related fields of computer science that can collectively enable machines to exhibit behavior resembling human intelligence (Magazzino 2024). These technologies are the foundation of the contemporary data-driven systems and contribute greatly to solving complex energy and environmental issues. Although AI is the general vision, the specific subsets, which enable systems to improve with time and learn information, are ML and DL. These technologies have evolved in their concept, and developed paradigms and architecture, which makes it necessary to analyze the role of this technology in sustainable development and the optimization of energy.

The following section will discuss the historical progress of AI, significant paradigms in the learning process under ML, major architectures in DL and a comparison between the traditional modeling and the DL-based techniques.

4.2.1. *Evolution of AI*

The idea of AI can be traced back to ancient times, when philosophers and scientists could contemplate the possibility of inanimate objects having the kind of intelligence that humans have (Ul Haq et al. 2022). Nevertheless, the development of AI as a scientific discipline started in the middle of the 20th century.

In 1956, AI was actually coined at the Dartmouth Conference held by John McCarthy, Marvin Minsky, Nathaniel Rochester and Claude Shannon. The initial aim of AI was ambitious, as it aimed to create machines that could reproduce the process of human thinking, problem solving and learning. The evolution of AI in different domains is shown in Figure 4.2.

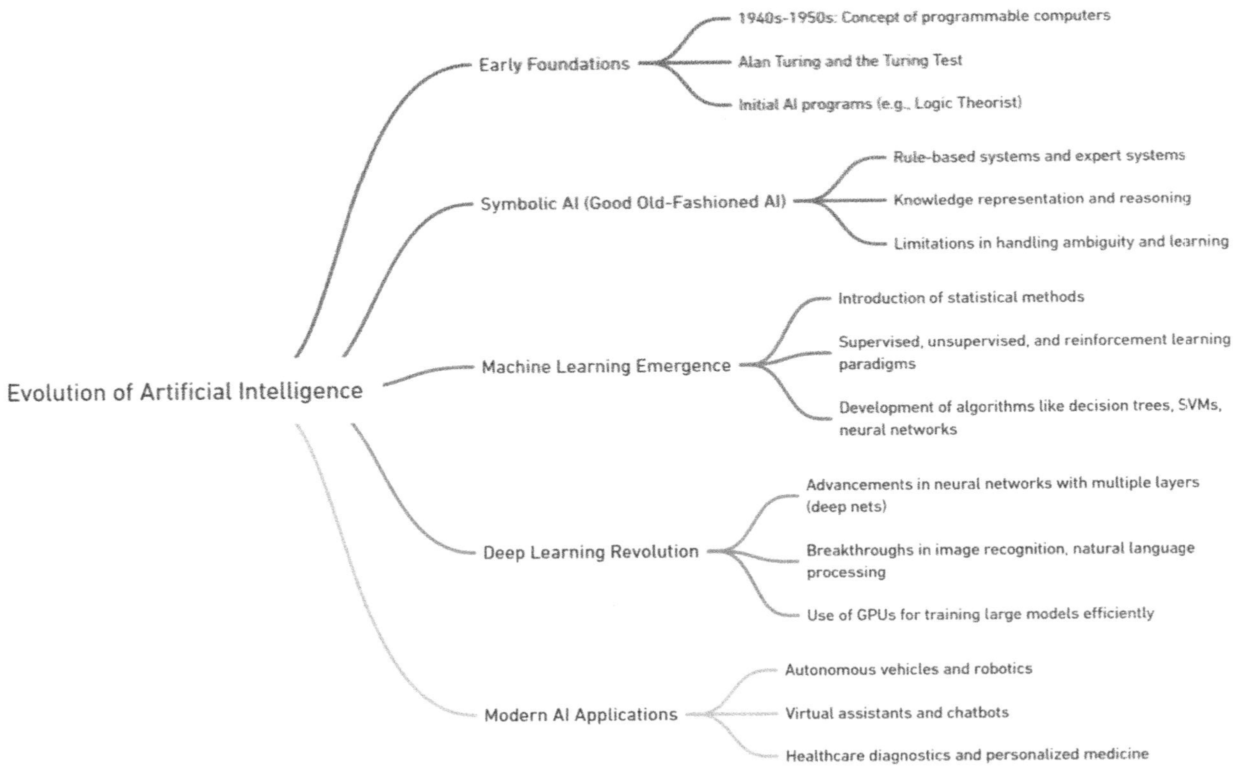

Figure 4.2. *Evolution of artificial intelligence. For a color version of this figure, see www.iste.co.uk/ulhaq/artificial1.zip*

The early years of AI (1950s and 1960s) saw mainly symbolic AI and rule-based systems. These early programs were based on rules and logical thinking to figure out or solve problems, like when playing chess or solving mathematical theorems. Even though the early performances showed prospects, such systems were not flexible and could not learn with experience, and they eventually failed in real-world situations.

The 1970s–1990s are sometimes called the AI Winter, as there was a decrease in funding and interest in research on AI as it did not live up to an unrealistic hype. However, in the background, there was a great advancement in the field of expert systems, which were based on specific, domain-oriented knowledge that aided in decision-making in medicine, engineering and finance.

Three key factors, namely, the explosive growth of digital data, increase in computational power (in particular, GPUs) and progress in ML algorithms, have contributed to the revival of AI in the late 1990s and early 2000s. The new period changed the emphasis on rule-guided programming to data-driven learning systems, which became the basis of modern ML and DL systems.

Currently, AI has developed as an interdisciplinary field including data science, neuroscience, robotics, linguistics and cognitive science. It is transformative in energy systems, environmental monitoring and climate modeling, where it can provide intelligent and adaptive solutions to the global challenge of sustainability.

4.2.2. *ML paradigms: supervised, unsupervised and reinforcement learning*

ML is a branch of AI that allows systems to learn trends based on data, and make decisions without being directed on how to do so. The ML algorithms do not only enhance performance through experience as opposed to pre-defined rules (Kaur and Ali 2024b). ML has three main learning paradigms, namely, supervised learning, unsupervised learning and reinforcement learning.

4.2.2.1. *Supervised learning*

This requires a model to be trained on a labeled set of data, where every input has a known output (Ul Haq et al. 2025c). The algorithm is trained to learn a mapping function of input to the output and applies this to forecasted outcomes of unknown, novel data. Supervised learning is also popular in classification and regression, and useful in predicting energy demand, estimating pollution or classifying the land use in satellite images. Widely used supervised learning algorithms are linear regression, logistic regression, support vector machines (SVM), decision trees, random forests (RFs) and neural networks.

4.2.2.2. *Unsupervised learning*

Unsupervised learning, in turn, works with unlabeled data. It aims to extract latent patterns, patterns or relationships in the input data (Kaur and Ul Hassan 2025). Unsupervised methods of learning include clustering and dimensionality reduction. K-means, hierarchical clustering, DBSCAN and principal component analysis (PCA) are common examples of algorithms used in environmental studies in order to cluster areas by similar climates, notice unusual sensor values or pinpoint pollution origins.

4.2.2.3. *Reinforcement learning (RL)*

It is a behavioral psychology-inspired approach that trains an agent to make a sequence of decisions by interacting with an environment (Ul Haq et al. 2025d). The agent also learns by trial and error, where the agent is rewarded or punished according to its behavior. It eventually learns the best strategy (policy) to maximize cumulative rewards.

Reinforcement learning has also been used in energy management systems where an agent can be trained to regulate energy consumption, balance workloads in a smart grid or optimize battery charging and discharging cycles in renewable energy storage systems.

These three learning paradigms offer different yet complementary methods of approaching real-life problems. They allow proper prediction, effective classification, automated control and dynamic optimization in the framework of energy and environmental systems.

4.2.3. *DL architectures: CNNs, RNNs, LSTMs and transformers*

DL is a special branch of ML, which involves applying multi-layered neural networks to approximate nonlinear relationships in data. They are modeled after the form and mechanism of the human brain and made of several layers of interconnected artificial neurons (Sharma et al. 2024a). DL has become incredibly popular because it has been shown to outperform other technologies in image recognition, natural language processing, time-series prediction and speech recognition.

CNNs are algorithms that are mainly applied to visual and spatial information, including images and videos (Ul Haq and Khanday 2025). They are variably structured in terms of convolutional layers that automatically detect meaningful features such as edges, textures and patterns. CNNs find application in environmental science to analyze satellite images to determine deforestation, urban growth, land use and polluted water bodies.

RNNs are modeled to deal with sequential data and time-series information by storing the memory of past inputs. This renders them applicable in tasks like weather forecasting and energy load forecasting, as well as air quality analysis. Nevertheless, the classical RNNs cannot overcome the long-term dependencies because of the vanishing gradient issues.

To address this weakness, long short-term memory (LSTM) networks were created. LSTMs have memory gates and special memory units to store and remember valuable information across a long sequence of data. They have become very useful in predicting renewable energy generation, studying climate trend and predicting demand patterns in intelligent energy systems.

More recently, transformers have gained strong performance as DL architectures based on attention mechanisms as opposed to sequence-based processing. Transformers are able to examine the relationship between large datasets in parallel and are quite efficient in capturing complex interactions. Transformer-based models have become more popular in energy and environmental studies because of the data fusion tasks in relation to multi-source issues, climate modeling and long-term forecasting activities.

These DL designs enable very precise and scalable solutions that are vital elements of new generation energy and environmental management systems.

4.2.4. Comparison of traditional models versus DL approaches

Traditional predictive modeling and classification ML models have been applied in predictive modeling and classification tasks to support vehicle and vehicle components, including linear regression, SVM, decision trees and k-nearest neighbors. Such models tend to be manually featured and domain knowledge in order to find the input features. They work well on small to medium-sized datasets and are less difficult to interpret and implement. Traditional models are often applied in the field of energy and environmental studies as they are easy to understand and follow. The comparison of traditional ML models vs. DL approaches are shown in Table 4.1.

However, traditional methods are mostly ineffective in handling high-dimensional, highly complex and unstructured data, for example, satellite images, sensor networks and extensive climate data. They are likely to perform poorly in situations where the relationships are not linear and when the data volumes are huge.

DL methods, on the other hand, are capable of automatically learning hierarchical feature representations on raw data and do not require significant amounts of manual feature engineering. They are also more accurate at processing large scale and unstructured information, meaning that they have much higher accuracy in image recognition, time series forecasting and pattern detection. In addition, DL models have the capability to incorporate various sources of data including weather data, sensor data and geographical information into a single predictive model.

In spite of their strengths, DL models have some weaknesses. They need huge data sets, immense computation and even more training. Also, they can be supposedly black boxes, which are more difficult to interpret and explain. This non-transparency may pose some ethical and practical issues in vital fields such as energy policy and environmental regulation.

Finally, there are strong and weak aspects of both the traditional and DL models. A smart hybrid system integrating traditional solutions, and DL structures may provide an effective and balanced solution to the complex energy and environmental challenges in the most efficient and responsible manner.

Aspect	Traditional machine learning models	Deep learning approaches
Feature engineering	Require manual feature extraction and rely heavily on domain knowledge	Automatically learn hierarchical and complex feature representations from raw data
Data requirements	Perform well on small to medium-sized datasets	Require very large datasets to achieve high performance
Ability to handle data complexity	Struggle with high-dimensional, unstructured and highly nonlinear data (e.g. satellite images and sensor networks)	Excellent at processing unstructured, high-dimensional and complex data such as images, time series and sensor streams
Model accuracy	Good accuracy for simpler, structured datasets	Typically higher accuracy, especially for image recognition, forecasting and pattern analysis
Interpretability	Easy to interpret, understand and explain	Often considered "black boxes" with low interpretability
Computational requirements	Low computational cost; fast to train and deploy	High computational cost; require GPUs/TPUs and long training time
Application domains	Suitable for straightforward tasks in energy and environmental studies where interpretability is important	Suitable for large-scale energy forecasting, climate modeling, sensor fusion and complex pattern recognition
Flexibility in data integration	Limited capability to integrate multiple heterogeneous data sources	High capability to combine weather data, sensor feeds, geographical data, etc., into a unified model
Strengths	Simple, interpretable, easy to implement; effective for small datasets	High accuracy, automatically learns features, handles complex data efficiently
Weaknesses	Poor performance on complex, nonlinear or massive datasets	Requires big data, heavy computation, hard to interpret; potential ethical and regulatory concerns
Overall suitability	Good for simpler and interpretable analysis; foundational baseline models	Best for advanced, complex and large-scale predictions requiring high accuracy
Ideal strategy	Limited for modern large-scale energy challenges	Works best when combined with traditional models in hybrid systems

Table 4.1. *Comparison of traditional machine learning models versus deep learning approaches*

4.3. Methodologies for environmental data acquisition

Intelligence systems on the environment are very dependent on the availability of big, wide and precise data. The quality, quantity and relevance of data under analysis determine the efficacy of AI, ML and DL models in solving environmental and energy dilemmas. Contemporary environmental monitoring systems combine the data on various sources including the IoT, satellite imagery, unmanned aerial vehicles (UAVs) and sensor networks. Such data are in turn analyzed by state-of-the-art big data platforms, preprocessed by cleaning and transforming data, and checked to make sure that they are reliable. This section discusses the key methodologies that are involved in data acquisition, data management and preparation of data in the environmental data so that intelligent analysis can be done.

4.3.1. *Data sources: IoT, satellite imagery, UAVs and sensor networks*

The contemporary environmental surveillance system rests on the large diversity of various data sources. Both sources present different insights and complete each other to form a comprehensive understanding of the environmental conditions at local, regional and global levels.

The IoT is also essential in real-time gathering of environmental data (Saini and Kaur 2025). Smart meters, weather stations, soil moisture sensors, air quality sensors and water level gauges are IoT appliances that are installed both in the city and in the countryside. These instruments constantly monitor the data on the parameters of temperature, humidity, rainfall, concentration of particulate matter, carbon dioxide level, noise pollution and indicators of water quality (pH, turbidity and dissolved oxygen). IoT devices can be linked to each other and transfer information in a wireless mode, allowing them to monitor the environment continuously and in real-time, creating the conditions under which an early warning system and adaptive management can work.

Another strong source of data in environmental science is satellite imagery. Sentinel, Terra, Landsat and MODIS earth-observing satellites give high-resolution images of the Earth surface on a regular basis. These images have become widely utilized in land use and land cover (LULC) mapping, deforestation surveillance, glacier melting research, ocean temperature research, urban growth detection and climate modeling. The global scale of satellite data makes it incredibly useful in the process of tracking large-scale processes of desertification, rise in sea level and forest fires.

Drones, technically referred to as UAVs, offer a medium scale between earth sensors and satellites. They are very agile and are able to fly at low altitudes in addition to take high resolution images and videos. UAVs are being applied in environmental surveys of inaccessible regions such as forests, wetlands, mountains and disaster-prone regions, among others. They assist in the use of applications over wildlife population, crop health, detecting illegal mining and oil spills.

Sensor networks are composed of distributed nodes, which are able to gather and relay information on a co-ordinated basis. The networks are commonly installed in forests, seas, rivers, farmlands and industrial areas. Indicatively, underwater sensor networks can be used to track ocean currents and the quality of water, whereas forest sensor networks can be used to track early wildfire indicators like changes in temperature and humidity. They can be used together with AI-based systems that will facilitate the mechanism of responding quickly to avoid catastrophic damage.

IoT devices, satellites, UAVs and sensor networks can be used together to create a multi-scale, multi-dimensional data infrastructure, around which intelligent environmental monitoring systems are built.

4.3.2. *Big data and cloud platforms for environmental analysis*

Modern monitoring systems produce large amounts of environmental data which necessitate high-order computing infrastructures to store, process and analyze. The technologies of big data and cloud computing platforms become significant.

Big data is normally categorized as environmental datasets because they are large. Single satellite imagery is capable of spawning terabytes of data every day, and IoT sensors generate a continuous stream of high-frequency data. The traditional system of data processing cannot handle such volumes. Large data systems like Hadoop and Apache Spark allow scalability in processing, which means that the information can be processed in a group of servers. The frameworks greatly cut down the time of computation and allow real-time or close-to-real-time analysis of environmental data.

Google Earth Engine, Amazon Web Services (AWS), Microsoft Arizona and IBM Cloud are some of the cloud computing platforms that have transformed the analysis of environmental data. Such systems can offer scalable storage capabilities, high-performance computing and geospatial analysis specialists. Policy makers and researchers can now have access to large environmental data without the need to invest in physical hardware infrastructure. Predictive models can also be built, trained and deployed effectively using cloud-based AI and ML services.

As an illustration, Google Earth Engine offers decades of satellite imagery and geospatial datasets, and also allows researchers to conduct complex environmental analysis on-site. In the same way, real-time dashboards on the environment that visualize air quality, weather and disaster warnings are supported by cloud services, helping decision-makers and the general public.

As big data and cloud computing become increasingly integrated, efficiency improves and sophisticated analytical tools become accessible, which enables smaller organizations and developing areas to participate in environmental data science projects.

4.3.3. *Data preprocessing and feature engineering*

Raw environmental data can tend to be noisy, incomplete and inconsistent such that they cannot be directly analyzed (Patil 2024). Thus, feature engineering and data preprocessing are essential for data preparation to be used successfully in AI and ML models.

Some of the important tasks that are involved in data preprocessing include data cleaning, missing values, outliers, normalization and transformation. Sensor information can be inaccurate because of failure of hardware or communication problems, whereas satellite images can be distorted by clouds, atmospheric penetration or sensor noise. Such errors should be rectified and then data can be relied upon.

Missing values can be interpolated, whereas outliers can be eliminated or fixed with the use of statistical tools. Normalization and scaling are useful to bring diverse features to a similar range, which is particularly significant for ML algorithms that are sensitive to data scale.

The process of deriving useful variables (features) of raw data that can be used to enhance model performance is known as feature engineering. An example is that, given temperature and humidity values, a heat index can be computed to indicate environmental stress situations more accurately. Spectral bands are used to calculate vegetation health in the form of vegetation indices, such as the normalized difference vegetation index (NDVI) in satellite imagery. Time-related characteristics like seasonal variations, daily averages and long-term variations are also elicited to facilitate prediction accuracy.

In complex systems with a large number of features, such as climate modeling, the integration of features between various sources, such as atmospheric data, ocean temperature, land use information and emission levels, can greatly enhance the reliability of the model.

The success of any successful AI-based environmental system is based on features engineering and effective preprocessing. Input data of poor quality, no matter how advanced the model, will result in unreliable output.

4.3.4. *Data quality, uncertainty and validation techniques*

Two of the most critical issues in environmental data analysis are ensuring the quality of data and coping with uncertainty. Any given environmental systems are complex and dynamic in nature and the data obtained contain different sources of error.

Data quality can be defined as the truth, wholeness, uniformity and trustworthiness of data. The quality of data is so poor that it may result in making misguided conclusions and unproductive environmental policies (Sharma et al. 2024b). Frequent verification of sensor functions, instrument calibration and verification of satellite data with ground-based measurements are necessary measures to ensure the quality of data.

The environment is uncertain because of errors in measuring, sampling, model assumptions and natural variability. For example, weather forecasts can be off because of turbulent weather or satellites may be covered by clouds or inaccessible because of sensor constraints. To deal with these uncertainties, statistical methods such as confidence intervals, probabilistic analysis and Monte Carlo analysis are typically applied. The uncertainty can be measured with these approaches and provide a set of possible outcomes instead of deterministic forecasts.

The validation methods make sure that AI and ML models provide generalizable and reliable results (Ul Haq et al. 2025b). Most common validation techniques are cross-validation, split-sample validation and against historical or real-world observations. The validation of environmental models is commonly done using an independent set of data that are gathered at various regions or times. An example is that an AI model that predicts air quality in a given city can be tested in a different place to descend its strength.

Environmental studies require collaboration with the domain experts at the validation stage. The findings are interpreted using expert knowledge to identify unrealistic trends, as well as improve the model design.

In general, the acquisition and processing of environmental data is rightful due to the integration of the latest sensing technologies, big data-based platforms, restrained preprocessing strategies and stringent verification methods. Such strategies include the fact that AI systems are designed using valid and useful data to accurately predict, make informed decisions and sustainably operate in the environment.

4.4. AI-based predictive modeling for environmental challenges

There is an increase in the nature of global warming, ecological devastation and unplanned industrialization, which have brought about the necessity of developing accurate and intelligent forecasting models. The traditional statistical models, though valuable, may be ineffective in giving non-line and highly complicated relations that may be present in environmental systems. ML, DL and AI can be utilized in producing accurate, versatile and scalable predictive models (Tang 2025). These technologies can process massive amounts of structured and unstructured data, establish hidden patterns and convert them into future projections that can be utilized in proactive decision-making.

Predictive modeling with the help of AI is significant in the context of predicting climate shifts, extreme weather events, estimating pollution rates and water management (Ukoba et al. 2024). AI would allow governments, environmental agencies, industries and communities to act in time and reduce environmental and economic harm by giving early warnings and dependable predictions. In this section, the authors discuss the key predictive strategies on addressing the main environmental issues by applying AI.

4.4.1. *Climate change and temperature forecasting models*

One of the most dangerous problems on our planet nowadays is climate change. Long-term climatic change has been manifested by rising global temperatures, changed precipitation patterns, meltdown of glaciers and rising sea-levels. Proper climate and temperature prediction is crucial in mitigation and adaptation planning.

The capacity to forecast future climate conditions has been greatly improved by AI and ML models. Physical equations and simulation-based traditional climate models demand enormous computational capabilities and fail to deal with uncertainties in chaotic climate systems. Conversely, AI models have the ability to end up learning historical climate data and discovering intricate temporal and spatial trends.

Temperature trends have been predicted with the help of ML algorithms, such as support vector regression (SVR), RFs and gradient boosting machines (GBM) with the help of past meteorological records. Such models study parameters such as surface temperature, greenhouse gases emissions, ocean temperatures, solar radiations and atmosphere composition.

RNNs and LSTM networks represent DL models that have recently been extensively used, particularly where long-term dependence in time-series climate data is required. The models are able to identify trends and variations by season across decades and predict a better forecast on change in temperature in the future.

Satellite images to analyze spatial climate patterns like ice melting, desertification and forest cover change are also analyzed using CNNs. Using the LSTMs and CNNs together, the hybrid DL models are able to extract both spatial and temporal information in climate data, thus producing highly accurate climate forecasting models.

Such AI-based weather prediction systems are significant in shaping environmental policies, planning infrastructure to harness renewable energy and educating agricultural activities. They also help in international climate plans because they provide realistic predictions regarding future climatic conditions.

4.4.2. *AI-based extreme event prediction (floods, heatwaves and cyclones)*

Climate change is causing extreme weather patterns such as floods, heatwaves, droughts, cyclones and hurricanes, which are growing in frequency and intensity. Such calamities lead to massive loss of life, infrastructure, ecosystems and stability of economies. Consequently, it is important to predict such events with timeliness and precision.

AI has come to create powerful instruments for creating sophisticated early warning systems. In flood prediction, AI algorithms take into consideration data of rainfall patterns, water levels in rivers, soil moisture, topography and past floods. XGBoost is an ensemble learning algorithm based on gradient boosting decision trees that has demonstrated impressive performance in flood risk assessment and water overflow prediction tasks.

Another field, in which AI has been useful, is heatwave prediction. Through the use of historical temperature data, humidity levels, wind patterns and the effects of urban heat islands, AI models can forecast the cause and intensity of a heatwave a few days or even weeks before it happens. Deep recurrent models and LSTM are especially useful in modeling these long-term temperature trends.

In cyclone and hurricane forecasting, AI systems are dependent on the imagery of the satellites, the tendency of atmospheric pressure, the temperature of the sea surface and the speed of the wind. DL models, and particularly CNNs, can identify the patterns of a storm in satellite images and forecast the movement, strength and area where the cyclones make landfall. By utilizing these AI-based models, meteorological agencies can provide timely warnings, evacuate vulnerable groups and reduce the effects of disasters.

Overall, it can be said that AI systems that have been created to forecast extreme events have proved to be more adaptive and quicker, as well as, more precise in some cases, compared to the conventional numerical weather prediction models.

4.4.3. *Air quality and pollution level estimation*

Air pollution is one of the major concerns with regard to our environment and people's health, especially in big cities and industries. The major pollutants include particulate matter (PM 2.5 and PM10), nitrogen dioxide (NO_2), sulfur dioxide (SO_2), ozone (O_3) and carbon monoxide (CO). They have a severe negative effect on our health and the surrounding ecological systems.

In order to address this problem, individuals are resorting to AI-based models that are useful in estimating and predicting the quality of air. They use multiple sources of data, such as air quality tracking monitoring stations, IoT sensors, meteorological stations, traffic activity and also satellite images. These data are subsequently run through machine-based learning models in order to forecast the level of pollution at various time periods.

This is because there are a number of methods available, such as regression models, support vectors machines, k-nearest neighbors and ensemble methods, which can assist in estimating the levels of these pollutants using both past and present data. Deep learning (DL) models, particularly Long Short-Term Memory (LSTM) networks and hybrid CNN–LSTM architectures, have gained significant attention due to their ability to effectively capture both temporal dependencies and spatial patterns in data. By integrating satellite imagery with weather observations and indicators of human activity – such as traffic congestion and industrial emissions – it is possible to generate detailed pollution maps that cover entire cities or even broader regional areas. Such visualizations are essential because they point out areas where the level of pollutants exceeds the safe level. These predictions have been used by governments and environmental agencies in making decisions, including enacting traffic regulations, regulating industrial emissions and making health advisories. In other words, AI-based air quality forecasting is not merely connected to ensuring environmental safety; it is also critical for controlling the health of the population.

4.4.4. *Water resource management and quality prediction*

Water plays a critical role in our existence and the growth of agriculture, industry and ecosystem health (Tandon et al. 2025). However, we have some major problems. As our populations continue to increase, climate change continues to cause havoc. Our water sources are being polluted, our management practices are not hitting the mark and we are experiencing the result of both water scarcity and poor water quality. When trying to overcome these difficulties, we are resorting more and more to the use of AI-based predictive models to work with our water resources in a more efficient manner. These models explore information pertaining to the rainfall, river flows, groundwater levels, reservoir storage, the rate of evaporation and consumption patterns. Through this information, AI systems can predict the future availability of water and assist in coming up with methods of allocating resources optimally.

Neural network models such as artificial neural networks (ANN) and LSTM networks are popular in the selection of predictors when it comes to forecasting river discharge, water demand and reservoir levels. The experiences of these projections are priceless; they are pertinent in flood management, drought control and irrigation planning. Regarding the quality aspect, a close examination of different parameters, such as pH levels, turbidity, dissolved oxygen, concentrations of heavy metals, and even the existence of the microbes themselves, is performed by the AI models. These models will be able to predict possible levels of contamination by using historical data and real-time sensor data. This prediction is critical in avoiding waterborne diseases and ensuring that drinking water is safe. Additionally, smart irrigation technologies are increasingly integrated with AI systems in modern agriculture. This integration ensures that crops receive the optimal amount of water based on soil moisture levels, weather forecasts, and crop type. As a result, it significantly enhances water conservation and improves overall agricultural efficiency. AI has indeed revolutionized the management of water. In conclusion, it has changed our mindset to be reactive rather than proactive and predictive because of the solutions presented by AI-based predictive modeling. The importance of AI in water management has never been as significant as it is now, whether it is predicting the effects of climate change, tracking the occurrence of extreme weather or checking the quality of water and air.

4.5. AI-driven energy system optimization

Replacement of the traditional energy systems based on fossil fuel usage with other cleaner and more sustainable sources has indeed escalated the need to seek smart, flexible and efficient energy management solutions. With ML, DL and reinforcement learning, AI-based systems will be able to work on the data without stopping, adapt to new circumstances and provide intelligent solutions to the problem of supply and demand. Here, we will go deeper into the roles of AI in changing all sorts of components of the energy ecosystem, particularly concerning the prediction of renewable energy, control of energy storage, supervision of smart grids and AI-supported trading of energy.

4.5.1. *Renewable energy generation forecasting (solar and wind)*

Sources of renewable energy such as wind and solar are somewhat unreliable in nature. This uncertainty is due to their dependence on the factors of the surrounding environment and weather. Having the capability to predict the amount of energy we can derive from these sources with accuracy is therefore vital in maintaining our power grids in steady operation and also in distributing energy in an efficient manner. In terms of making such predictions, AI-capable models of forecasting are very efficient. They are more likely to perform better than the older, traditional methods that generally assume statistical or physics-based methods, particularly in cases where there are nonlinear and quickly changing weather patterns. ML models such as SVM, RFs and gradient boosting are used to achieve the best possible results. The algorithms examine the meteorological conditions, including solar irradiance, wind speed, cloud cover, humidity and temperature, and are associated with past power output data. Interestingly, what is remarkable about those models is that they can reveal complex relations hidden behind huge data sizes, and thus they are able to predict the future generation of energy with an even greater level of precision.

DL methods, especially CNNs and LSTM, also enhance prediction capabilities. However, LSTMs have been popular due to their ability to capture temporal dependencies; therefore, LSTM networks are particularly suitable for time-series prediction of energy output, while Convolutional Neural Networks (CNNs) are effective for processing satellite imagery to detect cloud formations. AI models rely on stationary weather stations, LiDAR sensors and anemometers that can predict the speed of wind and turbine output at various time intervals. This reduces the backup generation of fossil fuel, curtailment and load distribution planning by caretakers of the grid. Solar power prediction with the help of AI models that process satellite images and sky cameras to notice real-time variations in solar irradiance is also helpful in achieving a higher level of renewable energy introduction, enhanced reliability of the grid and minimization of operational uncertainty.

4.5.2. *Energy demand and storage prediction models*

The amount of energy demanded varies at all times due to weather, time of day, industries and humans. Accurately estimated, it allows the planning of the resource, improved management of renewable resources and reduction of energy wastage. AI-based demand forecasting models, in this respect, examine the past trend of consumption, as well as other exterior factors such as temperature, population density, economic activity and seasonal pattern.

Both long-term and short-term energy demand forecasting are widely carried out with the help of regression models, neural networks and ensemble learning techniques. Different complex architectures can learn more complicated temporal connections in high-dimensional data, including LSTMs and transformers, so they are especially well-suited to learn time-dependent energy consumption. Such models would allow utilities to more accurately forecast the overall periods of peak load during the day to avoid overloading the grid and use a more efficient energy consumption.

Energy storage, especially in battery form and pumped hydro storage, is one of the most important roles in counterbalancing fluctuations of renewable energy. In the contemporary world, AI models are utilized in the optimization of charging–discharging cycles of the batteries. Reinforcement learning techniques have the ability to enable the energy storage system to make real-time decisions based on price signals, grid demand and renewable availability. By acquiring optimum strategies through continuous interaction with the energy environment, the systems prolong battery life, lower operational costs, and thus the entire system becomes more efficient. AI-led predictive maintenance is also used to detect the initial signs of battery degradation, hence preventing failures and managing assets efficiently.

4.5.3. *Smart grid management and load optimization*

Smart grids will be the future of energy systems that will combine the latest devices, sensors and communication systems to support two-way information flow between the providers and users. AI plays a critical role in managing and optimizing such grids to permit real-time tracking, reactive operation and automatic decision-making. Load optimization is one of the applications of AI in smart grids. Analyzing previous data with the help of smart meter AI technologies can enable us to predict demand patterns and adjust power supply on-the-fly. This helps grid managers to distribute electricity efficiently and predict changes in consumption and production. ML algorithms will be able to identify abnormalities, such as electricity theft, and deficiencies in the transmission or malfunction of devices to improve the reliability and safety of the grid (Ul Haq 2024).

Reinforcement learning will be a particularly suitable method in grid management, since the systems will evolve ideal methods of energy distribution in various situations. The agents can be trained to reduce power losses, match supply and demand, and reduce system instability. Also, AI enables management on the demand side by motivating consumers through automated mechanisms to redirect their consumption to off-peak hours. This eases congestion on the grid at peak periods and increases the utilization of renewable energy. In addition, AI aids fault detection and self-healing with smart grids. Through constant measurement of the voltage, frequency and current changes, AI algorithms can quickly identify faults and will automatically bypass power using other routes, which will greatly decrease the time of outage. Such self-contained features render resilience, robustness and efficiency to the current power infrastructure.

4.5.4. *AI-based energy trading and demand response systems*

AI-driven agents are able to automatically make decisions on when to purchase, sell or store energy depending on price projections, system constraints and local demand. Demand response programs make consumers alter their energy consumption during peak periods. These programs are highly enhanced by AI. The analysis of user behavior, appliance usage trends and energy pricing information can also be analyzed by AI systems, so that it can recommend a certain action, such as reducing use, relocating use to off-peak hours or utilizing stored energy. AI-based smart home systems are capable of automatically controlling the work of appliances, including air conditioners, electric vehicle chargers and water heaters to save money and ensure fewer loads on the grid.

In peer-to-peer (P2P) energy trading scenarios, AI assists in automating the process of negotiations between purchasers and merchants within local communities of energy. Combined with blockchain technology, AI allows the transactions of energy to be clear, secure and efficient. These intelligent platforms encourage the use of local renewable energy, reduction of transmission losses and accessibility of energy markets. Altogether, AI-based energy trading and demand response systems can not only enhance economic efficiency, but also contribute to environmental sustainability due to the promotion of the use of renewable energy sources and the decrease in dependence on conventional power sources.

The future of energy systems optimization using AI forms the basis of constructing sustainable, resilient and efficient energy infrastructures. The roles of AI include predicting renewable generation, demand, smart grids and automated energy markets. It provides answers to the variability, complexity and uncertainty problem in modern energy systems. AI contributes to the transition to a cleaner, more reliable and sustainable energy future for the world by offering real-time information, flexible control and smart decision-making.

4.6. Smart agriculture and precision forestry

Agriculture and forestry are two of the most important resources and environmentally important sectors. Traditional ways of farming and forestry use wide-brush methods that fail to recognize differences in soil quality, moisture, plant health and pest activity (Pipliya et al. 2025). Smart agriculture and precision forestry use AI, IoT and remote sensing technologies to oversee specific, data-driven decision-making in order to increase productivity while minimizing environmental damage. In smart agriculture, AI models analyze data collected from sensors in soils, weather stations, satellites and drones. They provide exact recommendations regarding irrigation, fertilization and pesticide treatments. These technologies help farmers apply the right amount of resources in the right time and place, which reduces waste, saves money and reduces environmental pollution. ML models can predict when a crop is likely to be more productive, recognize plant diseases and determine the optimal planting times depending on a climate pattern. As a result, smart agriculture helps in enhancing food security and promotes sustainable agriculture. Precision forestry also employs AI systems to monitor tree growth, detect illegal logging and monitor forest health. Satellite imagery and drone sensors give detailed information, which is used by AI algorithms to classify vegetation types, detect areas with pests or wildfire issues and estimate biomass. These smart systems help forest managers to plan thinning operations, reforestation and fire management strategies. By improving the use of forest resources and early threat detection, AI-based forestry systems aid in carbon storage and biodiversity protection.

Overall, smart agriculture and precision forestry are a step away from the homogeneous methods of treatment toward specific, intelligent management. This shift helps to boost efficiency and also causes an interesting reduction in environmental impact.

AI is also used to aid habitat mapping and ecological modeling, and forecast the impact of climate change on species distribution. In this way, biodiversity monitoring via AI provides instant insights into complex biodiversity, which aid in informed decisions about preserving ecosystems and the sustainable management of land.

4.6.1. *Real-time anomaly detection in environmental data*

Environmental problems, such as an abrupt increase in pollution, a toxic spillage, a sudden jump in temperature or a change in water quality, may have a serious negative impact on ecosystems and human health if they are not quickly addressed. Traditional monitoring systems are not able to detect these events in real time because of their limited processing power and in ability to handle large amounts of continuous data. AI-powered systems of anomaly detection are able to overcome these challenges and provide constant monitoring and quick responses.

ML models such as neural networks, or unsupervised models such as clustering and autoencoders can learn normal patterns of the environment based on data from the past (Pipliya et al. 2025). Once these baseline patterns are established, the system is able to detect deviations that could indicate abnormal events. For example, there may be instances where a sudden increase in the pollution levels of a river or a strange air quality reading in an industrial area will get immediate alerts for investigation and corrective action. These are real-time anomaly detection systems being adopted in urban air quality monitoring, industrial waste management, marine ecosystem and climate observation stations. When combined with IoT devices and edge computing, AI models can be applied at the data source (Pipliya et al. 2025).

In addition, alert systems powered by AI can also be used to automatically alert authorities, industries and the public.

4.7. Challenges and ethical considerations

While AI, ML and DL solutions can transform the way we manage the environment and optimize energy use, their adoption presents a number of challenges and ethical issues (Razak et al. 2025). The application of systems, using intelligence, in areas that address the concern of sustainability, should be guided by technological effectiveness, and the exercise of responsible governance by fairness, transparency and environmental awareness. Concerns such as data quality, Blackbox models, algorithmic bias and regulatory limits can impact the reliability and acceptance of AI-based environmental solutions. This section takes a hard look at key challenges and ethical issues associated with the use of AI in environmental and energy systems.

4.7.1. *Data availability and quality problems*

Setting up AI systems that focus on the environment and energy is quite challenging, and to tell the truth, the data makes it the most complicated (Vudugula and Chebrolu 2025). These systems need huge amounts of data which are not only reliable, but also clean and properly structured. However, in many locations, especially in areas that are remote and less developed, there is insufficient equipment for collecting such data. In situations where there is no proper infrastructure, the records are not only incomplete, but there are also all kinds of gaps that interfere with the extent to which AI can perform its tasks. Next, environmental data are derived from various sources, such as satellites, IoT sensors, weather stations, drones and government databases. Each one has its own way of communicating. The formats, the accuracy and even the frequency of updates are different for each source. For example, satellites may give you a global view of the situation over a period of time, but it may not contain the latest details. On the other hand, sensors on the ground may be able to tell you what is going on right at that moment, but only in a very small area. Trying to combine all these sources is a nightmare from a technical perspective, starting from the data cleaning stage and ending at the process where all the data from different sources are merged in a single system.

4.7.2. *Explainable AI and model transparency*

Most successful AI models, particularly deep neural networks, are often referred to by critics as black boxes, that is, it is almost impossible to read or understand how they make their decisions (Vanitha and Narasimhan 2025). DL models can be highly accurate when it comes to climate forecasting and predicting pollution, but they lack explanations of their results. A lack of transparency in these models casts suspicions on their credibility, particularly in situations where their application is in cases of managing disasters, energy allocation or policy making.

In environmental science, AI-based predictions can be used to make decisions related to evacuation strategies in case of a natural disaster, long-term urban planning policies or national carbon reduction policies. If the stakeholders fail to comprehend the reason behind a particular forecast, they may be hesitant to trust or follow AI-driven recommendations. This issue is particularly critical to policymakers, environmental scientists and governing bodies, as they have to provide the public and other stakeholders with logical reasons for their decisions. Explainable AI (XAI) represents a viable alternative to this problem. Different methods such as feature importance analysis, Shapley values and LIME (Local Interpretable Model-agnostic Explanations), as well as interpretable models like decision trees or rule-based systems, are being utilized in AI systems to make them more transparent. Nevertheless, there is usually a compromise between the accuracy of the model and its interpretability. The most accurate models are usually the most complex ones and therefore less interpretable, while simpler models provide insight but are less precise in their predictions.

Determining the adequate level of explainability without largely affecting the performance of the model is a very important problem, which is the case particularly in the environmental and energy sectors where transparency and accountability are of utmost importance.

4.7.3. *Bias, fairness and environmental impact*

AI systems are highly dependent on the nature of the data they are exposed to, in terms of bias. If the training data lack the representation of some geographical regions, social groups or environmental scenarios, the model's outputs may reflect that bias. For instance, climate models based mainly on data from developed countries may not be accurate in developing areas where the environment is different and the challenges are new. In the same vein, an AI-driven emergency response system may focus on urban areas that are better-equipped for monitoring, thus leaving out the less accessible communities, and thereby amplifying the existing inequalities.

The use of AI models that are affected by bias can mean that resources are not fairly distributed, leading to different environmental protection measures, and the occurrence of injustices among vulnerable groups that are the ones suffering the most because of climate change. The use of AI raises ethical issues of this kind since it can be an unintentional vehicle for environmental injustice if not properly addressed. Measures aimed at securing AI system fairness go through varied and representative datasets for training and also through monitoring of model performance from different demographic and geographical perspectives.

Besides the negative social effects of AI, the technology itself is costly for the environment. The process of training large-scale AI models is very demanding in terms of computational power, thus making it energy-intensive and causing carbon emissions to increase. The situation presents a paradox in which AI is the tool utilized to fix environmental problems, while simultaneously being one of the causes of environmental degradation. The implication of this issue is that the term "Green AI" is becoming increasingly important. It stands for energy-efficient models, efficient training methods and environmentally friendly computing practices. Developers and researchers should be socially responsible and ecologically conscious when working on AI projects.

4.8. Future directions and emerging trends

As the world faces growing environmental damage, climate crisis and higher energy demand, AI is bound to have an even greater impact on building a sustainable future. Rapid developments in AI technology, along with emerging digital tools such as the Internet of Things (IoT), blockchain, edge computing and autonomous systems, are creating new opportunities for environmental protection and intelligent energy management (Mariappan et al. 2025). These trends not only contribute to the accuracy and efficiency of monitoring and forecasting systems, but also make it possible to develop decentralized, transparent and flexible strategies to address global sustainability issues (Zhu and He 2025). This section considers the most important future directions that will shape the development of AI in environmental and energy systems.

4.8.1. *Autonomous environmental monitoring systems*

The introduction of autonomous monitoring systems using AI is revolutionizing the way environmental data are collected and evaluated (Du et al. 2025). Autonomous monitoring systems do not require as much human input to collect and evaluate environmental data as traditional methods do. Autonomous monitoring systems can collect environmental data continuously and consistently from the largest, most remote and inaccessible locations (such as oceans, forests and glaciers), with the development of autonomous drones, underwater vehicles, robotic sensors and satellite-based platforms.

AI vision systems can also provide computer vision and image recognition capabilities, and be used to identify environmental concerns (e.g. deforestation, endangered wildlife movements, illegal mining, oil spills, coral reef damage and land use changes) in real time. The same technologies found in many autonomous monitoring systems are used in monitoring technologies such as drones and autonomous underwater vehicles. Autonomous drones can monitor forest fires and endangered species, and also monitor ecosystem health with little human involvement. In the oceans, autonomous underwater vehicles equipped with AI can measure and record pollution levels, detect plastic waste and monitor changes to marine biodiversity.

4.8.2. *Green AI and energy-efficient algorithms*

While AI provides powerful tools for addressing climate and environmental challenges, the computing power required to train large AI models also consumes significant amounts of energy, often relying on non-renewable sources (Vaduganathan 2025). This has raised concerns about the carbon footprint of AI itself. As a response, the concept of Green AI is emerging – one that is centered around designing algorithms, models and hardware that are energy-efficient, environmentally friendly and optimized for computation. Green AI focuses on lowering resource consumption of AI systems through introduction of lightweight model, energy aware AI training and data processing strategies. Techniques like model pruning, quantization, transfer learning and federated learning help reduce the computational load without compromising on high levels of accuracy. In addition, specialized low-power hardware such as neuromorphic chips and edge-based processors are being developed that will be able to run AI models using far less energy. Another promising trend is the use of AI to increase the energy efficiency of its own infrastructure. For instance, AI technology can be used by AI in data centers to optimize cooling and balance loads across servers and anticipate peak usage times, resulting in less overall power consumption. Companies are also moving toward renewable energy-powered data centers to ensure that AI development will not contribute to carbon emissions. The future of sustainable AI is in a balanced approach – an approach where the environmental benefits of AI applications far outweigh their ecological costs. Green AI can be expected to become a central research topic where intelligent technologies would develop in harmony with the environment.

4.8.3. *AI for climate resilience and policy making*

Climate resilience planning and environmental policy is also one of the most significant new applications of AI. Predictive analytics has become a growing trend by government and institutions worldwide to prepare against climate-related risks such as rising sea-levels, droughts, extreme heatwaves and vulnerability of infrastructure. With the help of AI, it is possible to simulate various scenarios and analyze a large portion of climate data, socioeconomic information and geographical patterns. This helps the policymakers to realize the effects of various strategies on them. In the time of environmental crisis, AI models will assist in the development of flexible urban infrastructure, enhance evacuation schemes, find climate-safe areas and allocate resources in a more efficient way. The tools can also help governments develop long-term policies that can align with sustainability objectives identified by the United Nations sustainable development goals (SDGs) and the Paris Climate Agreement. Also, AI makes it possible to evaluate environmental regulations in real time. Governments can measure the effectiveness of policies by studying the level of pollution, the use of energy and the alteration of ecosystems to improve on the current policies. This evidence-based practice enhances good governance and makes the environmental protection process possible. Communities can share data, report environmental issues and participate in the sustainability planning by having public participation platforms that utilize AI. Such exchange of information leads to transparency and group-appropriate decisions. It renders the action on climate more just and closer to the local concerns. With further development of AI, it will probably turn into a critical instrument in the strategies of global climate. It will assist the societies in shifting reactive action plans to proactive, resilience-based programs.

4.9. Conclusion

Essentially, this chapter has demonstrated that AI, ML and DL are transforming the world by offering opportunities for correct prediction, effective resource management and smart decision-making, thereby addressing the urgent energy and environmental issues. With the help of these technologies, the solution to the problems may be provided directly by means of numerous different and innovative applications, including climate forecasting and air quality, optimization of renewable energy, smart grids, adaptive agriculture and environment monitoring in real time.

However, the concerns the chapter has raised on the quality of data, transparency, ethical concerns and the governance of such systems, are equally crucial in terms of the need to introduce AI to the world of cutting-edge technologies (IoT, satellite sensing, digital twins and blockchain), which are likely to support the sustainability agenda in a scalable manner. The roadmap in front of us represents what still needs to be done to see AI become one of the key innovative drivers of the environment. It entails, among others, the development of energy-efficient algorithms, system autonomy and decentralization, and partnership between policy-makers, researchers and industry stakeholders. By ensuring that technological innovations are accompanied by strong ethical standards and environmental concerns, AI can become a key driver of environmental strength, sustainable progress and a cleaner world for future generations.

4.10. References

Du, S., Zou, J., Zheng, X., Zhong, P. (2025). Solar radiation prediction based on the sparrow search algorithm, convolutional neural networks, and long short-term memory networks. *Processes*, 13(5), 1308.

Kaur, I. and Ali, A. (2024a). A complete study on machine learning algorithms for medical data analysis. In *Fog Computing for Intelligent Cloud IoT Systems*, Banerjee, C., Ghosh, A., Chakraborty, R., Elngar, A.A. (eds). John Wiley & Sons, Hoboken, NJ. doi: 10.1002/9781394175345.ch7.

Kaur, I. and Ali, A. (2024b). An in-depth exploration of machine learning algorithms and performance evaluation approaches for personalized diabetes prediction. In *Proceedings of the 2024 International Conference Emerging Innovations and Advanced Computing (INNOCOMP)*, Sonipat. IEEE. doi: 10.1109/INNOCOMP63224.2024.00093.

Kaur, I. and Ali, A. (2025). Unveiling the power of prediction: A comprehensive guide to learning techniques, from data preparation to model interpretability for early prediction of diabetes and effective management. In *Artificial Intelligence and Optimization Techniques for Smart Information System Generations*, Ali, A., Chakraborty, R., Alharbe, N. (eds). CRC Press, Boca Raton, FL [Online]. Available at: https://www.taylorfrancis.com/chapters/edit/10.1201/9781003592969-1/unveiling-power-prediction-inderdeep-kaur-aleem-ali.

Kaur, I. and Ul Hassan, I. (2025). A bibliometric analysis and management of big data and machine learning research. In *Emerging Trends in Industrial Engineering and Management*, Kumar, A., Kumar, P., Phanden, R.K. et al. (eds). CRC Press, Boca Raton, FL [Online]. Available at: https://www.taylorfrancis.com/chapters/edit/10.1201/9781003512585-11/bibliometric-analysis-management-big-data-machine-learning-research-inderdeep-kaur-inzimam-ul-hassan.

Magazzino, C. (2024). The impact of deep learning on environmental science. *BMC Environmental Science*, 1, 4. doi: 10.1186/s44329-024-00003-5.

Mariappan, Y., Ramasamy, K., Velusamy, D. (2025). An optimized deep learning based hybrid model for prediction of daily average global solar irradiance using CNN SLSTM architecture. *Scientific Reports*, 15(1), 10761.

Patil, K. (2024). Enhancing climate change monitoring and prediction through machine learning. *International Journal of Scientific Research in Computer Science, Engineering and Information Technology*, 10(7) [Online]. Available at: http://www.ijsrcseit.com/paper/CSEIT2410727.pdf.

Pipliya, S., Kumar, S., Gupta, R.K., Das, R.S., Meena, D., Srivastav, P.P., Tiwari, B.K., Garcia-Vaquero, M. (2025). The future of algal proteins: Innovations in extraction and modifications, functional properties, and sustainable food applications. *Future Foods*, 11, 100549.

Razak, T.R., Ismail, M.H., Darus, M.Y., Jarimi, H., Su, Y. (2025). Artificial intelligence in renewable energy: A systematic review of trends in solar, wind, and smart grid applications. *Research and Reviews in Sustainability*, 1(1), 1–22.

Saini, G.K. and Kaur, I. (2025). Navigating risk. In *Artificial Intelligence in Remote Sensing for Disaster Management*, Dahiya, N., Singh, G., Singh, S., Sharma, A. (eds). John Wiley & Sons, Hoboken, NJ. doi: 10.1002/9781394287222.ch8.

Saini, G.K., Kaur, I., Sharma, H. (2024). A comprehensive review and analysis of landslide detection through advanced image analysis techniques. In *Proceedings of the 2024 5th International Conference for the Emerging Technology (INCET)*, Belgaum. IEEE. doi: 10.1109/INCET61516.2024.10593354.

Shahverdi, N., Saffari, A., Amiri, B. (2025). A systematic review of artificial intelligence and machine learning in energy sustainability: Research topics and trends. *Energy Reports*, 13, 5551–5578. doi: 10.1016/j.egyr.2025.05.021.

Sharma, A., Kaur, I., Goel, P. (2024a). Enhanced classification of gravitational wave images using CNN model. In *Proc. 2024 7th International Conference on Circuit, Power and Computing Technologies (ICCPCT)*, Kollam. IEEE. doi: 10.1109/ICCPCT61902.2024.10673399.

Sharma, A., Kaur, I., Goel, P. (2024b). Detection of gravitational waves using machine learning. In *Proceedings of the 2024 5th International Conference for the Emerging Technology (INCET)*, Belgaum. IEEE. doi: 10.1109/INCET61516.2024.10593087.

Tandon, A., Awasthi, A., Pattnayak, K.C., Tandon, A., Choudhury, T., Kotecha, K. (2025). Machine learning-driven solar irradiance prediction: Advancing renewable energy in Rajasthan. *Discover Applied Sciences*, 7(2), 107.

Tang, K.H.D. (2025). AI and digitalization in energy and environmental management. *Recent Progress in Science and Engineering* [Online]. Available at: https://www.lidsen.com/journals/rpse/rpse-special-issues/ai-digital-energy-environment-manage.

Ukoba, K., Onisuru, O.R., Jen, T.C. (2024). Harnessing machine learning for sustainable futures: Advancements in renewable energy and climate change mitigation. *Bulletin of the National Research Centre*, 48. doi: 10.1186/s42269-024-01254-7.

Ul Haq, I. (2024). Diagnosis of neurological disease using bioinspired algorithms. In *Bio-Inspired Optimization for Medical Data Mining*, Srivastava, S., Anand, A., Kumar, A. et al. (eds). John Wiley & Sons, Hoboken, NJ.

Ul Haq, I. and Khanday, A.M.U.D. (2025). Exploring the role of explainable AI in women's health: Challenges and solutions. In *Explainable Artificial Intelligence in the Healthcare Industry*, Kumar, A., Kumar, T.A., Das, P. et al. (eds). John Wiley & Sons, Hoboken, NJ.

Ul Haq, I., Kumar, N., Koul, N., Verma, C., Eneacu, F.M., Raboaca, M.S. (2022). Machine learning techniques for result prediction of one day international (ODI) cricket match. In *The International Conference on Recent Innovations in Computing*. Springer, Singapore.

Ul Haq, I., Kaur, G., Rather, A.H. (2024). Fruit leaf classification using transfer learning for automation and industrial applications. In *Deep Learning Techniques for Automation and Industrial Applications*, Rathore, P.S., Ahuja, S., Burri, S.R. et al. (eds). John Wiley & Sons, Hoboken, NJ.

Ul Haq, I., Kumar, A., Rathore, P.S. (2025a). Machine learning approaches for wind power forecasting: A comprehensive review. *Discover Applied Sciences*, 7(10), 1139.

Ul Haq, I., Malhotra, J., Rawat, V., Kumari, J., Kaur, G. (2025b). Machine learning approaches for early detection of cervical cancer: A comparative study of classification models. In *Targeted Chemotherapy with Personalized Immunotherapy: An AI Approach*, Kumar, A., Das, P., Rathore, P.S. et al. (eds). John Wiley & Sons, Hoboken, NJ.

Ul Haq, I., Nandal, V., Uppal, H. (2025c). Blockchain applications in aviation securing transactions, streamlining operations, and improving passenger experience. In *Blockchain in the Tourism Industry: A New Era of Secure and Transparent Travel Solutions*, Kumar, A., Abreu, A., Batta, P. et al. (eds). Springer, Cham.

Ul Haq, I., Shah, H.A., Rufai, S.Z. (2025d). Enhancing water security through automation: Case studies and technical advancements in water quality management. In *Computational Automation for Water Security*, Dubey, A.K., Srivastav, A.L., Kumar, A. et al. (eds). Elsevier, Amsterdam.

Vaduganathan, D. (2025). Edge-AI powered multispectral drone mapping for ultra-high accuracy crop stress prediction. *Journal of Environmental Sustainability, Climate Resilience, and Agro-Ecosystems*, 2(1), 8–15.

Vanitha, M. and Narasimhan, D. (2025). Empowering urban planning with accurate air quality index prediction: Hybrid learning models for smart cities. In *Deep Learning and Blockchain Technology for Smart and Sustainable Cities*, Subramaniyaswamy, V., Revathy, G., Ravi, L. et al. (eds). Auerbach Publications, New York.

Vudugula, S. and Chebrolu, S.K. (2025). Quantum AI-driven business intelligence for carbon-neutral supply chains: Real-time predictive analytics and autonomous decision-making in complex enterprises. *American Journal of Advanced Technology and Engineering Solutions*, 1(1), 319–347.

Zhu, J. and He, Y. (2025). A novel photovoltaic power probabilistic forecasting model based on monotonic quantile convolutional neural network and multi-objective optimization. *Energy Conversion and Management*, 323, 119219.

5

AI in Renewable Energy Technologies

Artificial intelligence (AI) is continuously reshaping the renewable resources by offering advanced methods for forecasting, optimization and integration. This chapter surveys state-of-the-art AI methods applied to solar, wind and distributed energy resources and synthesizes results from recent comprehensive reviews and case studies. The discussion explores the applications of AI based in four main areas: solar energy forecasting and optimization, wind power systems, hydro/ocean/bioenergy and hydrogen with energy storage integration, along with various techniques such as machine learning (ML), deep learning (DL), reinforcement learning and explainable AI. These techniques are emphasizing their role in addressing technical challenges such as irregular supply, data uncertainty, system optimization and resource allocation. AI is used due to its proficiency in making forecasts and in ensuring more accurate control. In addition, it also makes renewable energy cheaper, better for the environment and more reliable, evidence of which is touched upon. The chapter ends by highlighting future research paths and policy measures needed for safe, reliable and large-scale adoption of AI technologies during the energy transition.

5.1. Introduction to sustainable energy systems

Energy is one most prominent resources of the present era. Energy is used in every part of our daily lives, from lighting our homes to running industries and transportation. However, the way in which we have been producing and using our resources for the past several decades has caused serious environmental issues. Most of the energy which has been utilized by humans comes from fossil fuels, such as coal, oil and natural gas. When these fuels are burned, they release harmful gases such as carbon dioxide (CO_2) and methane (CH_4), along with other pollutants such as nitrogen oxides (NO_X),

Chapter written by Jagdeep KAUR, Vidhi GUPTA and Aditi RAJ.

sulfur dioxide (SO_2) and carbon monoxide (CO), which cause pollution and climate change (Shoaei et al. 2024).

Energy is only called sustainable energy if it can meet the needs of the present generation without compromising the needs of future generations. This system focuses on generating and using energy wisely with full responsibility. Renewable resources are those resources directly generated from natural processes that are continuously replenished and are key components of sustainable systems. Renewable resources include solar energy, wind energy, geothermal energy and biomass. These resources do not generate any harmful substances (Ul Haq et al. 2025a).

Figure 5.1 shows some major renewable energy types. The figure shows how efficient renewable energy is and in what ways it can be used.

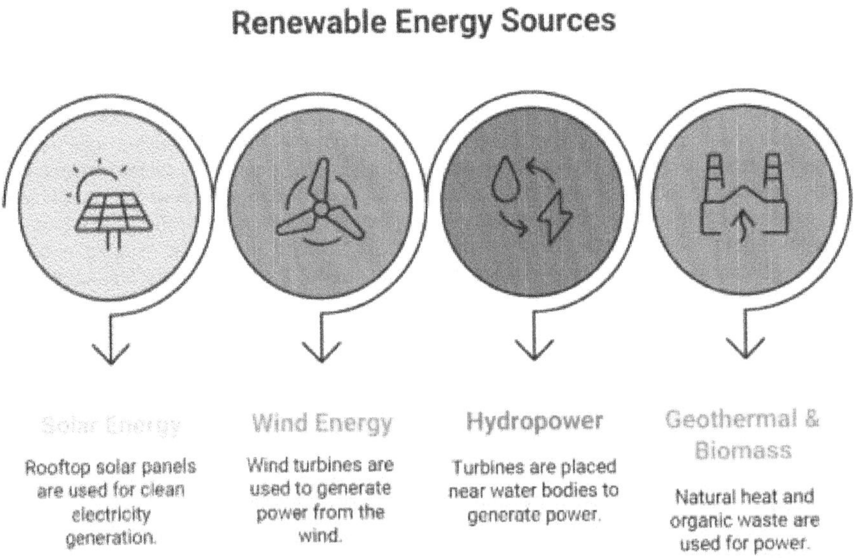

Figure 5.1. *Major renewable energy types. For a color version of this figure, see www.iste.co.uk/ulhaq/artificial1.zip*

For example, many homes today have installed rooftop solar panels to generate electricity. These systems not only reduce dependence on the main power grid, which is generated from fossil fuels but also cut down the emission of harmful substances containing carbon. Similarly, near bodies of water, energy can be generated using turbines, which help produce clean hydropower on a large scale. Countries such as China, Brazil, the United States, Canada and Russia are some of the largest producers.

Sustainable energy not only focuses on utilizing renewable resources like solar or wind, but also on using the current energy resources more efficiently to minimize waste and obtain maximum output. For example, using LED lights instead of traditional bulbs helps save a lot of electric power; driving electric vehicles instead of petrol or diesel cars helps reduce harmful smoke in the environment; or designing buildings that consume less power for cooling and heating so that electricity consumption will be less (Ul Haq et al. 2025c). Using renewable energy and following sustainable habits can help us move toward a cleaner and safer planet for the future.

5.1.1. *Global energy crisis, climate change and sustainability principles*

The world is facing a global energy crisis mainly because of the depletion of fossil fuels. These fuels take millions of years to replenish, yet we are consuming them rapidly as the demand for a continuous energy supply keeps increasing in parallel with the population and technology advancements. However, the supply of fossil fuels is limited and extracting them causes serious harm to the environment. This imbalance between demand and supply has resulted in rising fuel prices, power shortages and economic challenges in many countries (Waghmare et al. 2025).

Moreover, the overuse of fossil fuels has severe, wide-ranging consequences for the environment, human health and the global economy. These non-renewable energy sources such as coal, oil and natural gas are being depleted at an unsustainable rate, accelerating climate change and causing numerous global problems to arise. When these non-renewable resources are burned, they release carbon dioxide (CO_2) and other greenhouse gases that trap heat in the atmosphere and cause a rise in global temperature, leading to more frequent and intense droughts, heatwaves, storms and other extreme weather events (Akande et al. 2025). Acid rain, smog and other respiratory diseases are caused by air pollutants, leading to millions of premature deaths. The report from the Global Climate and Health Alliance (GCHA), along with other recent studies, states that the overuse of fossil fuels is driving a global health emergency, causing serious and long-term health problems to people at every stage of life.

To resolve these challenges, the concept of sustainability comes into practice. Sustainability means utilizing the resources carefully, keeping the current needs in mind without compromising future generations' ability to meet theirs. The key principles of sustainability are as follows: environmental protection, social equity and economic viability. The environmental sustainability principle entails the responsible use of natural resources, reducing waste and pollution, along with the conservation of ecosystems. The social sustainability principle highlights the importance of providing access to basic needs, education, healthcare and opportunities for personal and professional growth. Economic sustainability revolves around cultivating a strong and flourishing economy that serves both the present and future generations. These three pillars work together to meet current needs (Xiong et al. 2025).

Nowadays, many countries are actively adopting these principles. For example, Japan has established itself as a leader in sustainability by implementing 50% new cars with zero emission within the next several decades and its major cities are targeting 100% carbon neutrality by 2050. The Netherlands is a leader in sustainability, with ambitious goals and innovative approaches. The country aims to achieve a circular economy and reduce greenhouse gas emissions to zero by 2050. This proves that balancing development with sustainability is possible in countries only when the government and people take the initiative (Ul Haq and Khanday 2025).

5.1.2. *AI for environmental and energy challenges*

At present, AI is playing a crucial role in the area of sustainable development. AI enables machines to think, learn and make decisions just like humans. Instead of following the fixed rules or instructions, AI helps by guiding us in how to use the natural resources wisely and also suggesting how to resolve environmental issues like air pollution, etc. AI analyzes the large amount of data, our old traditional patterns, finds hidden paths and makes faster and improvised decisions to build the smarter systems with a future perspective. Humans utilize a lot of time to perform tasks that can be done by AI in a few seconds (Ul Haq and Khanday 2025).

One major application of AI is in optimizing energy production and distribution. For example, AI can be used to predict weather conditions by analyzing the pattern of the current weather, or to predict how much energy will be required by people on a daily basis. By following these methods, we can reduce the energy wastage and ensure that resources are utilized wisely.

AI also contributes to various fields like sustainable agriculture. Sustainable agriculture means growing crops and raising animals in such a way that it does not harm the environment, saves our natural resources and ensures long-term productivity. Agriculture is one of the most important sectors in the world as it provides raw materials and food for everyone. However, traditional methods require a lot of water along with insecticides and pesticides. AI analyzes all of these methods and data and suggest more sustainable methods, which are environmentally friendly while also improving productivity (Akande et al. 2025).

These examples prove that AI is not just a technological tool, it works in partnership with us to create a sustainable and environmentally friendly future.

5.1.3. *Overview of AI, ML and DL applications in energy and sustainability*

All of the fields such as AI, ML and DL are interconnected with each other. These fields play a vital role in promoting efficiency and sustainability. AI refers to a branch of computer science that allows machines to think, learn and make decisions just like humans. ML allows the computers to learn from different sets of data without being explicitly programmed. DL is also a subset of ML, which uses neural networks to analyze large amount of data. The function of DL is similar to the function of the human brain (Khouili et al. 2025).

AI technology acts as a revolutionizing technology in the case of energy management. AI helps make an electricity system smarter and more efficient by introducing smart grids. It is used to deliver the energy in a better way, detect faults and reduce the wastage of electricity. In this system, ML is used to predict how much renewable energy will be available so that operators can use it wisely. DL is used to predict the weather conditions by analyzing the patterns that help scientists prepare for extreme weather conditions, like storms and heatwaves.

From this information, we can conclude that AI, ML and DL together can create a more energy-efficient and eco-friendly world that supports both development and environmental balance (Akande et al. 2025).

5.1.4. *Conclusion*

Shifting and adapting toward clean and renewable energy is a big challenge but a great opportunity for our planet. Sustainable energy not only involves using renewable resources such as solar and wind but also includes using these resources wisely with full planning so that the needs of our future generations are not affected. Putting this thought into practice, we can use AI to help make the system smarter, cleaner and easier to manage.

This goal can be achieved easily with collective effort. Governments should create clean energy rules, industries should use eco-friendly technologies and people should save energy and reduce waste in their daily lives. Every small action will help us create a green and healthy planet.

5.2. Introduction to AI in renewable energy technologies

Renewable energy has emerged as one of the most prominently discussed areas when it comes to the topic of sustainable development. However, often inefficient energy generation and management has been observed, mostly caused by the unpredictability of the renewable sources such as solar, wind and hydropower. In order to find a solution to these challenges, AI is being incorporated to ensure an improvement in prediction accuracy, performance and to increase the reliability of renewable energy systems. ML, DL, fuzzy logic and reinforcement learning are types of AI technologies that help provide strong analytical and decisiveness capabilities. These technologies gain the upper-hand over other types of technologies due to their ability to self-learn the systems, identification of various patterns and to make predictions, which do not require human assistance (Xiong et al. 2025).

Benefits of incorporating AI into renewable energy are as follows:

– increased accuracy of forecasting energy generation and demand;

– optimal power plant performance;

– automated energy storage;

– maintenance and fault detection enhancement;

– optimal integration of hybrid energy systems into power grids.

5.2.1. *AI for forecasting solar energy and its optimization*

5.2.2.1. *Solar energy system*

Solar energy is considered to be one of the most reliable renewable energies and has the most futuristic scope in terms of being a good renewable resource due to its availability, flexibility and scalability. It is used through two major methods, which are commonly termed photovoltaic (PV) systems and solar thermal systems.

PV systems are responsible for converting sunlight into other forms of energy, such as electricity. Solar thermal systems convert sunlight to generate heat.

1) PV systems consist of solar panels that are made from semiconductors with the partial conduction of electricity ensuring that the PV effect is possible. These materials include crystalline silicon or CdTe and CIGS that are thin-film compounds. Direct current is produced whenever photons excite protons after the striking of sunlight on the surface. This current is further converted into alternating current, which is used in the grid. Key parameters influencing performance include solar irradiance, temperature, tilt angle, orientation and shading. Engineers employ performance ratio analysis and I-V curve tracing to monitor efficiency.

2) Solar-thermal systems, especially concentrated solar power (CSP) plants, use mirrors or lenses to focus sunlight onto receivers that heat fluids to produce steam for turbines. Thermal energy storage – commonly molten-salt systems – enables electricity generation even during the night.

3) To ensure grid stability and financial planning, it is important to forecast the solar irradiance, which is the power per unit area of sunlight that reaches the surface. Satellite imaging, sky cameras and numerical weather prediction models are a few methods used for the forecasting mentioned above. Apart from that, autoregressive models and time series analysis serve

as statistical approaches that provide reliable predictions regarding the unavailability of complex AI models.

5.2.2.2. *Requirement of AI in solar energy systems*

The generation of solar energy mostly depends on the availability of sunlight, because it is the fundamental source of energy. However, there are chances of fluctuation because of weather, change in seasons and varying atmospheric conditions, all of which can hinder the process of predicting power output and maintaining grid stability. Previously, traditional mathematical or statistical forecasting methods were used to capture such data but their efficacy fell short due to their inability to capture nonlinear patterns. However, AI-based models can use their self-learning ability to ensure the accuracy of predictions.

Sunlight serves as the main source of energy for PV systems. Solar irradiance has an intermittent nature that is caused by fluctuating weather conditions, seasonal variations, atmospheric pollution and cloud movement – leading to significant variability in power output. To forecast solar power output, historical data, real-time satellite images, meteorological inputs and sensor data are all utilized. Artificial neural networks is an AI technique, which is used to determine complex parameters such as temperature, humidity and energy output.

Linear regression or autoregressive models, which are considered traditional mathematical or statistical forecasting methods, were initially chosen to predict solar power generation. These methods were able to fulfill the need for stability under weather conditions but they had the disadvantage of not being able to handle complex and nonlinear patterns, which were considered to be inherent in meteorological data. Furthermore, such models fail to adapt dynamically to environment changes and inefficient grid operations.

Recurrent neural networks (RNN) and long short-term memory (LSTM) are used to capture dependency, which are temporal and provide additional help in improving short-term forecasting. Forecasts are typically divided into the following:

– very short-term forecasting: minutes to an hour ahead, used for grid balancing and inverter control;

– medium- and long-term forecasting: days to months ahead, used for maintenance planning and energy trading.

Accurate forecasting reduces reserve requirements and helps utilities manage power fluctuations efficiently.

5.2.2.3. *Wind power systems*

Wind energy is another form of energy, which is responsible for the conversion of kinetic energy from moving air into electricity. Wind power efficiency depends upon location, wind speed and turbine designs:

1) System components and operation:

The turbine consists of four main components: blades, a rotor, a generator and a tower. The rotor performs the function of spinning the generator whenever wind moves the blades, which generates electricity. The control system performs the function of not only protecting the turbines during extreme weather conditions but also capturing a maximum amount of energy.

2) Site assessment and design:

Performance is affected by various factors that include average wind speed, air flow pattern, land type and also distance from power lines. Winds are stronger and steadier in the offshore wind farms but they are costly if compared to onshore farms that are cheaper and give easy access but face land use issues.

3) Performance monitoring and optimization:

Data records of wind-speed and turbine performance is further used by engineers to estimate output in terms of power. Early detection of faults and reliability is ensured with the help of regular maintenance, and monitoring using sensors and SCADA systems. Vibration and temperature checks ensure smooth operation and reduce breakdowns.

Wind power systems are thus important because they ensure conversion of energy from another form into electricity, which can further be used accordingly. However, the efficiency of the output given by these systems depends upon various factors (Ul Haq et al. 2025b).

5.2.2.4. *Hydropower, ocean energy and bioenergy*

5.2.2.4.1. Hydropower

Hydropower is responsible for converting hydro energy into electricity. The water that is stored in large dams is released through turbines that help generate power with a high rate of efficiency. Hydropower not only offers reliable energy but also supports the stability of the grid and storage of power with the help of pumped storage. The problem of ecological damage or displacement is reduced with the changes in design, which are more futuristic, promoting small or micro hydropower systems that provide power while keeping in mind the ecological factors.

5.2.2.4.2. Ocean energy

Ocean energy includes tidal and wave power. Tidal energy uses the rise and fall of tides through barrages or underwater turbines. Wave energy captures the motion of sea waves using floating or oscillating devices. Although still in the developmental stages, ocean energy is predictable and consistent, making it a valuable asset for coastal regions in the future.

5.2.2.4.3. Bioenergy

Bioenergy is produced from organic materials such as crop residue, wood waste or animal manure. The main conversion methods include:

- combustion: direct burning for heat or electricity;
- gasification: converting biomass into gas for fuel;
- anaerobic digestion: producing biogas through microbial activity.

5.2.2.5. *Hydrogen energy and energy storage systems*

Hydrogen is considered one of the most important clean energy carriers, as it can store and transport renewable energy.

a) *Production methods*: electrolysis can be defined as the splitting of water with renewable electricity to create green hydrogen. Steam methane reforming is considered a cheaper but less effective method as it emits gray hydrogen or carbon. Biomass gasification is cleaner if combined with carbon capture (blue hydrogen).

b) *Storage and transport*: as hydrogen has a low density, it must be compressed, liquefied or stored in metal hydrides. Developing safe pipelines and refueling systems is still a challenge.

c) *Applications*: hydrogen, due to its dynamic properties, is used not only in fuel cells but also vehicle industries and most importantly in power storage. It helps balance renewable energy when solar or wind output is low.

d) *Energy storage technologies*: energy storage helps maintain stable electricity supply.

Table 5.1 shows how hydrogen energy is stored and the concepts related to it.

	Aspects	**Points**
1.	Production	Electrolysis (green), SMR (gray), biomass gas
2.	Storage	Compression, liquefaction, or metal hydrides
3.	Applications	Fuel cells, vehicles, power backup, grid balance
4.	Technologies	Battery, thermal, hydro and hydrogen storage
5.	Challenges	High cost, safety issues, efficiency loss

Table 5.1. *Hydrogen energy and storage (Ejiyi et al. 2025)*

5.3. Smart grids, IoT and AI for energy management

In the present era, energy management has become a major challenge due to the increasing population and its rising demand for energy. Traditional electricity grids were designed to supply energy to consumers. This system was like a one-way communication, which will only supply energy to consumers without any intelligent control or a feedback system. Figure 5.2 is a descriptive flowchart showing digital technologies, which are used for energy management, which is a very important concept related to renewable energy. With the advancement of technology, the need for more innovations and adaptive systems increased as there were rapid changes in the energy consumption method. These advanced systems can monitor, control and optimize energy flow efficiently. This is where smart grids, the Internet of Things (IoT) and AI comes in.

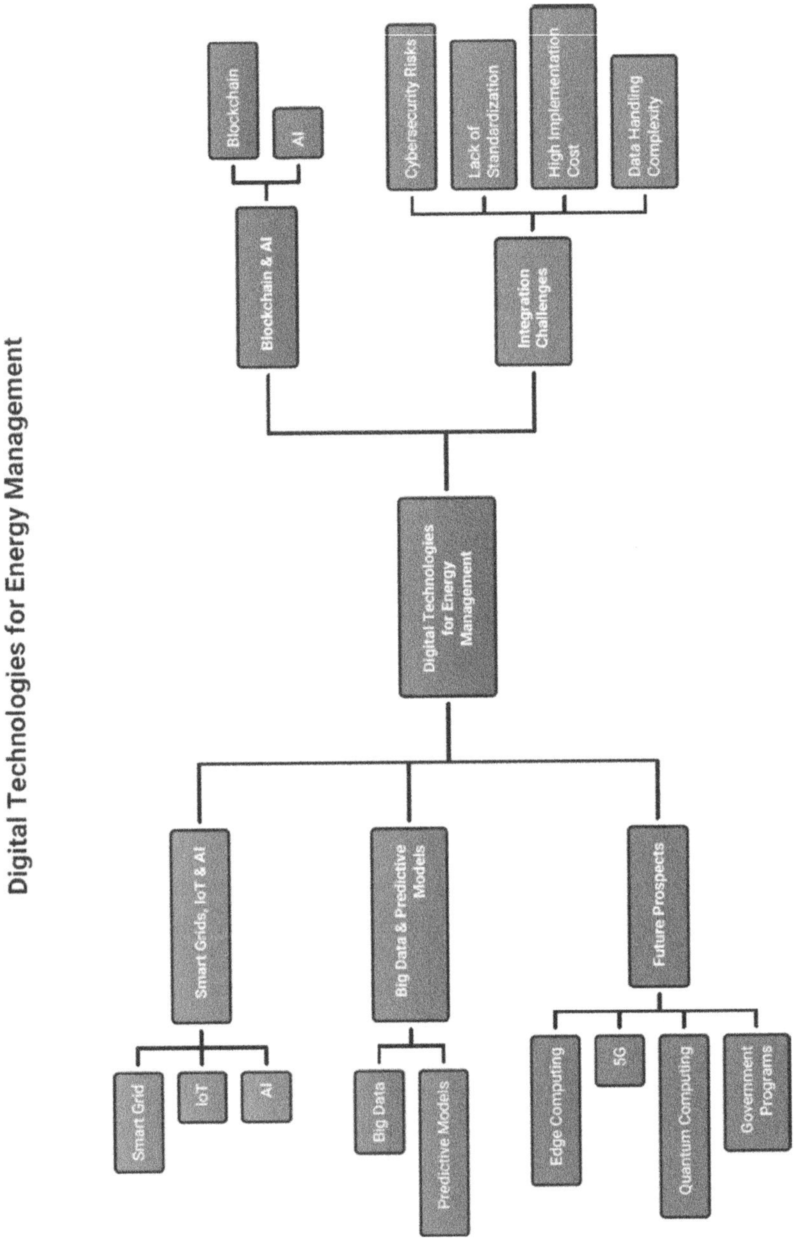

Figure 5.2. *Flowchart of digital technologies for energy management. For a color version of this figure, see www.iste.co.uk/ulhaq/artificial1.zip*

A smart grid is like a network that uses energy distribution and digital communication technology simultaneously as a two-way communication. It allows both data and electricity to flow in both directions, helping us to use energy more efficiently and reliably. It also enables utility companies to optimize the generation, transmission and distribution of electricity along with real-time monitoring, efficient power distribution and quick recovery from faults or outages. With the help of a smart grid, consumers can easily understand the energy they use, and even the energy they produce and store with the help of solar panels or EV batteries (Ul Haq and Khanday 2025).

The IoT is a smarter grid that helps connect various devices, such as IoT sensors that help us to detect risks early, redistribute power to decrease outages and balance loads without direct intervention by operators. Sensors can also be used to detect mechanical problems and perform simple troubleshooting and repairs, notifying technicians only when necessary – before anything actually breaks down. It also measures voltage, current, temperature and other parameters and then sends collective information to a central system for analysis.

AI acts as the brain for the smart grid, processing massive amounts of data to think, analyze and make better decisions. AI is used to analyze the data patterns, detecting faults in the grid from the information collected by the IoT sensors. It also suggests preventive maintenance actions by analyzing the current situation and past experiences, so that the suggested measure is an improved version of the present one.

One of the best examples of an AI and IoT-based smart grid is in the UK, which has one of the world's most ambitious climate change targets: to reduce greenhouse gas emissions to net zero by 2050. To achieve this target, they have to decarbonize the high emitting sector, such as residential and commercial building. 30% of the energy is used here only. To meet this target, some technologies were introduced, such as the IoT to enhance efficiency, reduce waste, improve reliability, and create a more flexible energy system.

Smart grids also promote renewable energy integration by predicting solar and wind energy generation through AI algorithms. For example, during cloudy days, AI predicts the drop in solar power output and compensates it by drawing power from stored energy or other renewable sources. This ensures stability in energy supply while minimizing wastage.

Overall, the combination of smart grids, the IoT and AI helps create a self-monitoring, self-healing and highly efficient energy network that supports the vision of a sustainable future (Dhungana 2025).

5.3.1. *Blockchain and AI for renewable energy trading*

Energy trading was largely controlled, according to the traditional methods, by central management like government utilities or large energy businesses. With the improvement of technology, most individuals know how to use renewable resources – similar to solar panels and small wind turbines – thus, a fair, transparent and safe market to deal in energy is necessary. It is here that blockchain and AI come in. AI is put into practice to bring revolutionary changes. Blockchain is a secure and transparent digital registry, which maintains the account of all of the transaction records. All transactions are stored in a block; they are arranged in a chain in such a way that these blocks have to be joined together, and this will not allow any alterations or tampering with the information.

Blockchain technology enables peer-to-peer (P2P) energy trading, allowing individuals and companies to exchange electricity directly without intermediaries. Small-scale energy producers can sell surplus electricity securely and efficiently to nearby consumers through decentralized trading platforms. The integration of AI with blockchain further enhances energy trading mechanisms. AI-driven models can forecast energy prices, determine optimal trading times, and support grid stability by predicting supply-demand fluctuations. By analyzing real-time data, AI systems can anticipate peak demand periods and identify cost-effective opportunities for buying or selling electricity (Hanif et al. 2025).

Most nations, especially in Europe, North America and Asia are applying blockchain and AI to innovate energy trading and management. All around the world, China and the United States are leading globally in energy blockchain research and development, whereas Germany and Singapore have emerged as leading adopters of this technology. These technologies enhance grid efficiency, facilitate peer-to-peer energy trading and help manage renewable energy sources. Here, people with rooftop panels can sell extra energy produced to their neighbors via a secure online marketplace enabled by blockchain. If they are using AI, they can also forecast how the energy is dealt with, how much power will be generated and used in large quantities and at what cost (Ul Haq et al. 2025b). It can also bring transparency to trading carbon credits, highlighting who is trustworthy. Carbon credits show the number of carbon dioxide emissions allocated to an organization or a person, kept track of by blockchain technology. Such credits are used to minimize fraud and also ensure that firms comply with environmental regulations. AI with blockchain may be very significant in the future, entirely automating energy trading. As an example, electric power could be done through smart contracts, dispositions on a decline of prices or with a surplus of energy produced by solar panels.

This would make the system more efficient and motivate people throughout the world to use renewable resources.

5.3.2. *Big data analytics and predictive models in energy systems*

The energy sector produces vast amounts of data every second, generated from power plants, smart devices and weather stations, etc. It is virtually impossible to handle this quantity of data manually. This is where data analytics and predictive models enter the picture, making the job easier and smarter. Big data analytics implies the use of highly developed computer tools to gather, process and comprehend vast amounts of data to uncover the latent patterns, correlations, market trends and other insightful information. These insights are useful in energy systems in a number of ways – such as the amount of energy that people will need, locating faults in the organization, designing energy production and cost-saving. Energy data analytics also enables utilities to detect inefficiency in production and delivery to minimize power generation by carbon-intensive peaker plants, reduce greenhouse gas emission and advance clean energy.

Predictive modeling is a method whereby highly sophisticated statistical methods are used and ML algorithms are applied to predict, with the help of historical data, what will happen in the future. In the case of energy management systems, these predictive models assist us with predicting the amount of energy that will be used or produced with the help of renewable resources, as well as when the system may fail as a result of the equipment. As an illustration, China is the largest electricity generator in the world, with

United States and India trailing after. Its system is widely based upon data analytics and anticipatory models within its energy systems as well as in its smart grid projects.

The State Grid Corporation of China (SGCC) offers services to over 1.1 billion customers who have been using advanced analytics, over a span of more than twenty years, to increase grid stability, reduce outages and maximize the use of renewable wind and solar energy sources. Their forecasting maintenance systems enable early detection of potential problems, which can be used to reduce downtime and enhance reliability. It is also motivated by the fast development of renewable energy in China, with the system favoring smarter grids, which will support its net-zero goals by 2060. Denmark is a country that uses data analytics to manage its energy network successfully, generating over half of its electricity using wind power. Predictive models are used to study the weather patterns and forecast the wind energy production, which helps grid operators ensure a balance is achieved between demand and supply in order to maintain stability even under variable wind conditions. This is a strategy that is compatible with the sustainability goals of Denmark, which seeks near zero carbon emission.

On the same note, the SGCC employs analytics in an effort to increase its massive renewable energy power up to 1,200 GW by 2024. The company forecasts solar and wind power generation to make the grids reliable for their 1.1 billion customers. Moreover, predictive maintenance is used as a means of minimizing downtime due to equipment issues. At the consumer end (for these two countries), smart meters capture detailed information and data of domestic energy consumption.

In Denmark, these data are used to provide utility customized energy-saving advice; in China, it helps to control peak demand through incentive, encouraging reduction of use during peak demand times. The approach reduces wastage and promotes sustainability efforts (Dhungana 2025).

In general, such analytics-based approaches increase efficiency and grid stabilization with renewable sources that are variable, and encourage more environmentally friendly kinds of energy systems through optimization of resources and reducing the environmental impact.

5.3.3. *Integration challenges and future prospects*

Technologies like AI, IoT, blockchain and big data can completely change how we produce, use and manage energy. These new technologies, however, pose a number of challenges when imposed upon existing technology.

Smart grids use millions of IoT devices for gathering and sharing information about energy usage; this, in turn, creates more vulnerabilities to potential cyberattacks or data theft. If hackers have access, they will steal personal data or disrupt the supply of electricity. Therefore, all of these data should be safeguarded and kept private for people to build trust.

Another challenge is interoperability. This means that different digital technologies and devices can communicate with each other efficiently and work together. Different companies make different devices and systems, and they do not always work well with one another. This is called a lack of standardization.

The cost for building the smart energy system is high. For developing countries, this high implementation cost acts as a barrier because new technology needs new equipment, software and trained workers. Moreover, smart grids and IoT devices produce a huge amount of data every second. Handling and analysis of such data requires powerful computers and large storage systems, which further add to the challenge.

Even though these problems exist, the future still looks bright with possibilities on the horizon. Emerging technologies such as edge computing, 5G networks and quantum computing are set to enhance the speed and security of data management. AI will be of help in making quick and intelligent decisions for smarter and greener cities, managing the usage of electricity or fault detection automatically.

Several examples demonstrate how governments and industries are progressing in this area. The European Union's Smart Grids Task Force is striving to establish a standard for digital communication and cybersecurity throughout Europe. The Indian government has rolled out the National Smart Grid Mission with the aim of furthering smart grid technology and digital energy management in both urban and rural areas. These initiatives reflect the growing recognition that digital technologies form the backbone of the future of sustainable energy systems.

5.3.4. *Conclusion*

The use of smart grids, IoT, blockchain and big data analytics is changing the present era by managing the use of energy and taking care of sustainability. These are, in essence, technologies that make energy systems smarter and more efficient. Their use will enable us to monitor energy in real-time, make better decisions automatically and create transparent systems whereby both consumers and producers can easily track and trade energy.

As soon as countries begin implementing these new technologies, their power savings and reductions in power cuts will increase, along with increased use of renewable sources like solar and wind. For the best outcome, we also need a very good government policy, public awareness and research, especially in AI-based energy systems.

By working with AI, these ranges of advanced technologies will absolutely change how we generate, sell and consume energy in this digital and eco-friendly future. That will be of value for creating a cleaner, smarter and more dependable world for future generation.

5.4. Global policies and AI-enabled energy strategies

With the increasing requirement for clean energy, government and global organizations have started to focus more on meeting this need for a brighter future. Policies have been introduced by the government to promote both renewable resources and integrate AI for smarted energy management. Industries and government both reap the benefits of reduced waste, optimized power and forecast demand due to this integration of AI. Many countries have adopted "AI for green energy" strategies that encourage research, funding and cross-border cooperation. Key international initiatives include the following:

– Paris Agreement (2015): this is signed by over 190 countries to limit global warming to below 1.5°C. In addition, the UN took the initiative to introduce SDG-7, which aims to ensure energy is available, accessible and affordable for all by the year 2030, only five years away from now.

– International Energy Agency (IEA): this is working on promoting global collaboration on clean technology and efficient energy systems. Apart from the European Green Deal, which emphasizes not only industrial decarbonization but also the integration of AI to enable smart grids and improve energy efficiency, several other global initiatives are promoting sustainable energy transitions.

– India's National Solar Mission and AI Mission: this mission focuses on encouraging the integration of solar power with AI for energy optimization.

Why should AI be implemented in policies?

AI massively helps in the prediction of renewable generation, which is based on weather data. Furthermore, as already discussed, smart grids make use of ML, which helps in controlling electricity flow and also in detecting faults automatically.

Due to its unique features, the government has also started to incorporate AI to help in the field of data analytics by tracking energy consumption patterns in order to ensure better tariffs. These policies aim for a balance between environmental sustainability, economic growth and technological innovation. As more countries adopt AI-based frameworks, energy systems are becoming more efficient, resilient and ecofriendly (Xiong et al. 2025).

5.4.1. *Economic models and financing sustainable energy*

A strong economic foundation along with advanced technology is required in order to ensure a good and reliable sustainable energy system. Effective financial models are essential for affordability and success of renewable energy projects that include solar farms, wind parks or hydroelectric stations, which are often considered to have high setup costs and also require long planning periods.

5.4.1.1. *Benefits of sustainable energy*

– The importance of financial support: it is important to note that heavy investment in terms of infrastructure, research and workforce training is required in order to help ensure a smooth transitioning from fossil fuels to renewable energy.

– Reliable funding: this is required to ensure that there is no hindrance to the operation of these energy systems. Apart from that, financial planning helps to regulate the process further by making these systems efficient and most importantly affordable for consumers or users. Without any proper financial planning, even the best projects can face delays or, in unfortunate cases, failure.

– Benefits of effective financing: these include more innovation due to encouragement. If proper financial support is ensured, companies or the parent accessor can focus on developing better technologies, which are both efficient and most importantly renewable.

– Reduces risk: stable financial models assure investors that their money will generate steady returns. Easy access for all such programs that help financially also ensures that renewable energy is accessible to all. More investment in clean energy reduces pollution and contributes to global climate goals.

5.4.1.2. *Challenges involved*

With all of its benefits, it is obvious that renewable energy is the need of the hour. However, challenges include the following:

– High initial cost: the initial setup of the renewable plants is considered expensive.

– Frequent policy changes: this can lead to discouragement for the investors, hence lack of financial funding.

– Lack of a skilled workforce: the technologies are considered advanced and specialist knowledge can be required.

– Limited access to capital: financial barriers are faced by developing countries, forcing them to rely on other more affordable options.

5.4.1.3. *Future discussions*

Countries should create energy policies that are consistent and clear in order to ensure that the above-mentioned challenges are solved to avoid hindrance. Furthermore, international cooperation should be promoted, and strong financial institutions established which specialize in sustainable projects. Encouraging private sector involvement and community participation can make the energy transition faster and more stable.

Developing nations can especially benefit from low-interest loans, technology sharing and capacity-building programs. When combined with supportive economic planning, renewable energy becomes not just an environmental goal but also a driver of employment (Michalakopoulos et al. 2025).

5.4.2. *Case studies: developed nations and developing nations*

The use of AI in energy systems is growing all around the world, but the level of progress is very different between developed and developing nations. Developed countries already have strong infrastructure, advanced technology and large investments that help them use AI effectively. On the other hand, developing nations face challenges such as limited funds, a shortage of skilled workers, and slower technological growth. But it is important to note that both sections are making steady prominent progress (Waghmare et al. 2025).

5.4.2.1. *Developed nations*

Taking Germany as an example, it makes use of Smart Grid Projects, in which AI integration balances out the energy flow between various parts and thermal power plants. This system is responsible for managing electricity efficiently and preventing power failure, using data analysis to reach this goal. In the United States, AI is used for optimizing wind turbines.

Apart from that, it also helps in monitoring electricity grids and improving battery performance. Well-known technology companies like Google have also taken steps to reduce the energy used in their data centers by integrating AI to reach the goal of saving not only power but also money. Japan has taken a unique approach by combining AI with robotics to maintain offshore wind and solar power systems. Countries like India, Brazil and Kenya have also started to incorporate AI for renewable energy. However, this integration is on a very small or experimental scale. Brazil applies AI to boost bioenergy production from sugarcane and agricultural waste, helping reduce waste and improve efficiency.

5.4.2.2. *Key features*

Developed countries make use of AI for predictive maintenance and smart grid automation, which are often considered advanced tasks. However, other countries, which are underdeveloped or still in the process of being fully developed, depend upon government programs to focus on forecasting and management of the grid. Despite these differences, developing countries are progressing quickly by using affordable and open-source AI tools.

These technologies help them skip older systems and move straight to modern, AI-driven energy solutions. In the future, as access to AI becomes easier, the gap between developed and developing countries in the energy sector will continue to narrow. Moreover, there is a big difference in the sectors on the basis of skills and affordability.

Underdeveloped or developing nations often tend to have a deficiency of AI experts which are well trained and hence end up facing higher costs in the initial stages of integrating these systems. However, developed countries do not face any such hindrances and therefore deal with issues that are related to privacy or, most importantly, ethical use of AI.

5.4.3. *Community and microgrid-based AI applications*

In many parts of the world, especially in villages and small towns, people are beginning to use their own local power systems, which are called microgrids. A microgrid is a small electricity network that can work either with the main grid or on its own. It usually runs on renewable energy sources such as solar panels, wind turbines, or small hydro systems. These systems are becoming popular because they provide reliable and eco-friendly electricity to areas that were earlier left without proper power supply.

5.4.3.1. *How AI supports microgrids?*

AI has a significant role in enhancing the functionality of microgrids. It assists in gathering and analyzing sensor and energy meter data and weather reports. These are currently being made using AI in smarter and more manageable microgrids. In the case of cloudy weather, the system can begin to store additional solar energy in batteries prior to the shortage occurring (Khouili et al. 2025). AI may also be used to control the distribution of electricity among households, schools, hospitals and shops. It ensures that power is assigned where it is required by the majority and that there is no part of the system overworked. Another helpful thing is that AI is able to spot little issues before they become big. For example, if a battery or turbine is beginning to malfunction, it can warn the technician in time.

5.4.3.2. *The importance of microgrids*

Microgrids powered by AI are frequent in places where humans usually experience power deficiency or lack regular power. Renewable energy sources, such as sunlight and wind, allow individuals to generate their own power rather than always relying on large power companies as the source. This not only saves money but also makes the environment clean. The energy generated by such microgrids is applied to illuminate houses, power schools and hospitals, and maintain little shops. The result is more convenience and comfort for the people residing in those regions. In some villages and towns, basic mobile apps can be applied to check the amount of electricity in use per day. This makes the people more aware of their energy practices and it reminds them to use power wisely and avoid waste.

These systems are operated by mostly renewable energy, and they also minimize pollution and combat climate change.

5.4.3.3. *Real-life examples*

In small power systems, AI has already been deployed in many countries. In India, solar microgrids are constructed in villages that previously did not have proper access to electricity. These microgrids are providing steady electricity to households, educational establishments and small industries.

Solar is managed in Kenya and Nigeria with the help of AI and IoT. The microgrids are utilized in remote regions that may not be easily linked to the main power grid. Smart microgrids are even being used in some towns and universities in the United States and Europe. In case of a storm, wild-fire or heavy snowfall, the main electricity grid is frequently interrupted. Nevertheless, hospitals, schools and other consumers are still able to receive power through microgrids, providing emergency shelter when it is required the most.

These smart microgrids are supported by AI. Systems, which determine the most beneficial times to store energy or to use it, reduce waste and lower costs. In countries such as Germany or Denmark, microgrids built around AI are also being applied to develop energy-efficient campuses and communities that operate mostly on renewable sources. Microgrids are used differently in each country in accordance with the local requirements. There are some areas where the goal is to make electricity available to the remote villages that have never had a stable power supply. In other regions, it is about the retention of basic services during times of emergency caused by natural disasters, or even economizing on the costs of energy. No matter where they are employed, the principle of these systems is the same – to render pure, uniform power with the assistance of intelligent technology, which is affordable for all. The growing use of microgrids reveals how the world is shifting toward more local and sustainable energy generation.

5.4.3.4. *Issues and future deliberations*

New technology in not readily affordable for many small towns and villages. They often rely on government assistance or gifts from other institutions to initiate such projects. Maintenance is another issue. A microgrid requires, even for installation, individuals with the necessary know-how to run it correctly. The microgrid needs substantial initial financial investment to purchase solar panels, batteries, correct wiring and control units. This is challenging for many small or rural communities, because these systems are not cost-effective and/or easily accessible. In the majority of cases, individuals are forced to rely on government initiatives or third parties for financial assistance and technical aid.

Another problem is the Internet connection. The majority of AI-based microgrids require a stable Internet connection to check the power circulation and identify issues. But in many rural areas, there is poor network coverage or no network coverage. As a direct result, the system is not always able to transmit or receive information in time, making it difficult to regulate the flow of power or monitor its faults. Nevertheless, despite all of these issues, the future of AI-driven microgrids is bright. Governments and social organizations are actively supporting the transition toward decentralized energy systems by offering training programs, low-interest loans, and technical assistance to help communities develop and maintain microgrids. In the future, microgrids are expected to become increasingly common in both urban and rural areas.

Microgrids will not only provide the country with a clean and stable electricity supply, but will also provide local technicians and engineers with new opportunities. Batteries are becoming stronger, and solar panels have become cheaper and longer lasting. When these little modifications are added to each other, they may produce a 150% change in the way individuals generate and distribute electricity. This puts communities in a better position to construct their own power systems without spending excessive amounts of money. In particular, microgrids provide individuals with the power to control their own energy, making life easier and more stable. They develop local areas, generating new jobs and enabling communities to become more self-sufficient. Finally, microgrids do not simply embody advancing technology; they also signify self-reliance, development and a true concern for the environment.

5.4.4. *Future trends in AI for renewable energy*

The use and production of renewable energy is gradually being transformed by AI. With the ongoing development of technology, AI will produce more power systems that are trustworthy, economical and environmentally friendly. By advising on the best times to keep and deliver energy to homes and industries, AI will aid us in the conservation of waste and ensure that power is equally distributed among power users. In the near future, smart grids and batteries may communicate with each other, balancing production and demand without any human assistance. One of the best future applications of this technology is forecast and planning.

The renewable energy sources, such as wind and solar, are entirely dependent on power production, which can vary on a day-to-day basis. With the help of AI, we can more readily foresee how much sunshine or wind a district may get. Through accessing past weather patterns and actual data, AI can direct energy stations to strategize on the quantity of power to be generated and stored in advance. Energy storage and distribution is another area where AI will come in handy. Managing when and how to utilize stored power is a large challenge in renewable systems.

AI can balance this process even more by regulating the times of electricity being stored in batteries and the time it ought to be directed to homes, schools and factories. It is able to maintain an unchanging monitor on the functioning of various machines and identify little problems in solar panels, wind turbines or batteries way before they lead to any major breakdown. This process can be controlled with the help of AI through analyzing the trends of supply and demand, fair pricing and connecting those with surplus energy with those who need it.

This strategy will unite people and motivate local communities to use clean energy more wisely. For developing countries, AI is able to create new opportunities, opening the door for progress. The other emerging concept is sharing energy using AI and trading.

Soon, individuals who are generating power through solar can either transfer or sell the additional energy that they produce to others.

	Trend	Description
1.	Smart grid automation	AI will balance energy production, reducing waste
2.	Advanced forecasting	Predicts sunlight, wind speed and power output
3.	Energy storage management	Controls when to store or release power
4.	Predictive maintenance	Detects early faults in solar panels before breakdowns
5.	Energy trading and sharing	Enables peer-to-peer energy exchange
6.	Support for developing nations	Promotes affordable AI-driven energy systems

Table 5.2. *Future trends of AI in renewable energy (Ejiyi et al. 2025)*

5.5. Future directions, pathways to net-zero: challenges, risks and future of AI in sustainable energy

Reduction to non-zero emission is one of the most radical and ambitious problems of the 21st century. Numerous governments, industries and research facilities are currently striving to ensure that the emissions of the greenhouse gases (GHG) are reduced to almost zero with the remaining emissions compensated by either carbon capture, renewable technology or other means.

AI is one of the key players in realizing this mission because it can analyze large sets of sophisticated data, predict results and streamline decisions (Akande et al. 2025). It has the potential to increase the effectiveness of renewable sources of energy such as solar and wind power, reduce energy wastage and help scientists to make more precise forecasts regarding climatic changes. On a darker note, there are also cases when AI-based systems accelerate emissions because they require a significant amount of data and electricity to operate. There are also threats of cybersecurity and ethical dilemmas over the use of data. Here, the focus will be on the various approaches that can be taken to achieve net-zero, the key obstacles and how AI can be utilized to make the world a clean and sustainable place (Ul Haq et al. 2025b).

5.5.1. *The global net-zero agenda*

The idea of implementing net-zero emission has taken root in the past couple of decades with the help of many efforts, such as the Paris Agreement, which is an international climate change treaty under the law. It targets reducing the growth in the mean global climate temperature to be significantly lower than 2°C above pre-industrial level, and has recently pursued efforts to reach 1.5°C by the end of the century.

Reaching these targets will entail a radical change in the manner of production, transmission and consumption of energy. AI can be the epicenter of this change. As an example, ML will be able to forecast the demand, obtain more stability in the grid and preemptively avoid power cuts due to system failure. In the UK, AI is enhancing meteorological forecasting precision, which is an important component that contributes to integrating wind energy into the power grid.

In India, on the same note, AI algorithms have been employed to monitor energy consumption rates in urban cities and to maximize the output performance of the solar-powered microgrids in rural areas.

5.5.2. *Role of AI in achieving net-zero*

AI supports the net-zero journey through several interconnected pathways.

AI is used to forecast the amount of solar and wind energy that will be made in the future, based on the past weather and power generation records for an area. AI also makes it easier to plan and manage the electricity grid in order to reduce energy wastage. Moreover, it assists power plants in operating more effectively and avoiding sudden drops or overloads in electricity. AI also improves storage systems of energy, for example, batteries, that accumulate additional energy when the supply is high and give it out when it is required. This enables renewable energy to be stabilized and makes it more reliable even in the absence of sunshine or when the wind is not blowing.

5.5.2.1. *Improving energy efficiency*

Today, industries and buildings are occupying giant portions of the world energy consumption. By detecting and fixing problems before they emerge, AI-driven energy can be saved by automation and analytics. One of them is the application of the DeepMind to Google, which applied AI in managing the cooling systems within its data centers. In summary, AI calculated the way to maintain the temperature at the best level with less energy consumption, which has reduced cooling expenses by approximately 40%. Similarly, these kinds of applications can be taken to other fields, include those that have factories, transportation and logistics, in order to make the machinery, routes and operations more efficient. This efficiency conserves energy, but also reduces harmful emissions, providing stakeholders with a major step toward a clean and sustainable future (Ul Haq et al. 2025a).

5.5.2.2. *AI in carbon capture and climate modeling*

Complex atmospheric conditions are addressed with the application of AI to optimize CCUS systems. Predictive models of ML are used to predict the optimal geological locations to store carbon, estimate the carbon storage capacity and track the risks of carbon leakage. Various startups are developing AI-based materials discovery tools capable of accelerating the design and optimization of advanced materials.

5.5.3. *Issues and potential limitations*

Although AI has brought about an absolute change in how we generate and control energy, it is also associated with several significant issues. What started as the process of simple forecasting and data analysis is currently being transferred over to intelligent systems that are able to make their own decisions, even to the point of repairing themselves when something goes wrong. These intelligent systems will unite renewable sources of energy to ensure that power flows smoothly all of the time, managing battery storage and demand times.

Other interesting trends that are beginning to emerge include the following:

– AI-based energy trading: in the near future, smart trading systems will begin to emerge, which are driven by AI with blockchain. Individuals will be able to purchase and sell renewable electricity directly within their communities, building fair and open local energy markets.

– Autonomous microgrids: villages, towns and campuses will soon have microgrids, which have the capability to regulate the creation and consumption of power automatically, guaranteeing a constant power supply even in case of main grid failure.

With the growing automation of systems, the traditional occupations in power will be eliminated and energy management or plants might begin to deteriorate. To manage this change, the workers will require training in how to use and handle the emerging technologies rather than letting themselves be ousted by them. Governments, companies and other parties should ensure that AI is applied appropriately with the collaboration of research. AI has brought tremendous changes in the way we conduct our affairs and use energy. However, it has some problems, which we must consider carefully.

One issue is over reliance on machines and the data they process. This may lead to inaccurate estimates of the electricity demand resulting in either shortages or redundant power generation. The other challenge is what is referred to as automation bias. When individuals put too much trust in computer results, they cease checking for accuracy manually. When an AI program is incorrect in its prediction and nobody checks it, that error may be diffused in the system before it is discovered, in turn causing incorrect results in other areas (Ul Haq et al. 2024).

5.5.4. *Smarter energy: how the future could look*

In the coming decade, technology will have a far greater impact on the manner in which we produce and consume energy. The future energy systems may not only assist us in planning and optimization, but they could also make small decisions independently and could even deal with minor problems before they escalate into larger ones. Local energy trading is one of the exciting possibilities.

Individuals could trade in renewable energy with one another, and it would resemble a small village trading market. This would allow the communities to utilize the energy they are generating in a better way and automatically control the supply and demand. These smarter systems would be able to integrate renewable energy and energy storage, changing electricity demand in real-time to ensure that the power remains reliable and consistent. It may become possible to have fewer blackouts, smarter energy consumption and a system that is more responsive to actual demands. At a larger scale, the additional power in one place could be distributed to areas that require it, thus making the use of energy more efficient and consistent in the regions (Wang et al. 2021; Hanif et al. 2025). This would assist communities in utilizing the energy they are generating to the fullest without depending fully on the large utility companies (Ul Haq and Khanday 2025):

– Mini self-managed grids: neighborhoods or towns would have their own small grids that would manage themselves.

– Monitoring carbon: technology can also simplify the process of monitoring the emission by companies. Proper and transparent tracking would enable them to improve more quickly and adhere to the environmental regulations more accurately.

5.6. Conclusion

Access is a major constituent of this advancement. Big cities or companies with ample funds should not be the only ones with access to advanced energy systems. They must also be available to small villages, remote locations, as well as developing communities. This has to be achieved by sharing knowledge, developing equitable policies and investing in adequate infrastructure. When there is fair distribution of energy tools, they will minimize waste, enhance efficiency and extend light and opportunity to where it has always been overlooked.

Smart energy systems can help usher in smarter and more secure energy sources. But they are only as valuable as our applications of them. It is not a machine or a new technology that can bring a cleaner energy future. Yes, they can assist, but it is up to people to change how they use this assistance. Our lifestyle, how businesses operate and the decisions that governments and societies make all determine the manner in which energy is produced, distributed and utilized in our lives.

With a basic smart system, a community can determine their specific optimal time to store additional power or utilize it when it is required. Such planning can help decrease the amount of energy wastage and save money. The factories are now capable of monitoring their real-time pollution rates in order to take immediate measures rather than wait until they receive long reports after a couple of weeks. Naturally, no system is perfect. There is a risk that technology may break down, information may fall into the wrong hands and not all people will have access to new tools or resources at the same time.

5.7. References

Akande, O., Okolie, J.A., Kimera, R., Ogbaga, C.C. (2025). A comprehensive review on deep learning applications in advancing biodiesel feedstock selection and production processes. *Green Energy and Intelligent Transportation*, 4(3), 100260.

Dhungana, H. (2025). A machine learning approach for wind turbine power forecasting for maintenance planning. *Energy Informatics*, 8(1), 2.

Ejiyi, C.J., Cai, D., Thomas, D., Obiora, S., Osei-Mensah, E., Acen, C., Eze, F.O., Sam, F., Zhang, Q., Bamisile, O.O. (2025). Comprehensive review of artificial intelligence applications in renewable energy systems: Current implementations and emerging trends. *Journal of Big Data*, 129(1), 169. doi: 10.1186/s40537-025-01178-7.

Hanif, M.F., Ahmad, R., Farooq, A.B., Liu, X., Ahmad, A., Iqbal, S., Mi, J. (2025). The solar AI nexus: Reinforcement learning shaping solar energy forecasting and storage control. *Wiley Interdisciplinary Reviews: Energy and Environment*, 14, e70012.

Khouili, O., Hanine, M., Louzazni, M. (2025). Evaluating the impact of deep learning approaches on solar PV forecasting: A systematic review. *Renewable Energy Reports*, 59.

Michalakopoulos, V., Zakynthinos, A., Sarmas, E., Marinakis, V., Askounis, D. (2025). Hybrid short-term wind power forecasting model using theoretical power curves and temporal fusion transformers. *Renewable Energy*, 256(C), 124008.

Shoaei, M., Noorollahi, Y., Hajinezhad, A., Moosavian, S.F. (2024). A review of the applications of artificial intelligence in renewable energy systems: An approach-based study. *Energy Conversion and Management*, 306, 118207.

Ul Haq, I. (2024). Diagnosis of neurological disease using bioinspired algorithms. In *Bio-Inspired Optimization for Medical Data Mining*, Srivastava, S., Anand, A., Kumar, A. et al. (eds). John Wiley & Sons, Hoboken, NJ.

Ul Haq, I. and Khanday, A.M.U.D. (2025). Exploring the role of explainable AI in women's health: Challenges and solutions. In *Explainable Artificial Intelligence in the Healthcare Industry*, Kumar, A., Kumar, T.A., Das, P. et al. (eds). John Wiley & Sons, Hoboken, NJ.

Ul Haq, I., Kaur, G., Rather, A.H. (2024). Fruit leaf classification using transfer learning for automation and industrial applications. In *Deep Learning Techniques for Automation and Industrial Applications*, Rathore, P.S., Ahuja, S., Burri, S.R. et al. (eds). John Wiley and Sons, Hoboken, NJ, 151–178.

Ul Haq, I., Kumar, A., Rathore, P.S. (2025a). Machine learning approaches for wind power forecasting: A comprehensive review. *Discover Applied Sciences*, 7(10), 1139.

Ul Haq, I., Malhotra, J., Rawat, V., Kumari, J., Kaur, G. (2025b). Machine learning approaches for early detection of cervical cancer: A comparative study of classification models. In *Targeted Chemotherapy with Personalized Immunotherapy: An AI Approach*, Kumar, A., Das, P., Rathore, P.S. et al. (eds). John Wiley & Sons, Hoboken, NJ.

Ul Haq, I., Nandal, V., Uppal, H. (2025c). Blockchain applications in aviation securing transactions, streamlining operations, and improving passenger experience. In *Blockchain in the Tourism Industry: A New Era of Secure and Transparent Travel Solutions*, Kumar, A., Abreu, A., Batta, P. et al. (eds). Springer, Cham.

Waghmare, A.V., Singh, V.P., Varshney, T., Sanjeevikumar, P. (2025). A systematic review of reinforcement learning-based control for microgrids: Trends, challenges, and emerging algorithms. *Discover Applied Sciences*, 7(9), 939.

Wang, Y., Zou, R., Liu, F., Zhang, L., Liu, Q. (2021). A review of wind-speed and wind-power forecasting with deep neural networks. *Applied Energy*, 304, 117766.

Xiong, B., Zhang, L., Hu, Y., Fang, F., Liu, Q., Cheng, L. (2025). Deep reinforcement learning for optimal microgrid energy management with renewable energy and electric vehicle integration. *Applied Soft Computing*, 176, 113180.

6

Big Data Analytics and Predictive Models in Energy Systems

Modern energy systems are increasingly a product of the convergence of smart grids and advanced sensing technologies, together with renewable resources at scales of astonishing volumes of heterogeneous data. It is important to leverage this information to enhance green energy management, ensure grid reliability and improve efficiency. As the emphasis is on the valuable sources of data, including smart meters, SCADA systems, Internet of Things (IoT) sensors, weather and market data and social behavioral data, this chapter provides an in-depth overview of big data analytics and predictive modeling in the energy systems. The entire pipeline of model creation, including preprocessing of data and feature engineering, training, validation and deployment are presented, as well as statistical, machine learning (ML) and deep learning (DL) models, including ARIMA, random forest, SVM, LSTM, convolutional neural network (CNN) and transformers highlighted: load management, demand forecasting, energy market analytics, smart grid optimization, predictive maintenance and renewable energy prediction. Besides the discussion of cybersecurity issues, this chapter also analyzes the role of IoT, edge and cloud technologies in real-time processing, scalable storage and simulations of digital twins. These strategies, their implementation and impact are shown in real life case studies and insights. The conclusion of the chapter is a review of the future research directions, regulatory issues and challenges, such as explainable AI, federated learning and compatibility with next-generation communication technologies. By combining theory, technique and programs, this chapter shows how big data and predictive analytics garner the possibility of revolution to design dependable, sustainable and efficient energy systems.

6.1. Introduction

The energy sector is currently experiencing one of the largest transformations ever recorded in its history (Mostafa et al. 2022). This

Chapter written by Biswajit DAS, Himanshu PABBI, Shweta SINGH, Monika MEHRA and Sanny KUMAR.

change is being driven by the urgency of the world to find ways of utilizing sustainable energy, the acceleration of technology and the large-scale digitization of infrastructure. The energy systems were constructed on the basis of the similar predictability of demand trends, power generation concentration and unidirectional power flows, but today, things have become much more complicated and dynamic. Energy distribution, its production and consumption have been evolving radically with renewable energy sources, power generation decentralization and introduction of smart technology (Ul Haq et al. 2025a). The new challenges that these changes have brought about are intermittency, uncertainty and grid volatility, which have highlighted an unknown opportunity to become creative and efficient.

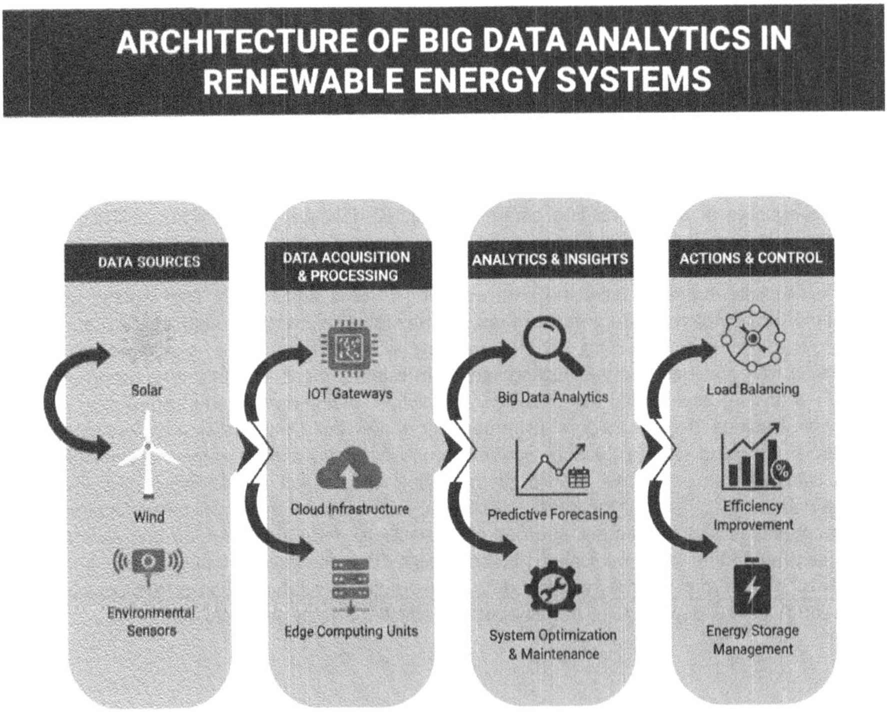

Figure 6.1. *Renewable energy system integrated big data analytics architecture. For a color version of this figure, see www.iste.co.uk/ulhaq/artificial1.zip*

As illustrated in Figure 6.1, the traits of this new energy age include an explosion of data, velocity, rate and diversity of data across all levels of the energy value chain, which has grown many times over, following the invention of smart meters, sensor-networked, industrial IoT devices and more complex supervisory control and data acquisition (SCADA) systems (Ayub et al. 2020). The industry has become a producer of tremendous volumes of different types of data every second such as weather forecasts and market trends, data on real consumption and grid performance indicators. This fact has been a rich source of information that can be used properly to contribute to the decision-making process, increase efficiency and reliability, and shift to more efficient and robust energy regimes (Ul Haq et al. 2024). It is not another by-product of activities in energy.

One of the most important problems of managing this shift is the big data analytics. This is reported to be a collection of sophisticated practices and tools, which will be utilized to collect, process, examine and decode big data in order to be in a position to get substantial knowledge and direct strategic operations (Ul Haq et al. 2022). The decision-making of the energy systems requires the use of big data analytics to prompt data to be used. As an example, utilities can predict peak demand based on consumption trends, operators can make a more efficient grid based on real-time and regulators can make a more effective energy policy based on data-driven models (Diamantoulakis et al. 2015). The capacity to transform raw data into practical wisdom is essential toward sustaining and protecting the energy infrastructure and also gaining a competitive edge.

Big data analytics are closely related to predictive modeling, which involves historical and current data collection, statistical and ML to predict future events and trends (Ul Haq et al. 2025c). Predictive models are useful in the energy systems, especially in cases where predicting is critical in the operations, planning and market participation. As an example, the accurate demand prediction assists utilities in resource allocation and avoids the costly supply and demand shortages (Ul Haq et al. 2025d). Predictive maintenance models can enhance the life of equipment by detecting the early signs of equipment degradation and reducing downtimes. Renewable energy based on forecast models through historical production estimates and weather forecasts can be used to enhance the integration of the grid and stabilization of power systems. The effect of predictive analytics is that it allows the stakeholders to adopt a proactive stance, that is, foreseeing the potential issues and mitigating them before they occur, as opposed to the reactive strategy, which assumes that they will occur and thus take action in response to the problem (Ul Haq and Khanday 2025).

The importance of the predictive modeling and big data analytics is also supported by the fact that the transformation of energy can often be characterized by the so-called 3D model of energy decarbonization, decentralization and digitalization (Chukwunweike and Salaudeen 2025). These trends have their own peculiar issues that need to be addressed with the help of data. The concept of decarbonization is motivated by the desire to reduce the issue of climate change as intermittent renewable power sources (wind and solar) become part of the grid, complicating the task of managing the grid.

Some of the new participants introduced through decentralization include prosumers, electric cars and microgrids; all of these add more complexity to the system. Digitalization connects millions of devices and sensors generating vast amounts of real-time data and creating issues of data governance, cybersecurity and interoperability (Nayyef et al. 2024). These elements collaborate with each other due to the use of big data analytics, which give the opportunity to predict, streamline and control the continuously evolving network of modern energy systems.

Another interesting application for big data and predictive analytics is grid resilience and reliability. Progressively more power systems are becoming vulnerable to disruptions because they are becoming more digitalized and connected (Ahmed et al. 2024). Such disruptions may include the extreme weather events and natural disasters as well as equipment and cyberattacks. Predictive analytics can increase resilience by providing preventive maintenance capabilities, real-time anomaly detection and vulnerability detection prior to its criticality (Oluokun et al. 2024). A transformer outage could be predicted by ML algorithms trained on historical failure data, and streams of real-time data could be examined to find anomalies that might point to a cyberattack. The competencies are required at a time where further challenges and risk are being encountered to ensure that energy infrastructure remains continuously running in an uninterrupted, reliable and consistent manner.

Both predictive modeling and big data analytics are the same as far as transformational economic and policy are concerned. The dynamic and competitive nature of the energy markets is also because of the changing supply and demand, the shifting pricing strategy and the growing involvement of distributed energy resources (Srinivas et al. 2025). The prediction models can be used to help the market players manage the risks, improve their bid strategies and forecast the price behavior. Conversely, policymakers can use information-based knowledge to develop policies that will facilitate grid modernization, promote the adoption of renewable energy sources and promote customer engagement. Also, by combining analytics and digital platforms, energy providers can increase customer satisfaction, offer personalized services and develop innovative business models on the basis of predictive data.

Technological progress in the fields of ML, artificial intelligence (AI) and high-performance computing (Ul Haq et al. 2025b) is also improving the potential of big data analytics in energy systems. The amount and diversity of energy data often simplify conventional analytical methods, yet modern algorithms, including ensemble models, deep learning, as well as reinforcement learning, are capable of handling high-dimensional data and can precisely discover complex patterns. RNNs and long short-term memory (LSTM) networks are very effective in time-series prediction (Al-Jumaili et al. 2023), and hence best suited to renewable generation or load demand prediction. Reinforcement learning algorithms can be used to dynamically optimize grid control strategies, and progressively more hybrid models that combine data-driven methods and physical simulations can be used to plan a system and predictive maintenance. These trends are widening the horizons of the potential of energy analytics (Zhou et al. 2017).

High-performance computing, AI and ML capabilities are improving the possibilities of big data analytics in energy systems. Algorithms such as deep learning, reinforcement learning and ensemble models can now be used to analyze high-dimensional data to identify complex trends in remarkable accuracy; however, traditional methods of analysis can often fail on the volume and complexity of the energy data. LSTM networks and recurrent neural networks (RNNs) are both also good at time series forecasting, which is why they are ideal at approximating renewable generation or load demand. Although progressively more hybrid models are being employed that combine data-driven models with physical simulations for predictive maintenance and system planning, reinforcement learning algorithms can be used to optimize grid control strategies in real-time. These developments are pushing the limits of energy analytics.

It is most likely that the incorporation of big data analytics and predictive models will shape the future of global energy industry in several aspects. This will necessitate the potential to produce actionable knowledge on big and complicated data since the systems are getting smarter, smarter and greener. IT technologies will streamline virtually every aspect of transformation of energy, such as the facilitation of the decarbonization process, resilience and smarter grids, and introduction of renewable energy sources. Lastly, the big data analytics and prediction models would introduce a paradigm shift in designing, operating and managing the energy systems that are not only technological advances (Igweonu 2024). They help the stakeholders predict the challenges, streamline the processes and make wise decisions in an environment that is becoming more complex and uncertain by converting raw data into strategic oversight. Trying to give a detailed critique, this chapter will examine the conceptualization behind the implementation of these paradigm-shifting technologies, their mechanisms and how they have been and may be used in future trends. In so doing, it will demonstrate how information-based tactics are enhancing the energy environment in the current times and how they are shaping up strong, intelligent and sustainable energy systems in the future.

6.2. Big data analytics in energy systems basics

The global energy industry is at risk of a digital revolution due to the exponential growth of data (Annapareddy 2021). The volumes of data previously unknown are being created throughout the entire energy value chain because of the advanced sensors, smart meters, IoT devices, and cloud platforms (Ul Haq 2024).

There is a shift in this evolution where real-time and analytics-based decision-making has replaced the traditional data collection and reporting mechanism. It has been revealed that the big data analytics have become an important tool in the modern-day energy system to learn the behavior of the system, enhance the efficiency of its operations, predict future trends, and aid the strategic planning.

Here, the fundamental principles of the big data analytics are briefly discussed in relation to the energy systems. The importance of real-time analytics in the development of resilient, scalable and intelligent energy networks is highlighted, as well as the meaning of big data, relevant characteristics of big data, the big data lifecycle and the infrastructure thereof.

6.2.1. *Big data*

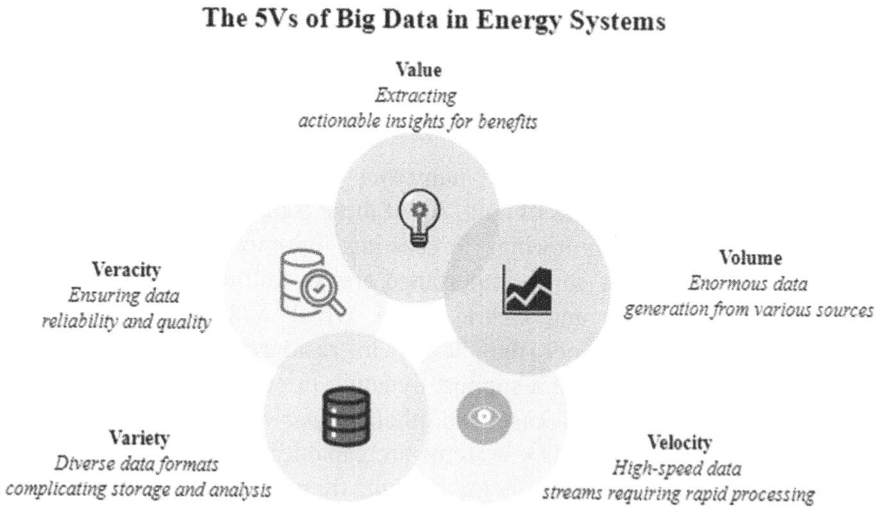

Figure 6.2. *The 5 Vs of big data in energy systems, which shows the main dimensions of importance of the big data, including value, volume, velocity, variety and veracity that determine the characteristics of the big data and play the role of energy analytics. For a color version of this figure, see www.iste.co.uk/ulhaq/artificial1.zip*

The big data term is used to refer to datasets that are too large, dynamic and diverse to be processed effectively using traditional data processing methods (Sonko et al. 2024). These data are available across a wide range of sources and are used in the energy industry to serve a diverse set of purposes, such as to manage assets, perform market research, predict demand and monitor the grid. The significant aspects of big data are often described in terms of the 5Vs model (Figure 6.2) that summarizes the key potential and issues regarding the large-scale data management: *Volume*: from sensors, meters, grid equipment and market activities, the contemporary energy systems generate tremendous amounts of data. Every day, utilities have to process terabytes or even petabytes of data to maintain operational visibility. *Velocity*: data streams are created at high speed particularly where real-time monitoring is required. Quick processing and analysis are required in order to make a timely decision. *Variety*: energy data can be of three types: semi-structured (event logs), structured, which is numerical reading, and unstructured, which is text, photos, or videos. The variability of these formats complicates the analysis and storage. *Veracity*:

the measurement errors, transmission delays, or noise can influence the data quality and reliability. The right data are required to make effective decisions. *Value*: the end objective of big data analytics is to have actionable insights that can enhance operations, economy or the environment (Njoku 2025).

6.2.1.1. *Sources of big data in energy systems*

The energy systems consist of numerous diverse components, each of which produces various types of data. All of these datasets are needed in order to achieve effective monitoring, forecasting, optimization and decision-making. The sources of some importance are as follows: AMI (advanced metering infrastructure) and smart meters, which collect intensive time-stamped data on consumer unit usage in residential, commercial and industrial markets. These data support dynamic pricing techniques, demand response programs, load forecasts and others. *Supervisory Control and Data Acquisition (SCADA)*: SCADA systems are capable of constantly supplying operational data streams on voltage, current, frequency and system state to monitor and control grid infrastructure. *IoT devices and sensor network*: sensors on transmission lines, transformers, turbines and other assets provide real-time information about the temperature and vibration, pressure and health of equipment. Fault detection and predictive maintenance would require such information. *Weather and environmental data*: the weather plays a major role in the production of renewable energy. Examples of meteorological data used in predicting the energy output and balancing the demand and supply include temperature, wind speed, sun irradiance and humidity (Balakrishna 2024). *Market and economic data*: the energy trading platforms, electricity markets and regulatory agencies produce price clues, volumes of trade and economic indicators. These data play a key role in market modeling and strategic planning. *Social and behavioral data*: to enhance load balancing and energy efficiency, the new demand-side management techniques utilize the information of user preference, mobility trends and consumer behavior. When these disparate data sources are married together, the issues of interoperability, synchronization and standardization are exposed, and opportunities to innovate and optimize a system are a previously unheard-of opportunity.

6.2.1.2. *The big data analytics lifecycle*

A sequence of stages, which are usually applied to organize the process of big data analytics in energy systems, is known as the data lifecycle. This lifecycle as shown in Figure 6.3 is the sequential evolution of turning raw energy system data into actionable data in five major steps, which include data acquisition, data management and storage, data preprocessing, data analysis and modeling, and visualization and decision support. Each of the steps is vital to converting raw data into valuable knowledge (Hamzat 2025). Data acquisition is concerned with the amassing of information on various platforms, devices and services so as to guarantee the full and ongoing data collection. Data management and storage is concerned with storing big data in an efficient way through cloud systems, distributed file system or data lakes that can store a variety of data. Data preprocessing involves cleaning, filtering and integrating data in order to eliminate noise, deal with missing values and normalize formats, which is of great importance in ensuring good quality analytics. Data analysis and modeling use statistical techniques, ML and optimization models to reveal trends, correlations and predictive information. Lastly, visualization and decision support shows the results of analytics in dashboards, charts or GIS to make real-time decisions based on data. Analytical outcomes, which are generated in energy operations and planning, are more accurate, reliable and applicable in systematic approach of this lifecycle.

Figure 6.3. *The big data analytics lifecycle in energy systems. For a color version of this figure, see www.iste.co.uk/ulhaq/artificial1.zip*

6.2.1.3. *Infrastructure and platforms for big data analytics*

Effective big data analytics require a solid technology base capable of processing large volumes of data with high velocity and complexity of the process. There are several key technologies that will form the analytics ecosystem in energy systems: Frameworks such as Apache Hadoop and Apache Spark enable big datasets to be processed in real-time, significantly reducing the time to compute and enabling the solution of challenging analytics problems. *Cloud computing*: it provides scalable, on-demand resources in terms of analysis, processing and storage (Ohalete et al. 2023; Adegoke and Obunadike 2025). They enable energy and utility companies to process the large volumes of data without necessarily engaging in the heavy investment in physical infrastructure. *Edge computing*: it provides benefits by reducing transmission delays and enhancing system responsiveness by processing data nearer to the source of the data, such as fault detectors or control signals. *Data lakes and warehouses*: it can be used to store both processed and raw data to be flexibly queried and analyzed. Data lakes specifically support schema-on-read methods that would be used with heterogeneous energy data. The choice of infrastructure depends on the requirement of the type of data volume, latency, security as well as the costs.

6.2.1.4. *Importance of real-time analytics*

Key applications include the following:

– *Grid stability and fault management*: continuous data analysis helps operators to detect anomalies, voltage variations and equipment faults before these causes of disruption can grow.

– *Predictive maintenance*: this is an asset health monitoring system, which is a real-time mechanism whereby it is planned ahead of any maintenance so as to minimize downtimes and prolong the life of the assets.

– *Demand response and load optimization*: the information of dynamic consumption boosts the economic performance and stability of the grid, which allows it to load balance and make dynamic pricing strategies.

Real-time analytics will be needed in order to establish the adaptive and self-repairing energy system that will be able to promptly adapt to the changing environment and move onto distributed and renewable energy sources. The digital revolution, which has dominated the energy industry, is founded on big data analytics. It provides the foundation of greater efficiency, reliability and intentional selection, since it is utilized for acquiring, information processing and interpretation of massive and bulky information (Igweonu 2024). This section has presented the fundamental concepts of the big data analytics, the key characteristics of this kind of analytics, the key sources of data and the premeditated lifecycle of converting the raw data into the form used. In addition, it has also denoted the necessity to support the infrastructure and the greater role of real-time analytics in helping intelligent, resilient and responsive energy networks. These are the higher predictive modeling techniques whose ground concepts shall be discussed in the following sections of this chapter.

6.3. Predictive modeling: concepts and techniques

Predictive modeling has become a vital component of the contemporary energy system to enable the utilities, grid operators and legislators to predict future development and optimize the system to make sound decisions. Unlike reactive measures, which react to the real-life events, predictive analytics offers a dynamic framework of knowledge and management of complicated energy systems. It processes historical and up-to-date data of various sources, such as smart meters, SCADA systems, IoT sensors, market services and weather services, to generate informational value (Jha et al. 2024). Several of the energy systems applications of predictive modeling include demand forecasting, renewable generation projection, equipment health monitoring, anomaly detection, as well as strategic planning. Its ability to forecast the future condition and trends will allow the stakeholders to effectively incorporate renewable resources, enhance operational efficiency, enhance reliability and reduce costs.

6.3.1. *Role of predictive analytics in energy systems*

There are several ways of applying predictive analytics to the contemporary energy systems. The first are primary applications where the models are employed to predict market prices, which are known as forecasting renewable energy supply or electricity demand. With precise load prediction, utilities are able to balance generation and demand, save operating costs and avoid grid instability. In the same way, renewable energy forecasting assists in the incorporation of intermittent resources such as wind and solar in order to ensure that supply remains constant with the demand despite weather changes. Another valuable application is optimization; predictive models guide the efficient utilization of energy resources, for example, load shifting under response to demand side programs, storage operations and generation scheduling. Predictive analytics are also necessary in order to identify anomalies in the performance of equipment, grid behavior, or consumption so that the operators can identify odd trends (Enemosah and Chukwunweike 2022; Hamdan et al. 2024). Predictive models prevent the occurrence of preventive interventions, reduction of downtime and costly interruptions by detecting deviations of normal operations. Finally, predictive modeling helps in decision-making by providing quantitative information that informs financial, operational and strategic decision-making in energy industry.

6.3.2. *Types of predictive models*

Energy systems predictive models are broadly categorized into statistical, ML and deep learning predictors of energy systems. The categories are characterized in different ways, benefits and drawbacks, which makes the categories applicable in any forecasting and analysis situations. Regression statistical models as well as autoregressive integrated moving average (ARIMA) are some of the common tools used in performing time-series forecasting and trend analysis. The models are highly effective in predictions that are short term, particularly when the data have linear trends or seasonal behavior. Their key advantages are that they are easy, easy to decipher and are quick to calculate, hence very expedient in simple prediction. However, they tend to fail in capturing nonlinear relationships that are complicated in nature of current energy systems. On the other hand, ML models have gained significant popularity due to their ability to detect complicated and nonlinear patterns in huge high-dimensional data. The reason is that such algorithms as random forest, support vectors machines (SVM) and gradient boosting are primarily deployed in applications such as energy demand prediction, predicting renewable energy, as well as fault detection. These approaches can learn by themselves using past information and adapt to the dynamic nature of the system, which offer more flexible and correct predictions than the classical models. In addition, the ensemble (e.g. gradient boosting and bagging) strategies combine the strength of multiple models and further improve the predictive accuracy. Despite their effectiveness, they might be quite less transparent and should be fine-tuned.

Deep learning models increase these capabilities with the assistance of complicated neural network constructions upon which the space and time dependencies of the data are modeled. The models are presented in Table 6.1, such as LSTM networks, which can easily generalize long-term dependence of time-series in predicting loads and renewable generation due to long-term trends, and therefore they are particularly useful in these fields. CNNs are beneficial regarding the spatial-temporal forecasting, which is the process of identifying the pattern in space and time.

As stated in Chukwunweike et al. (2024) and Ukoba et al. (2024), predictive analytics in big data uses statistical, ML and deep learning methods to derive actionable information using large volumes of data. They conducted a systematic review of 109 studies and categorized applications in the industrial, smart energy and urban sectors, as well as highlighted the increased significance of data-driven forecasting and decision-making. Despite being highly predictive models, deep learning models are computationally intensive and require massive training data in most instances.

The most significant predictive modeling methods, their typical application case, their advantages and limitations are outlined in Table 6.1.

Technique	Category	Typical use case	Advantages	Limitations
ARIMA	Statistical	Short-term load forecasting	Simple, interpretable	Struggles with nonlinearities
Random forest	ML	Energy demand prediction	Handles high-dimensional data	Less transparent
SVM	ML	Fault detection, load forecasting	Good generalization	Parameter tuning needed
LSTM	Deep learning	Time-series forecasting	Captures long-term dependencies	High computational cost
CNN	Deep learning	Spatial-temporal forecasting	Good pattern recognition	Data-intensive
Ensemble models	ML/hybrid	Price forecasting, load prediction	High accuracy	Complexity in deployment

Table 6.1. *Predictive modeling techniques and applications*

6.3.3. *Model development process*

The development of predictive models is done in a systematic way to ensure that they are applicable, generalized and reliable in energy systems. The initial step is the data preparation, which involves data collection, data cleaning, data standardization and amalgamation. To ensure integrity of the dataset, this step addresses outliers, missing values and inconsistencies. The second step is feature engineering, which entails the selection or construction of relevant input variables in order to enhance the performance of models. Examples of features are the historical load trends, weather conditions, market indicators and time factors such as the time of the year or the season. The next step is model training where the algorithms are trained to identify patterns within previous data. This is also commonly used to prevent overfitting, and hyperparameters are influenced to mean maximum performance. To ensure that the model has good generalization in new situations, model validation checks the model accuracy by using unseen data. Finally, deployment involves integration of the predictive model into decision-support or operational platform systems. Performance should be sustained through regular retraining and constant monitoring to meet the system conditions, data quality and operational requirements as conditions alter.

6.3.4. *Evaluation metrics*

The performance of predictive models should be assessed with the help of appropriate assessment measures, which evaluate robustness, accuracy and reliability. Regression problems are frequently measured by the coefficient of determination (R^2), mean absolute error (MAE) and root mean square error (RMSE). RMSE enlightens the size of forecast errors, whereas MAE provides an average deviation of observation. R^2 provides a goodness-of-fit, which is a percentage of the explained amount of variance of the model. Measures such as precision, recall and the F1-score are commonly used in the detection of anomalies or classification. The F1-score is used to determine the proportion of true positives discovered and the proportion of correct positive response; F1-score is a balance between precision and recall. They are the evaluation measures that should be closely considered to identify the strengths and weaknesses of the model and also how applicable it is in specific use of energy.

6.3.5. *Challenges in predictive modeling*

Some of the problems that can cause significant problems in the performance of a model are loss of numbers, sensor malfunctions and irregular format, which are related to data quality. Overfitting is a frequent issue, especially in models of deep learning and ML in which the model may select noise rather than latent pattern, hence reducing the capacity to generalize. Interpretability has also remained relevant and may be a serious problem with deep neural networks and other simplistic models; these are often black boxes that operators may struggle to gain insight into how the model got the answers. Lastly, scalability is transforming reality since the amount of data generated by the energy systems is enormous and requires a considerably large amount of processing power to operate and train the model. These issues require strong data pretreatment, model selection methods, interpretable methods and scalable computer infrastructure.

Predictive modeling is a revolution in the energy system of today whereby we are now capable of making decisions in advance, managing operations and enhancing reliability. Being used in forecasting, optimization, anomaly detection and decision support, it has statistical models such as ARIMA and regression; ML models such as random forest, SVM and gradient boosting; and advanced models such as LSTM, CNN and transformers. The methodological aspects in the development process include data preparation, feature engineering, model training, validation and deployment.

6.3.6. *Dataset description and experimental setup*

In this study, the smart grid real-time load monitoring data set is comprehensive time series data generated as a collection of energy management, forecast and fault detection datasets in smart grids. It consists of more than 50,000 records (fifteen minutes in-between) that are rich in temporal granularity and are ideal to analyze in real-time. It also contains renewable energies such as the use of solar and wind power along with the important parameters of smart grids such as the voltage, current, power consumption and reactive power. Such properties also feature the detection of faults, which indicate conditions of overloading, faults in transformers and the environmental conditions such as temperature, humidity and fluctuations of electricity prices. Predicted load (kW) is the target variable of the dataset, and with its help, ML and deep learning algorithms can make very accurate predictions regarding the energy. It hence suits research on smart grid analytics and real-time energy optimization as it offers a plethora of applications, such as fault/anomaly detection, energy demand forecasting, investigation of integration of renewable energy sources and dynamic pricing research. A comparative study was carried out to model smart grid load forecasting with six different models, namely, random forest regressor, support vector machine (SVM), LSTM, CNN, the statistical time-series model ARIMA and a predictive ensemble model. The data were preprocessed: missing values treatment and relevant numerical features selection. The column "Predicted Load (kW)" was used as the target variable, and the dataset was split into training and testing sets in an 80:20 ratio. All of the deep learning models were trained to learn complex relationships within the data. They were thoroughly tested using the standard metrics for performance evaluation: mean absolute error (MAE), mean squared error (MSE), and R^2 score.

Model	MAE	MSE	R^2 score
ARIMA	35.7890	1800.1234	0.9200
Random forest	15.1234	350.5678	0.9850
SVM	25.4321	980.6543	0.9600
LSTM	18.7654	490.3456	0.9800
CNN	20.0987	550.9876	0.9780
Ensemble	17.5432	400.8765	0.9830

Table 6.2. *Model performance comparison*

Results across Table 6.2 clearly indicate that the random forest model achieved the highest accuracy among all other individual and ensemble approaches, with the highest R^2 score of 0.9850, coupled with the least error metrics, MAE of 15.1234 and MSE of 350.5678. The integration of a number of learning paradigms enhances strength and provides a high load forecasting accuracy as seen in the second-best ensemble model in terms of R^2, which is 0.9830. The application is a good illustration of how different predictive analytics applications can utilize multivariate data to produce highly accurate load predictions, which enhances grid stability, smart energy management and energy demand prediction. A comparative approach of this magnitude provides a solid experimental foundation of predictive analytics in energy systems of the present time.

This intensive analysis examines the performance of various ML and deep learning algorithms in predicting smart grid load based on a powerful evaluation framework that consists of mean absolute error, mean squared error and the R-squared (R^2).

The study includes a statistical time-series model as well as deep learning models such as LSTM or CNN and the traditional ML models such as random forest or SVM. To exploit the complementary properties of both models, an ensemble strategy, which integrated the predictions of random forest, SVM and LSTM, was also considered. It was found that the performance profile of each model is different. The random forest model was repeatedly found to be the best at predicting a mean absolute error of the lowest value (15.12), a mean squared error of the lowest (350.57) and a maximum R^2 of 0.9850. This shows its amazing ability to detect nonlinear complex relations in the smart grid data. The ensemble model also exhibited great results under all of the metrics (MAE: 17.54, MSE: 400.88, R^2: 0.9830), which emphasized the benefits of combining multiple predictive clues. Two deep learning models, CNN (MAE: 20.10, MSE: 550.99, R^2: 0.9780) and LSTM (MAE: 18.77, MSE: 490.35, R^2: 0.9800), also showed impressive performance, which makes it possible to note that neural networks are capable of working with complex time-series data. Nevertheless, the ARIMA model (MAE: 35.79, MSE: 1800.12, R^2: 0.9200) and the SVM (MAE: 25.43, MSE: 980.65, R^2: 0.9600) had much higher error rates. ARIMA demonstrated the lowest R^2 and the highest MSE, which is probably because it is a univariate time-series model with a more constrained scope.

The visual analysis provides additional support for these conclusions. Figure 6.4 compares the MAE and R2 for each model. It is clear that the random forest leads both metrics, with the ensemble model coming in second.

The random forest performs better than the other models, as evidenced by the fact that its error magnitude is much smaller, while ARIMA has the highest MSE, according to a bar chart created specifically for MSE (Figure 6.5).

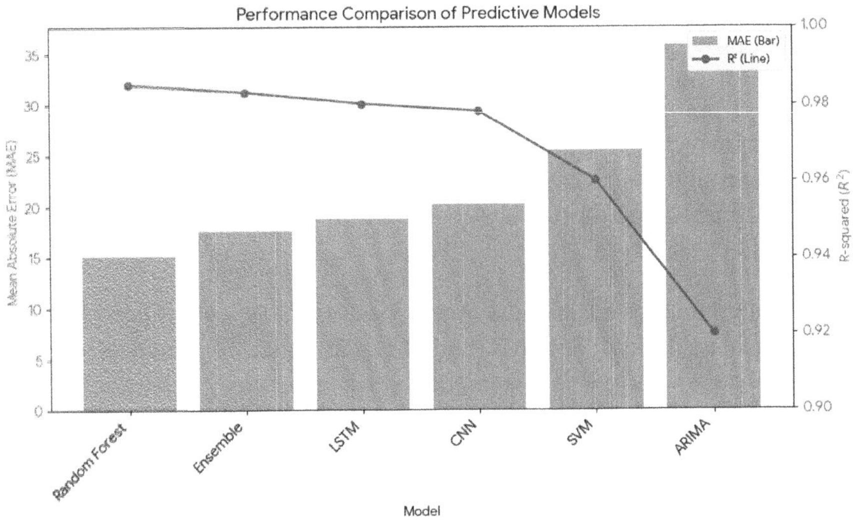

Figure 6.4. *Performance comparison of predictive models (MAE and R^2). For a color version of this figure, see www.iste.co.uk/ulhaq/artificial1.zip*

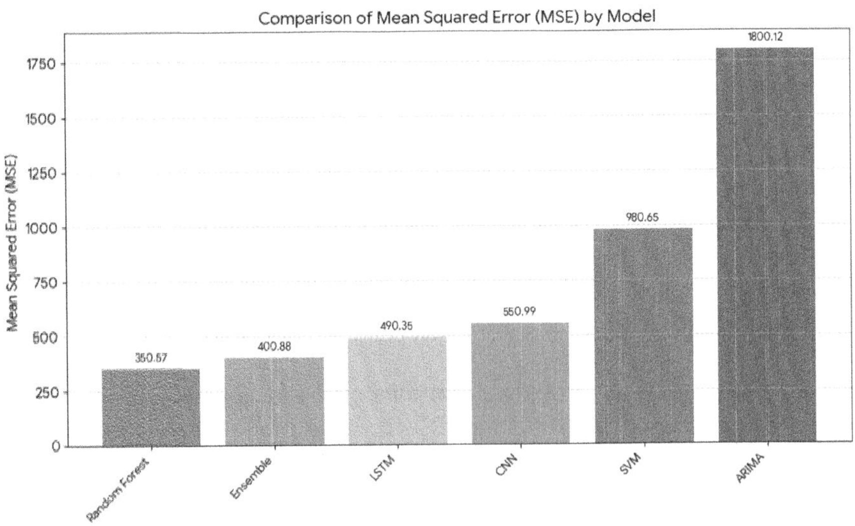

Figure 6.5. *Comparison of mean squared error (MSE) by model. For a color version of this figure, see www.iste.co.uk/ulhaq/artificial1.zip*

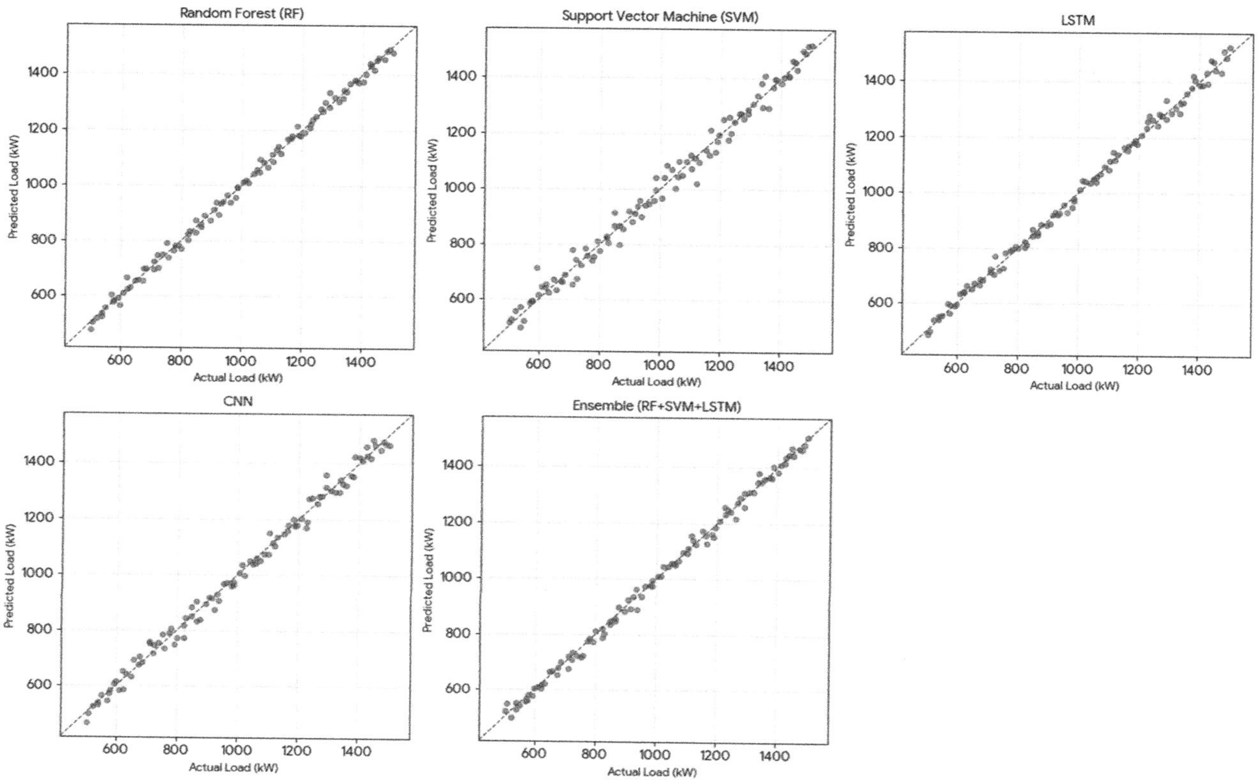

Figure 6.6. *Actual versus predicted load scatter plots for all models. For a color version of this figure, see www.iste.co.uk/ulhaq/artificial1.zip*

Lastly, a scatter plot comparison of the actual and predicted load for each model is shown in Figure 6.6. With their higher accuracy and dependability across the range of load values, the random forest and ensemble models' predictions cluster most tightly around the ideal y = x line (perfect prediction), as this visualization makes evident. Larger deviations from actual values are indicated by models with a wider spread, such as SVM.

6.4. Applications of big data analytics in energy systems

Big data analytics, therefore, has become an important tool for strategic planning, optimization and decision-making, considering that the increasing digitization of the energy sector has not only opened up new operating methodologies but also changed the old ones. Utilities and energy management can gain actionable insights from the large and varied information emanating from smart meters, sensors, grid devices, weather stations and market platforms to better system performance, reliability and sustainability for improving the performance of the systems. Due to the emerging need for predictive and prescriptive tactics in addition to the traditionally preferred reactive problem-solving, modern dynamic energy networks, integrated with renewables, depend upon big data analytics. Some of the primary applications of big data analytics to energy systems, examined in this area, are demand forecasting, renewable energy estimation, load management, predictive maintenance, smart grid optimization and energy market analytics.

6.4.1. *Demand forecasting*

A significant application of big data analytics is demand forecasting to provide an understanding of the power consumption trend that is necessary in capacity planning, operation efficiency and strategic decision-making. The short term, medium term and long term are three forecasting horizons, and each of them fulfills a different role. Short-term forecasting, covering a few minutes to a few days, forms the basis of real-time grid management and scheduling of the generation resources. Medium-term forecasting supports procurement, load balancing and maintenance planning and extends over a period of several weeks to months. Long-term forecasting, usually in years, is a support in investment planning, development of infrastructure and policy making. ML algorithms have radically transformed the nature of demand forecasting by extracting natural nonlinear correlations in both past and current data on consumption. Common algorithms applied to predict regions of load at the regional, municipal and industrial levels include algorithms such as the random forest, gradient boosting and SVMs. Case studies also prove the effectiveness of these models. Indicatively, ensemble ML methods have been used by utilities in North America and Europe to optimize energy procurement, improve peak load management and reduce forecasting errors. These predictive models create incredibly precise and thorough demand forecasts that are necessary for dependable grid operation by combining weather data, calendar effects and socioeconomic indices.

6.4.2. *Renewable energy forecasting*

Due to the naturally intermittent and meteorologically dependent nature of especially solar and wind renewable energy sources, accurate forecasting is an important aspect in maintaining grid stability and efficiency in energy utilization. Big data analytics make renewable energy more predictable by combining historical generation data with meteorological data such as temperature, wind speed, solar irradiance and cloud cover. Some of the sophisticated ML and deep learning algorithms that have been effective in capturing both temporal and spatial dependencies for the purpose of accurate short-term and day-ahead predictions include the convolutional models and LSTM networks.

For example, in the solar power forecasting of large-scale photovoltaic farms, high-resolution satellite images and ground-based weather sensors are used to forecast the probable output and fluctuations in irradiance (Ukoba et al. 2024). Similarly, the prediction of wind energy relies on high-frequency information obtained from local weather stations and wind turbines. Besides enhancing energy dispatch planning, accurate renewable predictions motivate market participation, reduce curtailment and enhance system efficiency (Thomas et al. 2023).

6.4.3. *Load management and demand response*

The use of big data analytics is an essential part of DR and load management programs as both are aimed at maximizing the utilization of electricity by adjusting user activity and grid demands. Advanced analytics can be used to offer dynamic pricing by dynamically adjusting the prices of electricity in relation to supply and demand, thus motivating consumers to shift their consumption outside of peak hours. To forecast the demand patterns and develop incentive-driven DR plans, predictive models consider demographic data, user patterns and past usage. Behavioral modeling is also commonly utilized in the quest to find the trend in consumption and tailor DR programs to meet the requirements of residential, commercial and industrial consumers. Depending on their habits of use, ML algorithms will categorize users into groups and predict their response to prices or automatic load control. These strategies enhance the reliability and effectiveness of energy networks by minimizing the peak loads and enhancing grid flexibility.

6.4.4. *Predictive maintenance and asset management*

The operation and maintenance of energy assets should be performed to provide system reliability and extend the life of the equipment. Big data analytics plays a role in predictive maintenance, which relies on the SCADA systems, IoT sensors and past maintenance history to constantly check the functionality of assets. Predictive analytical models are used to predict the probability of component failure, initiate the early manifestations of wear or failure and detect anomalies in the normal operation of the components (Enemosah and Chukwunweike 2022; Hamdan et al. 2024; Ukoba et al. 2024). Condition-based maintenance scheduling through predictive analytics will enable utilities to plan any intervention beforehand, which will result in lower costs of maintenance and unscheduled outages. As an example, ML models and vibrations in transformers or turbines are able to predict possible failures days or weeks before they occur. This is also the case for predictive models in storage systems, power lines and switchgear, which allow the detection of anomalies much earlier, allowing them to be repaired in time and enhancing the reliability of a system (Sankarananth et al. 2023; Ukoba et al. 2024).

6.4.5. *Smart grid optimization*

Smart grids are based on the big data analytics to get insights and improve the resiliency, dependability and efficiency of the system. Real-time load balancing, peak shaving and outage prevention are achievable through utilities that scan high-frequency data streams of meters, sensors and grid devices. Dynamical balancing is performed based on the supply and demand of power to ensure loss reduction and avoid overloading. Predictive modeling makes peak shaving techniques possible, minimizing the peak generation capacity which is expensive by promoting off-peak commercialization or by switching on energy storage devices. Fault detection with the application of analytics is also beneficial in improving outage prediction and avoidance. ML patterns will identify trends related to system malfunctions and enable proactive mitigation measures to prevent small issues before a big breakdown occurs. Other such frameworks are demand-side management and DERs; with analytics, smart grids are allowed to coordinate such complex, multi-layered networks without losing stability or effectiveness.

6.4.6. *Energy market analytics*

The analytics of big data has revolutionized the workings of the energy market by enabling proper predictions of prices, evaluation of risks and optimization of the trading strategies. In predicting the future market, predictive models will take into account the historical price information, the market trends, regulatory changes and the generation demand trends (Amini and Rohani 2024; Fowosere et al. 2025). These data are used by utilities, traders and policy-makers to create superior plans to participate in the market, hedge against changes of the price and improve their bidding process. Risk assessment models based on analytics identify the most likely operational and financial consequences of unforeseen events, regulatory changes and market variation. In addition, predictive analytics also helps facilitate the inclusion of renewable energy into the market by forecasting the profiles of generating and aligning the trading strategies and forecasted production. This incorporation of analytics in the functioning of the markets makes them more productive, less risky financially and simpler to make better decisions in the competitive energy markets.

The analytic (Thomas et al. 2023; Ishola and Abdulbasit 2025) advancement of big data has become an enabling game-changer in every part of the energy systems in terms of sustainability, dependability and efficiency (Beckley 2025; Fowosere et al. 2025). It has been used in some of its applications to predict demand, load, predictive maintenance, optimizing a smart grid, energy market analytics and predicting renewable energy use. Proactive, dynamic approaches to optimizing operations, reducing costs and enhancing resiliency of systems can be applied by utilities and energy managers using both historical and real-time data. Techniques of statistical and hybrid ML and deep learning methods offer the foundation of correct prediction, anomaly detection and supporting decision making (Je et al. 2021). As the complexity and decentralization of energy systems continues, the incorporation of big data analytics will be important in the creation of intelligent, flexible and sustainable energy networks.

6.5. Integration of IoT, Edge and cloud technologies

Because cloud, edge computing and IoT technologies allow better monitoring, real-time analytical, predictive modeling and strategic decision-making, they are becoming the driving force behind the modernization of energy systems. These technologies turn traditional energy networks into highly efficient, intelligent and adaptable networks that are capable of managing increased complexity induced by distributed energy sources, adoption of renewable energy sources and evolving consumer needs. With the help of distributed compute, scalable storage and networked equipment, energy operators can optimize costs and resource utilization and gain greater visibility, operational efficiency and resiliency (Devaraj et al. 2021; Ogunkoya 2024). This section examines the uses of these technologies in energy systems in data gathering, real-time processing, scalable storage, simulation and cybersecurity.

6.5.1. *Role of IoT in data collection*

IoT connecting digital analytics systems and physical infrastructures also makes energy system real-time data collection possible. Smart meters, sensors and intelligent monitoring equipment are IoT-enabled devices that constantly measure the energy consumption, voltage, current, temperature, vibration and equipment health. Smart meters are estimated by installing in residential, commercial and industrial settings, and the data are accurate and time-stamped, which allows load forecasting, dynamic pricing and demand response systems. Transformers, turbines and distribution lines have sensors that measure the operating parameters to avert failure and faults through predictive maintenance and fault detection. The use of large-scale IoT device usage is the foundation of modern energy intelligence, and it increases the level of observability of the systems and produces the high-resolution data sets required to perform advanced analytics and ML.

6.5.2. *Edge analytics for real-time processing*

Although IoT devices can produce large volumes of data, there is a latency and bandwidth limitation issue that may make it difficult to transmit all data to central systems. Edge analytics circumvents such problems by working with data where it is generated, with less latency, less bandwidth and real-time decision-making. Edge computing machines process streaming information on the edge and identify abnormal conditions, initiate automated control and produce summary information to be analyzed in central machines. Edge analytics enhances grid stability and operational safety by enabling timely reaction to critical occasions in applications like predictive maintenance, load balancing and defect detection. Communication can be maximized by distributing computation among the edge nodes and can provide insights faster, thus with more responsiveness and resilience introduced into the energy system.

6.5.3. *Cloud computing for scalable storage and processing*

Cloud computing enhances edge analytics by supplying the scalable processing and storage of the large volumes of data produced by IoT-enabled energy systems. Cloud platforms facilitate high-volume, high-velocity and high-variety data management by enabling the integration of the disparate data sources, using the data lakes and distributed storage systems offered by utilities. State-of-the-art cloud-based analytics platforms provide scenarios analysis, predictive models and decision support with the assistance of ML pipelines, visualization tools and parallel processing capabilities.

Due to the flexibility and elasticity of cloud infrastructure, energy operators will be able to perform complex simulations, scale resources according to demand and keep historical archives that can be used to plan long-term and comply with regulations.

Consequently, cloud computing provides the foundation of the integration of the big data analytics, ML and operational intelligence throughout the far-spreading energy networks.

6.5.4. *Digital twins and simulation*

Digital twins represent another use of IoT, edge and cloud technology and represent a real-time, virtual image of real energy assets, systems and networks. These digital models can be used to simulate operating conditions, analyze system behavior and predict possible problems after combining sensor data, previous performance history and prediction algorithms. As an example, a digital twin of a power plant or a microgrid can forecast the impacts of changes in the load, the unpredictability of renewable energy or the degradation of equipment, and facilitate preventative maintenance and optimization of operations. Simulation enables asset lifecycle management, strategic planning and energy market participation by enabling operators to investigate the benefits of the "what-if" scenario without undermining actual infrastructure. Digital twin is a feasible and effective predictive analysis and intelligent decision-making tool due to the synergistic use of edge-based preprocessing, the power of cloud-enabled computing and the information gathered by the IoT.

6.5.5. *Cybersecurity considerations*

A combination of cloud, edge and IoT technologies has created new cybersecurity and privacy issues for energy systems. Due to their considerable connectivity and data exchange, energy networks are vulnerable to cyberattacks, data breaches and unauthorized access, and can affect the reliability and safety of operations. Securing device-to-device connectivity, ensuring data integrity and more robust authentication protocols should be done to ensure system resilience. There are also issues of privacy, especially with smart metering and demand-side management where the information on customer consumption could disclose personal information. Moreover, practices such as network segmentation, encryption, intrusion detection systems and incident response planning are essential to reduce cyberthreats and guarantee the stable and safe functioning of the contemporary energy systems. These problems have to be resolved to build trust and achieve the maximum potential of cloud, edge and IoT integration in energy management.

IoT, edge and cloud convergence are making energy systems smart, data-driven networks that are adaptively controlled and have real-time monitoring and predictive analytics. IoT devices enable continuous and fine-grained data collection that gives information regarding the performance of the assets, patterns of consumption and environmental conditions. Although cloud computing offers the power of computation and scalable data storage to the complex analytical and ML solution in addition to historical data management, edge analytics cuts down on the communication overhead and latency in order to enable the processing and decision-making to be made immediately. Digital twins integrate these technologies to develop the real-time virtual models of predictive analysis, simulation and strategic planning. Nevertheless, cybersecurity and privacy should also be carefully considered to implement such technologies with a goal of guaranteeing the resilience and reliability of interconnected energy systems. Collectively, these technological developments render intelligent, sustainable and efficient energy networks that can adapt to the dynamic needs of the contemporary power systems.

6.6. Case studies and real-world implementations

Energy systems transitioned from a pure concept of research to vast practical applications of big data analytics, predictive modeling and advanced areas of computing technology. These developments are employed by utilities, grid operators and energy firms everywhere across the globe in order to achieve sustainability, reliability and efficiency in operations. A few case studies and real applications will be considered in this section, which would assist in visualizing some of the lessons learnt, technology strategies and outcomes of smart grids, demand response systems, predictive maintenance, renewable energy forecasting and energy market analytics.

6.6.1. *Smart grid implementations*

Smart grids are one of the most well-known usages of big data and combination of IoT within the energy systems. The Netherlands Smart Meter Program has installed millions of smart meters in Europe, which have enhanced the management of the grid, dynamic pricing and real-time monitoring. Collecting information on precise consumption, such meters facilitate the demand-side management programs and the short-term load predictions. The smart grid technology that is implemented by PG&E in the United States includes IoT sensors, automated switches and advanced distribution management systems. All of these enable load balancing between the urban and rural networks, predictive maintenance of transformers and real-time outage detection. Asian examples include the TEPCO smart grid projects in Japan, which guarantee that when the power gets to the maximum, there is guaranteed maximum power delivery to the isotope and the reliability of the grid remains constant, as the AI-based predictive analytics are combined with renewables. The combination of these projects indicates that smart grids can lower operational expenses and cut environmental outages and grow customer satisfaction.

6.6.2. *Renewable energy forecasting projects*

Accurate renewable generation prediction is critical to grid stability and economical energy control. Most utility-scale solar and wind forecasting systems have found big data analytics to be helpful. At the solar forecasting station of Fraunhofer ISE in Germany, they apply meteorological information, satellite images and ground sensors in order to predict the quantity of PV production at a high spatial and temporal resolution. The same methods have been applied to predict wind farm output on the NREL of the United States to enable grid operators to plan and balance such dynamic sources of energy. Renewable forecasting tools are used in India to supplement energy dispatch on enormous solar and wind farms with past history production data and real-time meteorological information. All of these efforts demonstrate that data-driven predictive modeling can be crucial to enhance grid stability by managing the uncertainty of renewable sources of energy.

6.6.3. *Predictive maintenance in power plants*

The efficiency of the modern power plants has been placed on predictive maintenance. Utilities can monitor the state of equipment in real-time and prevent issues before they occur using IoT sensors, cloud computing and ML. In the United States, Duke Energy has installed AI-based monitoring systems in its power stations, which are coal fired and gas fired. They analyze vibration, temperature, pressure and operating data to identify the first indications of equipment wear and enable maintenance personnel to act in advance. The EDF Energy has installed predictive maintenance systems in its nuclear and thermal reactors in Europe, which use digital twins to simulate equipment operations and draw attention to possible issues.

Long equipment life, lower operation costs and less downtime are the reasons why predictive maintenance would make a strong business case in industrial energy operations.

6.6.4. *Demand response systems*

Real-time analytics and predictive modeling are increasingly being utilized by demand response programs to enhance patterns of energy use. Automated demand response systems utilized by ISO New England in the United States dynamically adjust commercial and industrial loads based on pricing signals and grid conditions. ML models predict periods of high demand and trigger DR events to prompt users to reduce their consumption. This involves integration of smart meters and predictive algorithms into real-time load control schemes so as to regulate residential and commercial energy usage in Italy by Enel X. Accordingly, in Japan, the TEPCO DR program that combines behavioral analytics with real-time pricing is used to lure customers to change their electricity consumption out of the peak hours. These case studies demonstrate how DR systems can be effective toward providing grid flexibility, minimizing peak demand conditions and improving energy efficiency.

6.6.5. *Energy market predictive analytics*

The energy industry has been changed by big data analytics and AI-based trading platforms. Forecast models are applied to price power, comprehend market risk and facilitate the trading strategy by utilities and energy traders. EPEX SPOT and Nord Pool in Europe run ML algorithms that predict the price of power in the short term and inform the participants in the market about the optimal price they should bid. The United States has a predictive analytics system that combines weather, generation and demand data in PJM Interconnection to optimize market operations and reduce volatility. The same is applied to renewable energy trades whereby proper forecasts of wind and solar energy will result in increased market penetration and reduced curtailment risk. The energy market analytics can therefore be described as a combination of big data, operations decision-making and predictive modeling in the dynamic and competitive environment.

Predictive modeling and complex computer technologies used in the practice in addition to big data analytics have made a significant contribution to the efficiency, reliability and flexibility of the contemporary energy systems. Europe, United States and Asian case studies indicate successful examples of smart grids that employ demand side management, automated control and real-time monitoring. Renewable energy sources have been maximized in the forecasts of the same to increase the stability of the system and decrease the risks caused by fluctuations. Predictive maintenance in the power plants has minimized unscheduled outages, increased the useful life of assets and lowered the operating expenses. The demand response systems used the dynamic pricing and use of real-time data to demonstrate how it could affect customer behavior and enhance load control. Lastly, predictive analytics allow the predicting of prices, managing risks and trading in energy markets. Taken together, all of these examples can imply how the collaboration of cloud, edge computing, IoT and ML technology could influence the future of energy in the world and transform it into an exemplar of strong, intelligent and sustainable energy networks.

6.7. Challenges, limitations and future directions

The use of big data analytics, predictive modeling and advanced computational technologies in energy systems creates new possibilities of sustainability, reliability and efficiency, which have never previously been discussed. Nonetheless, many barriers and restrictions in the areas of data management, technical implementation, policy concerns and regulatory standards have to be tackled before it could become acceptable to broadly adopt these technologies. The intelligent energy networks can only be developed further by overcoming these challenges, and the scalability, security and sustainability of future solutions will be ensured. This section provides an opinion on what the most pressing issues are and identifies some of the hot opportunities for research that can define the future of energy analytics.

6.7.1. *Data-related challenges*

The foundations of predictive modeling and energy analytics are based on data, yet the management of energy data is challenging due to its heterogeneity, quality and integration requirements. Energy systems generate large amounts of structured and unstructured data, including weather or market data, sensor data on IoT devices, operational records on SCADA systems and time-series data on smart meters. It is not an easy task, as such datasets can often be of different formats, resolutions and update rates. Moreover, inadequate or absent data may significantly worsen the work of the model, which leads to incorrect forecasting and suboptimal decisions. Such methods as data cleansing, normalization and imputation are essential, yet may be computationally expensive and add uncertainty. Also, being compatible with a plethora of hardware, software platforms and suppliers remains a challenge that requires robust data governance strategies and standardized frameworks.

6.7.2. *Technical challenges*

In addition to data-related problems, predictive analytics experiences colossal technical constraints in implementation and scale in energy systems. Scalability problems include the ability to accommodate high volumes of data at exceedingly high expenditures with no performance drop as the datasets expand in size and complexity. Large-scale deep learning and ML models are often computationally intensive, and so require parallel computing, distributed computing systems and special computer hardware. The model interpretability is another important challenge. Although more complicated models, such as deep neural networks and ensemble methods, are highly accurate in prediction, they are black-box; therefore, operators cannot understand how their decisions are made, nor can regulators. This may result in a lack of trust, particularly in safety-sensitive applications, and will not help in widely adopting it. Moreover, real-time analytics may be difficult to implement due to latency problems, the necessity of processing edges and synchronizing analytics on distributed energy resources. These technological issues have demonstrated how vital the development of effective, transparent and responsive analytical frameworks of the current energy networks are.

6.7.3. *Regulatory and policy issues*

Energy analytics should also conquer regulatory and policy hurdles in order to operate safely, lawfully and ethically. Among the areas of special interest is the problem of data privacy in the context of smart meters and IoT devices, which can capture data related to user usage on very fine scales. Such data should be encrypted, anonymized and communicated in a way that will not allow it to be abused or accessed without appropriate permission. Data management and storage are significantly more complicated when it is seen through national and international boundaries, as in the case of the GDPR in Europe or national energy regulations in other nations. These governance models are expected to define the roles, responsibilities and accountability on data, model deployment and decision-making. The implementation of analytics-based energy systems could be hindered by the lack of specific policies, operational uncertainty, mistrust among the population and legal risks.

6.7.4. *Future research directions*

New technologies open up wonderful possibilities to remove current limitations and bring energy analytics nearer to the world of increased size, efficiency and transparency. Explainable AI is also becoming a crucial method required to enhance model interpretability and assist the operators in comprehending why predictions are provided and developing trust in automated decision-making. By facilitating the optimization of energy systems on a large scale, complex simulations and speedy processing of data quantum computing can revolutionize predictive analytics. Federated learning and privacy-preserving models have been in the spotlight as they allow training of ML models on distributed energy assets jointly and provide data privacy and lessen security and regulatory risk. Combining distributed ledger technologies like blockchain with next-generation communication technologies like 6G will additionally improve the security, transparency and real-time information exchange among decentralized energy networks. The upcoming trends will lead to stronger, independent and adaptive energy systems that will eventually keep up with the increasingly challenging nature of modern grids and the introduction of renewable sources.

Edge AI or implementing AI algorithms directly on the devices at the network edge is gaining progressively more importance in energy forecasting and decentralized energy management. Edges AI, in contrast to cloud-based analytics, need not transmit raw data to centralized servers, such as with cloud-based analytics, and therefore, edge AI can respond quickly with low latency and less bandwidth consumption. This is particularly convenient in very distant renewable energy facilities and microgrids where connectivity can be weak or unreliable. In energy forecasting, edge AI is capable of taking input in the form of incoming weather, sensor measurements and consumption history to provide precise short-term localized predictions. These projections allow the smart control of the generation and storage units, including changing the blade position of wind turbines or discharge schedules of a battery. The edge AI devices can adjust to the constantly changing environmental conditions and optimally control the flow of energy in an autonomous, constantly updated function with input of new information. Edge AI enhances the resiliency of a system by enhancing fault detection and anomaly recognition of key components in the system like inverters and switchgear to reduce the potential downtime. Edge AI is a federated learning supplemented by the contribution of distributed model training and retention of sensitive data on-premise. In renewable energy systems that become increasingly complex, edge AI can be utilized in rapid and smart decentralized decision-making in energy systems that are both off-grid and grid connected.

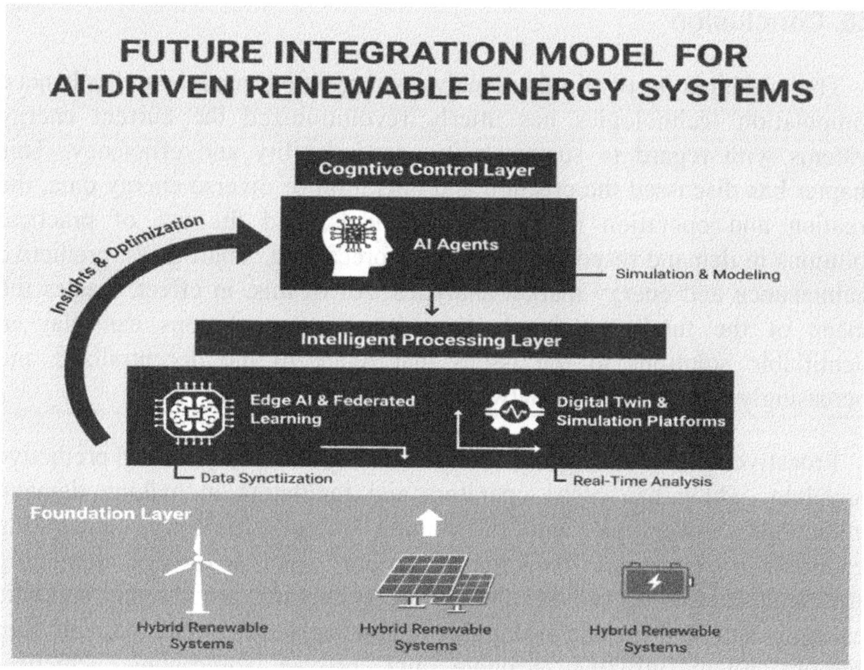

Figure 6.7. *Hierarchical AI-based renewable energy system architecture*

Although the benefits of the big data analytics and predictive modeling in the energy systems are numerous, so are the challenges. Even though technical challenges comprise scalability, interpretability and real-time processing, limiting the realistic implementation, heterogeneity, missing values and integration issues can affect model performance. The deployment is also complicated by regulatory and policy issues associated with information privacy, compliance and governance. New technologies such as explainable AI, quantum computing, federated learning, 6G and blockchain are proposed as revolutionary possibilities to overcome these restrictions in the future. By addressing these challenges with the help of research, innovation and regulatory frameworks, energy systems will be able to become ultra-intelligent, efficient and secure networks that will match the requirements of the contemporary energy space and contribute to the rapid global shift toward sustainable energy to occur.

6.8. Conclusion

The combination of big data analytics, predictive models and enhanced computation technologies has utterly revolutionized the current energy systems with regard to sustainability, dependability and efficiency. This chapter has discussed the creation and operation of diverse energy data, the creation and operation of predictive models, and the use of practical solutions in demand response, renewable forecasting, smart grids, predictive maintenance and energy market analytics. All of this, in effect, creates the image of the fundamental role that data-driven solutions can play in identifiable solutions to the issues that relate to the decentralized and increasingly intricate energy networks.

Proactive energy management is built on big data analytics and predictive modeling, which can assist operators and regulators in making demand predictions, generating and distributing more efficiently, integrating renewable resources and reducing operational risks. IoT, edge computing and cloud computing provide the ability to capture, process and simulate real-time data with the use of digital twins, whereas statistical, ML and deep learning allow utilizing scalable and precise forecasting. Practical application in Europe, the United States and Asia has shown practical benefits such as lower operating expenses, system dependability, maximization of assets utilization and demand-side flexibility.

In spite of these developments, there are challenges nonetheless. Multiple operational and technical problems exist in terms of quality, heterogeneity and data integration, and scalability, interpretability and real-time processing problems hamper the use of complex models.

Legal and regulatory issues related to data privacy, security and compliance must be taken into consideration to develop safe, analytics-driven energy systems, which are moral and sustainable. New directions and concepts in research (explainable AI, quantum computing, federated learning and integration with next-generation communication networks such as 6G) offer opportunities to overcome these limitations and reach new performance and resilience levels. Big data and predictive models are the keys to the formation of a sustainable, reliable and effective energy future in the strategic perspective. With advanced analytics, energy operators can incorporate huge percentages of renewable energy, optimize resource use and keep the grid steady during times of rising demand and environment-imposed limitations.

Policy frameworks are also needed to allow the sharing of data, standardization and secure operations in order to fully reap the potential value of intelligent energy systems. The combination of AI, digital technology and energy analytics will enable even more innovation in grid management, energy markets and consumer interaction. Research in explainable and privacy-protecting models and scalable computing infrastructures will result in far more autonomous, versatile and resilient energy networks. Academia, business and politics collaboration will remain the most critical when transforming technical progress into sustainable, economically viable and socially responsible solutions in terms of energy systems in the future.

Ultimately, the issue of big data analytics and predictive modeling is not only a technology – it is a paradigm changer that is at the core of intelligent management in the current energy systems. Predictive insights could be incorporated into the operational decision-making to enhance greater efficiency, reduce cost and enhance sustainability for all stakeholders involved. The case studies and discussions in this chapter will therefore stimulate more research continuity, innovation and policy formulations in the pursuit of a more intelligent, greener and far more resilient energy landscape in future generations.

6.9. References

Adegoke, S.O. and Obunadike, T.C. (2025). Global tariff shocks and U.S. agriculture: Causal machine learning approaches to competitiveness and market share forecasting. *Int. J. Res. Publ. Rev.*, 6(4), 16173–16188. doi: 10.55248/gengpi.6.0425.16109.

Ahmed, M.S., Tanim, S., Hussain, S. (2024). Artificial intelligence in public project management: Boosting economic outcomes through technological innovation. *Int. J. Appl. Eng. Technol.*, 6, 47–63.

Al-Jumaili, A.H.A., Muniyandi, R.C., Hasan, M.K., Paw, J.K.S., Singh, M.J. (2023). Big data analytics using cloud computing based frameworks for power management systems. *Sensors*, 23, 2952.

Amini, M. and Rohani, M.B. (2024). The role of machine learning and artificial intelligence in enhancing renewable energy through data science. *World J. Technol. Sci. Res.*, 12(7), 2341–2365.

Annapareddy, V.N. (2021). Transforming renewable energy and educational technologies through AI, machine learning, big data analytics, and cloud-based IT integrations. *International Journal Of Engineering And Computer Science*, 10(12), 25572–25585.

Ayub, N., Irfan, M., Awais, M., Ali, U., Ali, T., Hamdi, M., Alghamdi, A., Muhammad, F. (2020). Big data analytics for short and medium-term electricity load forecasting using an AI techniques ensembler. *Energies*, 13, 5193.

Balakrishna, R. (2024). SCADA: Need for data analytics and time series analysis for effective load forecasting. *J. Electr. Syst.*, 20(11s), 552–560.

Beckley, J. (2025). Advanced risk assessment techniques: Merging data-driven analytics with expert insights to navigate uncertain decision-making processes. *Int. J. Res. Publ. Rev.*, 6(3), 1454–1471. doi: 10.55248/gengpi.6.0325.1148.

Chukwunweike, J. and Salaudeen, H.D. (2025). Advanced computational methods for optimizing mechanical systems in modern engineering management practices. *Int. J. Res. Publ. Rev.*, 6, 8533–8548.

Chukwunweike, J., Lawal, O.A., Arogundade, J.B., Alade, B. (2024). Navigating ethical challenges of explainable AI in autonomous systems. *Int. J. Sci. Res. Arch.*, 13(1), 1807–1819. doi: 10.30574/ijsra.2024.13.1.1872.

Devaraj, J., Madurai Elavarasan, R.M., Shafiullah, G.M., Jamal, T., Khan, I. (2021). A holistic review on energy forecasting using big data and deep learning models. *Int. J. Energy Res.*, 45(9), 13489–13530.

Diamantoulakis, P.D., Kapinas, V.M., Karagiannidis, G.K. (2015). Big data analytics for dynamic energy management in smart grids. *Big Data Research*, 2, 94–101.

Enemosah, A. and Chukwunweike, J. (2022). Next-generation SCADA architectures for enhanced field automation and real-time remote control in oil and gas fields. *Int. J. Comput. Appl. Technol. Res.*, 11(12), 514–529. doi: 10.7753/IJCATR1112.1018.

Fowosere, S., Obofoni, C.E., Namboozo, S., Anwansedo, F. (2025). The role of artificial intelligence in green supply chain management. *Int. J. Latest Technol. Eng. Manag. Appl. Sci.*, 14(2), 325–331. doi: 10.51583/ijltemas.2025.14020033.

Hamdan, A., Ibekwe, K.I., Ilojianya, V.I., Sonko, S., Etukudoh, E.A. (2024). AI in renewable energy: A review of predictive maintenance and energy optimization. *Int. J. Sci. Res. Arch.*, 11(1), 718–729.

Hamzat, L. (2025). Real-time financial resilience and debt optimization for entrepreneurs. *Int. J. Adv. Res. Publ. Rev.*, 2(5), 202–223.

Igweonu, C.F. (2024). Molecular characterization of antibiotic resistance genes in multidrug-resistant *Klebsiella pneumoniae* clinical isolates. *Int. J. Eng. Technol. Res. Manag.*, 8(8), 241. doi: 10.5281/zenodo.15536913.

Igweonu, C.F. (2025). Validation of cleanroom microbial monitoring techniques using rapid molecular methods in biopharmaceutical production. *Int. J. Comput. Appl. Technol. Res.*, 13(2), 58–74. doi: 10.7753/IJCATR1302.1007.

Ishola, A.B. and Abdulbasit, A.O. (2025). A review on the use of biomarkers for early diagnosis of sepsis and associated hemostatic abnormalities. *Open J. Clin. Diagn.*, 15, 46–70. doi: 10.4236/ojcd.2025.152004.

Je, S.M., Ko, H., Huh, J.H. (2021). Accurate demand forecasting: A flexible and balanced electric power production big data virtualization based on photovoltaic power plant. *Energies*, 14(21), 6915.

Jha, D., Gupta, V., Hiran, K.K., Bhargava, S., Barua, T. (2024). Empowering renewable energy: A comprehensive analysis of big data analytics in innovation, efficiency, and sustainability. In *Proc. Int. Conf. Emerging Trends in Networks and Computer Communications (ETNCC)*. IEEE.

Mostafa, N., Ramadan, H.S.M., Elfarouk, O. (2022). Renewable energy management in smart grids by using big data analytics and machine learning. *Machine Learning with Applications*, 9, 100363.

Nayyef, Z.T., Abdulrahman, M.M., Kurdi, N.A. (2024). Optimizing energy efficiency in smart grids using machine learning algorithms: A case study in electrical engineering. *SHIFRA*, 46–54.

Njoku, T.K. (2025). Quantum software engineering: Algorithm design, error mitigation, and compiler optimization for fault-tolerant quantum computing. *Int. J. Comput. Appl. Technol. Res.*, 14, 30–42. doi: 10.7753/IJCATR1404.1003.

Ogunkoya, T.A. (2024). Smart hospital infrastructure: What nurse leaders must know about emerging tech trends. *Int. J. Comput. Appl. Technol. Res.*, 13(12), 54–71. doi: 10.7753/IJCATR1312.1007.

Ohalete, N.C., Aderibigbe, A.O., Ani, E.C., Ohenhen, P.E., Daraojimba, D.O., Odulaja, B.A. (2023). AI-driven solutions in renewable energy: A review of data science applications in solar and wind energy optimization. *World J. Adv. Res. Rev.*, 20(3), 401–417.

Oluokun, O.A., Akinsooto, O., Ogundipe, O.B., Ikemba, S. (2024). Leveraging cloud computing and big data analytics for policy-driven energy optimization in smart cities. *International Journal of Multidisciplinary Research and Growth Evaluation*, 5(1). doi: 10.54660/.IJMRGE.2024.5.1.1022-1034.

Sankarananth, S., Karthiga, M., Suganya, E., Sountharrajan, S., Bavirisetti, D.P. (2023). AI-enabled metaheuristic optimization for predictive management of renewable energy production in smart grids. *Energy Reports*, 10, 1299–1312.

Sonko, S., Adewusi, A.O., Obi, O.C., Onwusinkwue, S., Atadoga, A. (2024). A critical review towards artificial general intelligence: Challenges, ethical considerations, and the path forward. *World Journal of Advanced Research and Reviews*, 21(3), 1262–1268.

Srinivas, B.V., Vikas, S.V., Satish, K., Kulkarni, K. (2025). Predictive analytics for energy demand and renewable resource optimization. In *Proc. Int. Conf. Intelligent and Innovative Technologies in Computing, Electrical and Electronics (IITCEE)*.

Suci, A.M., Amini, R., Asri, A.K., Martin, N. (2025). Artificial intelligence in renewable energy: A review of predictive maintenance and energy optimization. *Journal of Clean Technology*, 2(1), 29–44.

Thomas, G.A.S., Muthukaruppasamy, S., Saravanan, K., Muleta, N. (2023). Revolutionizing smart grids with big data analytics: A case study on integrating renewable energy and predicting faults. In *Data Analytics for Smart Grids Applications: A Key to Smart City Development*, Sharma, D.K., Sharma, R., Jeon, G., Kumar, R. (eds). Springer, Cham, 179–198.

Ukoba, K., Olatunji, K.O., Adeoye, E., Jen, T.C., Madyira, D.M. (2024). Optimizing renewable energy systems through artificial intelligence: Review and future prospects. *Energy & Environment*, 35(7), 3833–3879.

Ul Haq, I. (2024). Diagnosis of neurological disease using bioinspired algorithms. In *Bio-Inspired Optimization for Medical Data Mining*, Srivastava, S., Anand, A., Kumar, A. et al. (eds). John Wiley & Sons, Hoboken, NJ.

Ul Haq, I. and Khanday, A.M.U.D. (2025). Exploring the role of explainable AI in women's health: Challenges and solutions. In *Explainable Artificial Intelligence in the Healthcare Industry*, Kumar, A. Kumar, T.A., Das, P. et al. (eds). John Wiley & Sons, Hoboken, NJ.

Ul Haq, I., Kumar, N., Koul, N., Verma, C., Eneacu, F.M., Raboaca, M.S. (2022). Machine learning techniques for result prediction of one day international (ODI) cricket match. In *The International Conference on Recent Innovations in Computing*. Springer, Singapore.

Ul Haq, I., Kaur, G., Rather, A.H. (2024). Fruit leaf classification using transfer learning for automation and industrial applications. In *Deep Learning Techniques for Automation and Industrial Applications*, Rathore, P.S., Ahuja, S., Burri, S.R. et al. (eds). John Wiley & Sons, Hoboken, NJ.

Ul Haq, I., Kumar, A., Rathore, P.S. (2025a). Machine learning approaches for wind power forecasting: A comprehensive review. *Discover Applied Sciences*, 7, 1139.

Ul Haq, I., Malhotra, J., Rawat, V., Kumari, J., Kaur, G. (2025b). Machine learning approaches for early detection of cervical cancer: A comparative study of classification models. In *Targeted Chemotherapy with Personalized Immunotherapy: An AI Approach*, Kumar, A., Das, P., Rathore, P.S. et al. (eds). John Wiley & Sons, Hoboken, NJ.

Ul Haq, I., Nandal, V., Uppal, H. (2025c). Blockchain applications in aviation securing transactions, streamlining operations, and improving passenger experience. In *Blockchain in the Tourism Industry: A New Era of Secure and Transparent Travel Solutions*, Kumar, A., Abreu, A., Batta, P. et al. (eds). Springer, Cham.

Ul Haq, I., Shah, H.A., Rufai, S.Z. (2025d). Enhancing water security through automation: case studies and technical advancements in water quality management. In *Computational Automation for Water Security*, Dubey, A.K., Srivastav, A.L., Kumar, A. et al. (eds). Elsevier, Amsterdam.

Zhou, Z., Xiong, F., Huang, B., Xu, C., Jiao, R., Liao, B., Yin, Z., Li, J. (2017). Game-theoretical energy management for energy Internet with big data-based renewable power forecasting. *IEEE Access*, 5, 5731–5746.

7

Smart Grids, IoT and AI: Transforming Energy Management for a Sustainable Future

Smart grids, Internet of Things (IoT) and artificial intelligence (AI) are being thrust into energy management systems as the global shift toward more sustainable and cleaner energy systems and generally smarter energy systems takes place. Smart grids enable bidirectional communication with electrical networks and provide active control capabilities, whereas the Internet of Things (IoT) facilitates continuous data acquisition from distributed energy resources, consumer devices and smart grid infrastructure. Blended with the forecasting and adjustive capacity of AI, a combination of these technologies will provide never-before-seen opportunities to optimize the balance between demand and supply, increase grid resiliency and minimize the carbon footprint. This chapter discusses AI-based analytics and machine learning models that enable real-time load forecasting, demand response and fault detection, as well as the integration of renewable energy into the smart grid. It also looks at how IoT sensors and edge devices help to form a decentralized and data-rich environment that enables intelligent decision-making on a scale. Moreover, emphasis is placed on the interaction among digital twins, energy storage, AI-identified optimization algorithms providing an opportunity for self-healing networks and the predictability of energy management. The chapter summarizes research and practice by synthesizing recent developments and implementation, as well as the promising opportunities of smart grids or IoT and AI toward sustainable, reliable and affordable energy ecosystems. Concerns such as interoperability, cybersecurity and data privacy are discussed, and the future of federated learning, blockchain-based energy trading and policy frameworks that can bring it to the mainstream are further discussed. The last but most important point is that when these technologies converge, they lead to the next generation of smart and resilient energy infrastructures, which are eco-friendly.

Chapter written by Khalid Hafiz MIR and Anzah BASHIR.

7.1. Introduction

Medical AI has been developing over the years, but agentic AI has caused a paradigm shift. Conventional AI technology is commonly developed to serve as a decision support system, and it is subject to direct human supervision. Conversely, agentic AI can make independent decisions, which means that it can handle clinical information, identify patterns, forecasts and even take up actions, without undergoing constant monitoring by a human. This increased ability is achieved through advanced techniques, including predictive modeling, pattern recognition, reinforcement learning and, in a few cases, natural language understanding, to allow AI systems to actively participate in clinical processes (Singh et al. 2020). The decision to implement agentic AI in healthcare is explained by its ability to revolutionize the way patients are handled, operational efficiency and medical research. As an example, detailed medical data, including imaging, lab results and electronic health records (EHRs), could be examined with a high level of accuracy to improve early diagnoses, minimize diagnostic errors and optimize the treatment plans by detecting minor patterns that a human clinician could easily overlook (Qureshi and Kajla 2016). Continuous monitoring of patient data enables agentic AI systems to predict potential risks, such as hospital readmission, disease progression and treatment-related complications. These predictive capabilities support proactive decision-making and enable timely allocation of healthcare resources. Besides the advancement of diagnosis and prediction of risks, agentic AI is also important in enhancing the functioning of the hospital. It is able to prioritize clinical workflows independently, schedule patients and allocate resources in a more efficient way, thus, systematically decreasing the administrative workload of healthcare providers, decreasing patient waiting time and simplifying the process within an organization. The other important applicability of agentic AI is that it is able to offer personalized treatment advice (Ul Haq et al. 2025b). However, incorporating patient-specific information, such as genomics, lifestyle choices and comorbidities, such systems may suggest treatment plans that are personalized to maximize the therapeutic effect and are less prone to cause side effects. This is a radical population-based medicine for custom care. The integration of agentic AI into healthcare workflows is illustrated through a schematic diagram that demonstrates its practical implementation. The process highlights how human oversight and AI autonomy are balanced and dynamically maintained in real-world clinical settings (Dewitte et al. 2021). It represents an adaptive paradigm whereby agentic AI does not solely improve the accuracy and effectiveness of clinical care, but works in tandem with human knowledge to make safe, ethical and effective decisions in the context of evolving modern healthcare.

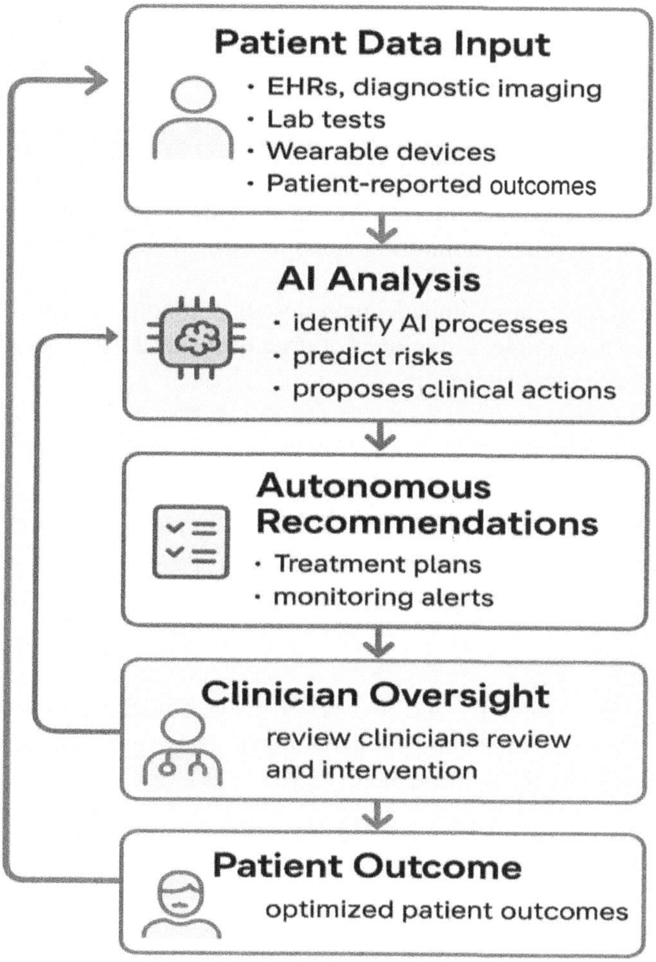

Figure 7.1. *The workflow of agentic AI in clinical practice. For a color version of this figure, see www.iste.co.uk/ulhaq/artificial1.zip*

Patient data input

They include EHRs, diagnostic imaging, lab tests, wearable and patient-reported outcomes as examples.

AI analysis

The agentic AI system processes the data based on machine learning algorithms, predictive models and pattern recognition techniques (Ul Haq et al. 2022).

The AI identifies the potential diagnoses and risks, and proposes clinical interventions.

Autonomous recommendations

– Depending on the analysis, the AI devises recommendations, which may be treatment plans, monitoring alerts or a diagnosis priority.

– In other machines, limited quantities of autonomous activity may be carried out, for example, a reminder of drug doses or a warning to clinicians of dangerous circumstances.

Clinician oversight

– Human clinicians review AI-generated recommendations and intervene when necessary (Soori et al. 2026). This human-in-the-loop approach ensures ethical and regulatory compliance by providing appropriate oversight while still leveraging AI autonomy.

Patient outcome

When both agentic AI and a decision by a clinician are incorporated, there will be an optimization of patient outcomes, increase in safety and effective care delivery (Ul Haq et al. 2024).

7.2. Ethical considerations

The ethical dimension of agentic AI use in medicine is a multi-dimensional phenomenon that must be approached with caution, such that innovation does not jeopardize patient safety, equity or trust. This section deals with the primary areas of autonomy and informed consent, accountability and liability, bias and fairness, privacy and data security. It is also possible to explain all these themes as an important issue that should be addressed to turn agentic AI into a consistent and morally sound aspect of clinical practice (Chandra 2022).

7.2.1. *Autonomy and informed consent*

Autonomy and informed consent are based on the premise that during a consultation, the practitioner must provide the patient with all essential information regarding the treatment and its potential outcomes. Informed consent and autonomy are based on the principle that healthcare practitioners are ethically and legally required to provide patients with complete and accurate information about the proposed treatment, including its potential benefits, risks and possible consequences (Ul Haq et al. 2025d).

Medical ethics are rooted in respect of patient autonomy, and the concept of informed consent has long played the role of keeping patients an active participant in decisions regarding their care. When applied to agentic AI, this postulate is complicated by the ability of the system to make or suggest non-intuitive and non-explainable decisions.

When compared to more traditional AI tools, which typically serve as decision-supporting tools, delivering insights that may be reviewed and discussed by clinicians with patients, agentic AI often goes beyond recommendation to action. Such a change lowers the openness and subsequently, the patients find it hard to comprehend the procedures that impact their treatment.

Informed consent, in this case, can be ensured only by disclosing the role of the AI, as well as explaining its limitations, uncertainties and possible risks. The consent forms may have to be redesigned to include specific statements on the availability of AI in clinical decision-making and whether the AI is working on its own or in collaboration with the supervision of a clinician (Park 2024). This improved disclosure process makes sure that the autonomy of patients is not affected, even in cases where the mechanisms of the AI decisions still remain technically complicated.

Feature	Traditional AI	Agentic AI
Decision transparency	High	Medium–low
Human oversight	Always	Optional
Explainability	Moderate	Challenging
Patient consent requirement	Standard	Requires enhanced disclosure

Table 7.1. *Comparison of traditional versus agentic AI in informed consent*

7.2.2. *Liable and responsible*

Another important ethical issue is the spread of responsibility that agentic AI generates. Accountability in a traditional healthcare context is a comparatively straightforward concept: decisions are made by physicians and the institutions are needed to provide the systems and safeguards to support such decisions. In agentic AI, however, responsibility is shared between a variety of stakeholders. The developers can be primarily responsible for system design issues, the institutions of improper deployment or monitoring and the level of reliance of the AI recommendations in the hands of clinicians (Ul Haq et al. 2025a).

The legal frameworks continue to struggle with the issue on how to place liability under circumstances where an AI-supported decision leads to patients being harmed. A potential solution is developer liability, where the blame is on the algorithm creators (Buiten et al. 2023). The other one is institutional responsibility, which focuses on the role played by the hospitals and the regulation bodies in promoting safe deployment. The third is a hybrid structure that shares the liability depending on the context of the mistake. No matter what model is used, accountability must be transparent, so that trust is not compromised and patient welfare is the paramount consideration.

$$E(H) = P(AI_{error}) \times C_{patient} + P(clinician\_error) \times C_{patient} \quad [7.1]$$

where:

– P = probability of error;

– $C_{patient}$ = cost of adverse patient outcome.

Liability and accountability are issues as agentic AI systems become part and parcel of clinical decision-making. AI-enabled care creates a new shared responsibility among various stakeholders, unlike traditional models where the major role of making medical decisions was carried out by clinicians. AI developers have the responsibility to design, safeguard and publish AI algorithms; clinicians must make use of professional judgment and supervision, and healthcare facilities are requested to guarantee adherence to regulations, support infrastructure and control (Ul Haq and Khanday 2025).

The following dispersion indicates the cooperative character of responsibility in AI health.

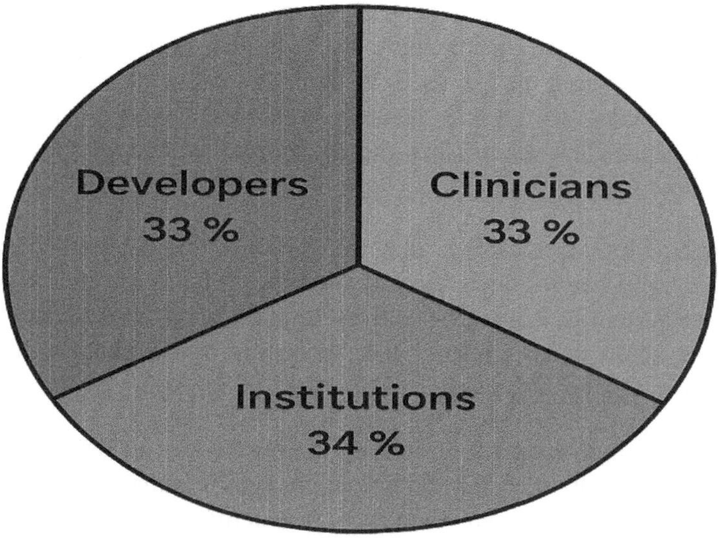

Figure 7.2. *Liability distribution in agentic AI-enabled clinical decisions. For a color version of this figure, see www.iste.co.uk/ulhaq/artificial1.zip*

The liability allocation presented in Figure 7.2 shows that there is no one stakeholder that can assert full responsibility in agentic AI-powered clinical care. This common model would promote teamwork; at the same time, it would undermine accountability where negative results were achieved.

To balance innovative incentives with patient safety, developers should make sure that their algorithms are transparent and rolled out without bias, clinicians should keep a skeptical eye on the results of AI execution and institutions should develop governance mechanisms. Such a tri-party distribution of responsibility ultimately aims to create trust in AI systems; yet, it also increases the demand for more explicit legal and ethical provisions to avoid an inability to be near or within the zone of clinical practice (Nouis et al. 2025).

7.2.3. *Bias, fairness and equity*

Perhaps one of the most important ethical issues of agentic AI implementation in medicine is the risk of bias that can vitiate justice and equity of patient care. The models of AI are also necessarily conditional upon the information to be used in training. When these datasets are historically unequal in terms of health care access, quality of treatment or population representativeness, then the AI system can also reinforce or even increase these inequalities.

To take a simple example, a diagnostic system that has been trained on data largely of urban residents can fail to predict patients of rural origin, and a predictor system based on a specific ethnic group can make less accurate predictions about other groups. These concerns need mindful and active actions in order to be addressed (Ul Haq et al. 2025c).

The inclusion of a variety of datasets guarantees the inclusion of various age, gender, ethnicity and socioeconomic groups. Systematic surveillance of model outputs can assist in identifying predictive discrepancies prior to impact on patient care, and routine audits can give an opportunity to re-tune models and address systematic biases present in the system. In combination, the strategies contribute to fair treatment and assist in retaining trust in AI-driven medical systems.

Figure 7.3 indicates that there are differences in the AI diagnostic accuracy between demographic cohorts of age, sex and ethnicity, and that bias on training datasets can compromise equity in healthcare. The figure indicates that younger patients and males are more likely to be diagnosed with higher levels of accuracy, whereas older patients, the female population and non-binary patients, in particular, experience a lack of diagnostic accuracy. In the same way, there are ethnic groups that have better performance, and the underrepresented groups have much lower accuracy. Such incoherence indicates that AI systems can be trained using non-representative or biased data, which will carry on the existing disparities in healthcare. The results show the significance of training data variety and representativeness, periodic auditing and bias tracking systems that help to reset models and make them fair. Such a practice will safeguard the sphere of justice and retain trust in medical systems based on AI.

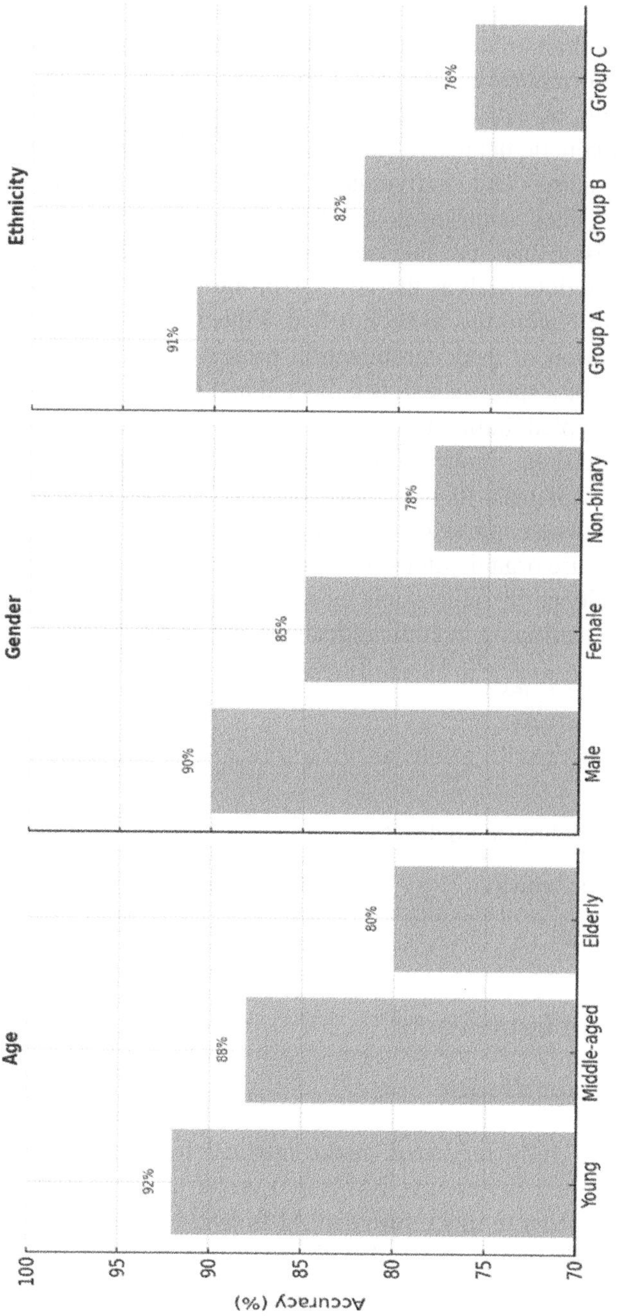

Figure 7.3. *The performance difference among demographic groups*

7.2.4. *Privacy and data security*

The ethical pillars of an AI in medicine are its privacy and security, given that medical information is sensitive. The agentic AI systems are founded on massive amounts of data collected by the use of EHRs, diagnostic images, wearables and genetic databases. Though it is feasible to engage in powerful predictive modeling and individual care because of such information availability, it also contributes to the increased risk of unauthorized information disclosure or misuse (Madrid-García et al. 2025). Data protection legislation, such as the HIPAA in the United States or the GDPR in the European Union, has to be fulfilled. Ethical deployment also requires the implementation of data minimization principles, ensuring that only the data necessary for a specific task is collected and processed. In addition, data should be encrypted both at rest and in transit to prevent unauthorized access. In addition, modern methods like differential privacy have mathematical assurances that no individual patient data can be deduced by AI output, even when aggregated data are analyzed. Focusing on privacy and security, healthcare organizations will not only defend patient rights, but also maintain confidence in AI systems as a tool that can be trusted and whose use is ethically justifiable in clinical decision-making.

$$\epsilon = ln \frac{Pr[M(D_1) \in S]}{Pr[M(D_2) \in S]}, \quad [7.2]$$

where

- D_1, D_2 = neighboring dataset;
- M = AI mechanism;
- S = output set.

7.3. Regulatory frameworks

7.3.1. *Current landscape*

AI is not yet fully regulated in the medical field, with bodies like the FDA in the United States, the EMA in Europe and the CDSCO in India being at the forefront to make sure that AI is safe, effective and accountable. These frameworks are concerned with certifying AI as a medical device, implementing transparency in the algorithm processes and installing post-market surveillance systems that will monitor the actual instrumental performance. These programs are used to find a balance between innovation and patient welfare.

Region	Regulatory body	AI guidelines focus
USA	FDA	Software as medical device and risk stratification
EU	EMA	CE marking, transparency and clinical validation
India	CDSCO	Clinical evaluation, risk management and data governance

Table 7.2. *Global AI healthcare regulatory highlights*

7.3.2. *Adaptive regulation*

Adaptive control methods are utilized in the design of learning systems to improve learning in computer simulation models. *Adaptive regulation of learning systems:* adaptive control techniques are applied to the design of learning systems to enhance learning in computer simulation models (Ul Haq 2024).

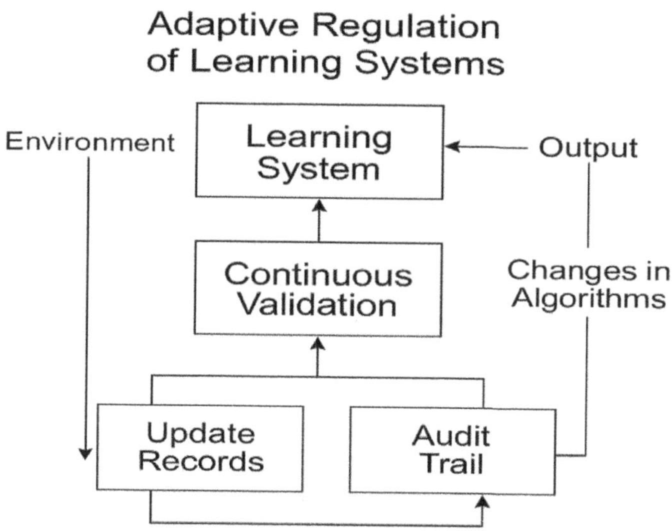

Figure 7.4. *Cycle of adaptive regulatory monitoring in the form of a circular flow diagram. It explains why regulatory supervision of agentic AI in the medical field is an iterative, evolving cycle, that is, deployment, surveillance, risk identification and audit, policy revision and re-deployment*

In contrast to non-agentic medical devices, agentic AI systems are not static, and they may be enhanced and advanced as a result of continuous learning. This flexibility requires regulatory frameworks that surpass fixed-point approval procedures. Adaptive frameworks are also focused on continuous validation, updating records and trail audit of changes that record changes in algorithms during deployment. This makes evolving AI very compliant, safe and effective clinically in the long term.

7.3.3. *Standardization and certification*

Other international initiatives are also in progress to create standards and certifications that will be able to harmonize AI practices across borders. New efforts, such as the ISO/IEC TR 24028 on trustworthiness in AI, the IEEE P7000 family of standards on ethical design of AI and HL7 FHIR on interoperable healthcare data exchange, add much needed consistency. These systems decrease the level of ambiguity, improve trust on a cross-border level and allow agentic AI to integrate into the clinical setting in a safer way.

7.4. Metrics for ethical and regulatory compliance

7.4.1. *Risk assessment metrics*

It is used to evaluate potential harm from AI.

$$Risk\ score = \sum_{i=1}^{n} probability \times severity \qquad [7.3]$$

7.4.2. *Explainability index*

It quantifies the transparency and interpretability of AI decisions:

$$Explainability\ index = \frac{Number\ of\ interpretable\ outputs}{Total\ outputs} \times 100 \qquad [7.4]$$

Metric	Threshold	Current value
Risk score	<0.05	0.03
Explainability index	>80%	85%
Bias index	<5%	3%

Table 7.3. *Sample compliance metrics for agentic AI systems*

7.5. Future directions

AI hospital ethics boards

Hospitals will form special AI ethics boards to manage the deployment, so that the rights of patients, patient safety and transparency maintain the primary role in clinical decisions. These boards will be in-house regulators, who will balance innovation with ethical responsibility.

Co-regulation across the border

Because AI systems cross national borders, it is essential to establish a global harmonization of regulations to achieve uniformity in the realms of safety, responsibility and interoperability. This kind of cooperation will allow quicker global adoption to be achieved and reduce legal and ethical contradictions.

Live AI audit systems

The next-generation structures will be concerned with real-time auditing of AI actions, which will allow constant monitoring of decision-making processes. This active monitoring will lead to the detection of errors or biases in a short period of time, minimizing risks in clinics with high stakes.

Elaboration with patient-centered AI governance

Patients will also be heavily involved in the governance models in such a way that they influence the way AI will be developed and used. The specified participatory approach will create trust and make AI more in touch with patient values and expectations.

7.6. Conclusion

The invention of agentic AI comes as a breakthrough in the current healthcare field, as it implies the introduction of autonomous decision-making, which can significantly improve the quality of diagnostics, personalization of treatment and efficiency. However, its advantages can only be achieved when development and deployment are on a well-established ethical and regulatory framework. The key pillars of trust and acceptance are the safeguarding of patient safety, fairness, accountability and transparency. It is only possible to progress through close cooperation among AI developers, clinicians, policymakers, regulators and patients, and combining technological progress with human values medical accountability to establish a healthcare ecosystem that is not only innovative, but also fair.

7.7. References

Buiten, M., de Streel, A., Peitz, M. (2023). The law and economics of AI liability. *Computer Law and Security Review*, 48, 105794. doi: 10.1016/j.clsr.2023.105794.

Chandra, I. (2022). Penentuan lokasi wireless device berbasis 3D access point location based. *Journal of Intelligent System and Computation*, 4, 1–6. doi: 10.52985/insyst.v4i1.215.

Dewitte, S., Cornelis, J.P., Müller, R. Munteanu, A. (2021). Artificial intelligence revolutionises weather forecast, climate monitoring and decadal prediction. *Remote Sensing*, 13, 3209. doi: 10.3390/rs13163209.

Madrid-García, A., Benavent, D., Merino-Barbancho, B. (2025). From chat to act: Large language model agents and agentic AI as the next frontier of AI in rheumatology. *EULAR Rheumatology Open*, 1(3), 147–156. doi: 10.1016/j.ero.2025.06.012.

Nouis, S.C., Uren, V., Jariwala, S. (2025). Evaluating accountability, transparency, and bias in AI-assisted healthcare decision-making: A qualitative study of healthcare professionals' perspectives in the UK. *BMC Med Ethics*, 26(1), 89. doi: 10.1186/s12910-025-01243-z.

Park, H.J. (2024). Patient perspectives on informed consent for medical AI: A web-based experiment. *Digit Health*, 10. doi: 10.1177/20552076241247938.

Qureshi, A. and Kajla, A. (2016). Intelligent face recognition. *International Journal of Computer Sciences and Engineering* [Online]. Available at: www.ijcseonline.org.

Singh, S., Karimipour, H., HaddadPajouh, H., Dehghantanha, A. (2020). Artificial intelligence and security of industrial control systems. In *Handbook of Big Data Privacy*, Choo, K.-K.R. and Dehghantanha, A. (eds). Springer, Cham. doi: 10.1007/978-3-030-38557-6_7.

Soori, M., Jough, F.K.G., Dastres, R., Arezoo, B. (2026). AI-based decision support systems in Industry 4.0, a review. *Journal of Economy and Technology*, 4, 206–225. doi: 10.1016/j.ject.2024.08.005.

Ul Haq, I. (2024). Diagnosis of neurological disease using bioinspired algorithms. In *Bio-Inspired Optimization for Medical Data Mining*, Srivastava, S., Anand, A., Kumar, A. et al. (eds). John Wiley & Sons, Hoboken, NJ.

Ul Haq, I. and Khanday, A.M.U.D. (2025). Exploring the role of explainable AI in women's health: Challenges and solutions. In *Explainable Artificial Intelligence in the Healthcare Industry*, Kumar, A., Kumar, T.A., Das, P. et al. (eds). John Wiley & Sons, Hoboken, NJ.

Ul Haq, I., Kumar, N., Koul, N., Verma, C., Eneacu, F.M., Raboaca, M.S. (2022). Machine learning techniques for result prediction of one day international (ODI) cricket match. In *The International Conference on Recent Innovations in Computing*. Springer, Singapore.

Ul Haq, I., Kaur, G., Rather, A.H. (2024). Fruit leaf classification using transfer learning for automation and industrial applications. In *Deep Learning Techniques for Automation and Industrial Applications*, Rathore, P.S., Ahuja, S., Burri, S.R. et al. (eds). John Wiley & Sons, Hoboken, NJ.

Ul Haq, I., Khanday, A.M.D., Shah, H.A., Rufai, S.Z. (2025a). Enhancing water security through automation: Case studies and technical advancements in water quality management. In *Computational Automation for Water Security*, Dubey, A.K., Srivastav, A.L., Kumar, A. et al. (eds). Elsevier, Amsterdam.

Ul Haq, I., Kumar, A., Rathore, P.S. (2025b). Machine learning approaches for wind power forecasting: A comprehensive review. *Discover Applied Sciences*, 7(10), 1139.

Ul Haq, I., Malhotra, J., Rawat, V., Kumari, J., Kaur, G. (2025c). Machine learning approaches for early detection of cervical cancer: A comparative study of classification models. In *Targeted Chemotherapy with Personalized Immunotherapy: An AI Approach*, Kumar, A., Das, P., Rathore, P.S. et al. (eds). John Wiley & Sons, Hoboken, NJ.

Ul Haq, I., Nandal, V., Uppal, H. (2025d). Blockchain applications in aviation securing transactions, streamlining operations, and improving passenger experience. In *Blockchain in the Tourism Industry: A New Era of Secure and Transparent Travel Solutions*, Kumar, A., Abreu, A., Batta, P. et al. (eds). Springer, Cham.

8

Digital Twins and AI for Predictive Maintenance of Renewable Energy Assets

Artificial intelligence (AI) and digital twin (DT) technology are fast becoming some of the most incredible mobile solutions in predicting and maintaining the reliability of renewable energy resources. Renewable energy sources, including wind turbines, solar farms and hydropowered plants, are experiencing issues such as component wear and tear, uncontrollable failures and expensive downtimes, which are interfering with their efficiency and upgradeability. DT, a dynamic, virtual, physical energy asset representation, provides the opportunity for real-time monitoring, simulation and optimization of the functioning of a system. Combining these virtual replicas with AI techniques, such as machine learning (ML), deep learning (DL) and reinforcement learning (RL), predictive maintenance strategies can be built and can predict failures, cut through maintenance schedules and alleviate risk of operations. In this chapter, we discuss the design and deployment of AI-based DT of renewable energy systems, emphasizing why they are useful in anomaly detection, fault diagnosis and remaining useful life (RUL) prediction. Applications and case studies are examined with a primary focus on wind, solar and hybrid energy systems, appropriating enhancement of multiple aspects of asset reliability, energy production and lifecycle. Moreover, the chapter explains the major challenges that encompass data integration, cybersecurity, interoperability and scalability, and provides the research directions that should be followed for deployment in the future. By combining DT with AI, the process of predictive maintenance is improved, and, more importantly, helps progress the global shift to more sustainable, resilient and cost-effective energy systems.

8.1. Introduction

The worldwide energy market is under resettlement due to the significant urgency of reducing carbon emissions and limiting global warming, as well as securing federal energy security. Alternatives to fossil fuels like wind, solar, hydro and biomass are also forming as possibilities, yet their

Chapter written by Abdul Malik ANSARI.

efficiency and reliability are also central issues (Madaminov et al. 2025). As opposed to the traditional systems, renewable assets are extremely susceptible to changes in the environment, physical overstrain and the dynamic nature of operations routines, leading to severe breakdowns, loss of functionality and expensive forms of downtime (Ul Haq et al. 2024).

The solutions to this are changing the current maintenance strategies toward predictive maintenance (PdM); this utilizes real-time information and analytics to predict future failures in advance, instead of relying on the reactive (after they have broken) and preventive (based on time and schedule) methods used historically. PdM does not only minimize downtimes and expenditures, but also increases the lifespan of the assets.

DTs and AI are two enabling technologies currently demonstrating disruptive potential in this field. DTs form a dynamic virtual representation of the assets with live data streams provided by IoT sensors and SCADA systems, providing operators with simulating behavior, forecasting failures and testing the "what-if" scenario without interfering with the operation (Rahman 2026). This is supplemented by AI that examines large volumes of data, uncovers complex patterns and provides precise predictive information. DT and AI create a self-educating learning system of intelligent, adaptive maintenance that has a synergy between them (Ul Haq et al. 2025a; Zaman et al. 2025).

The integration of digital twin (DT) and artificial intelligence (AI) in wind energy systems enables predictive maintenance, including the detection of gearbox and blade failures. In solar farms, this approach can monitor and predict faults in photovoltaic (PV) modules, while in hydropower plants it supports turbine health monitoring. Such strategies help reduce operational expenditures (OPEX), improve system stability and enhance sustainability. However, challenges related to data interoperability, cybersecurity, model interpretability and computational cost must be addressed to enable large-scale implementation.

This chapter discusses the uses of DTs and AI in predictive maintenance of renewable energy assets with some backgrounds integration schemes, industrial practices, examples of their application, challenges, and future prospects of introducing smarter, resilient and more sustainable energy systems (Rana 2025; Zaman et al. 2025).

8.2. DTs in renewable energy

DTs, being a core technology in Industry 4.0, ensure the bridge between physical and digital worlds. Originally implemented in manufacturing and aircraft, DTs are finding immense application in renewable energy so that they can have real-time telemetry, fault diagnosis and performance control (Ul Haq et al. 2025c).

8.2.1. *Digital twin*

A DT is a computer-generated model of an actual object, technology or procedure that evolves in real-time as data provided by sensors and control systems arrive (Sghiri et al. 2025). Unlike the non-evolving models, DTs move with their physical counterparts, giving the operators actionable information to analyze, predict actions and act optimally. They are smart mirrors in renewable energy that can resemble turbines, PV arrays, hydro turbines or complete plants (Al-Shetwi et al. 2025; Ul Haq et al. 2025d).

8.2.2. *Architecture of a renewable energy DT*

Figure 8.1 illustrates the conceptual framework, which provides the end-to-end architecture of DT in terms of the asset sensing viewpoint to analytical insights.

A DT typically comprises the following (Ul Haq et al. 2025c, 2025d; Sghiri et al. 2025):

– *Physical layer*: it consists of the tangible object (turbine, panel, hydro unit) that has embedded IoT/SCADA sensors.

– *Data layer*: it processes various types of data (vibration, weather, strain and logs) (Sghiri et al. 2025).

– *Modeling layer*: this relies on physics-based models, AI-based models or hybrid models to model the behavior of assets (Ul Haq et al. 2025d).

– *Analytics layer*: the first layer is designed for detecting anomalies, predictive expectations and optimization (with XAI to explain) (Al-Shetwi et al. 2025; Ul Haq et al. 2025d).

– *Visualization layer*: it includes visualizing interface dashboards/AR applications providing predictive maintenance and decision-making (Al-Shetwi et al. 2025).

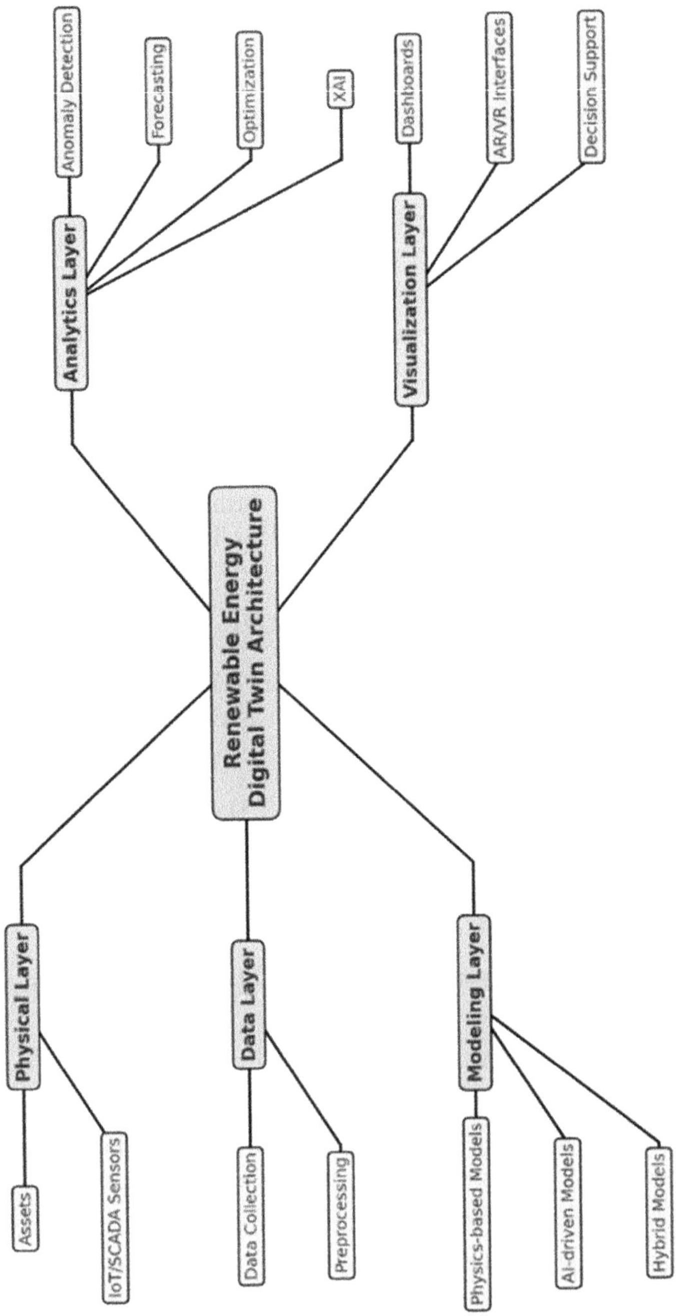

Figure 8.1. *Architecture of a renewable energy digital twin. For a color version of this figure, see www.iste.co.uk/ulhaq/artificial1.zip*

This multi-layered structure enables energy operators to perform "what-if" analyses, optimize control parameters and schedule maintenance proactively (Ul Haq et al. 2025d).

8.2.3. *AI for predictive maintenance*

AI can be considered the key for predictive maintenance, transforming input data about the sensors into valuable information. Based on ML and DL tools (Al-Shetwi et al. 2025), AI models are able to analyze time-series data of renewable energy sources, identify anomalies and predict a pre-specified failure before its appearance.

The most common approaches involve regression models to predict RUL, classifiers to detect faults and unsupervised learning to detect anomalies (Ul Haq and Khanday 2025; Kavousi-Fard et al. 2025). The more sophisticated algorithms, such as auto-encoders, recurrent neural networks (RNNs) and convolutional neural networks (CNNs), progress the degree of accuracy in order to capture nonlinearity and time-varying relationships.

Active learning AI predictive maintenance considers real-time data and past records to optimize inspection schedules, unplanned downtime and maximize lifetime, thus guaranteeing improved energy output and reduced maintenance expenditure.

RUL prediction

The RUL of an asset at time t can be mathematically expressed as:

$$RUL(t) = T_{fail} - t \quad [8.1]$$

where T_{fail} represents the predicted time of failure and t denotes the current operational time (Abdessadak et al. 2025).

Advanced models such as auto encoders, recurrent neural networks and convolutional neural networks capture nonlinear temporal dependencies in wind-turbine and photovoltaic (PV) datasets (Ul Haq and Khanday 2025; Kavousi-Fard et al. 2025). When embedded within DTs, these models enable self-learning maintenance schedules that minimize downtime and operational costs (Abdessadak et al. 2025).

8.2.4. *Adoption trends*

Industry adoption of AI-enabled DTs is rapidly growing. GE renewable energy employs DTs to predict gearbox and blade degradation, while Siemens Gamesa applies them for turbine yaw-alignment optimization (Al-Shetwi et al. 2025). Solar-farm operators use DT–AI combinations to monitor panel soiling and hotspot development, achieving measurable efficiency gains (Al-Shetwi et al. 2025). These trends highlight DTs as strategic tools for achieving resilient and cost-effective renewable-energy operations (Al-Shetwi et al. 2025).

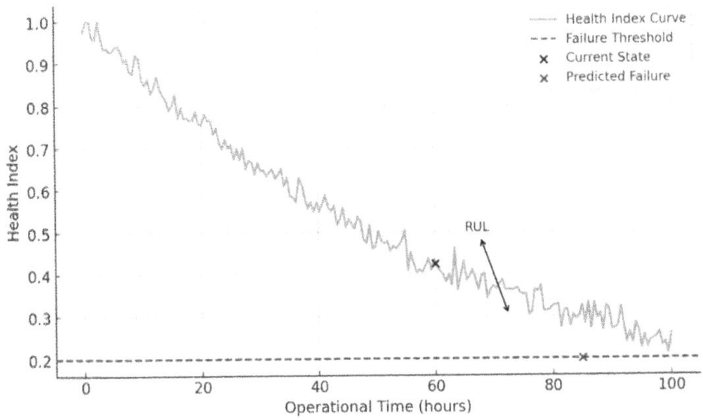

Figure 8.2. *Remaining useful life (RUL) prediction curve. For a color version of this figure, see www.iste.co.uk/ulhaq/artificial1.zip*

Figure 8.2 illustrates the RUL prediction curve, which reveals that as the health index of the asset decreases, the health index approaches the failure threshold and, as such, the predicted failure point is presented.

– *Health index curve*: it shows the asset condition degrading over time.

– *Failure threshold*: it includes the critical limit indicating failure risk.

– *Current state*: it includes the present health level of the asset.

– *Predicted failure*: it includes the forecasted point where the asset reaches the threshold.

– *RUL*: it includes the time left between the current state and predicted failure.

Major players such as *GE Renewable Energy* and *Siemens Games* are integrating DTs into wind turbines, while solar operators employ AI-enabled twins for PV performance modeling. These trends confirm DTs as a *strategic enabler* of resilience and sustainability in renewable energy.

8.3. System architecture of DT–AI integration

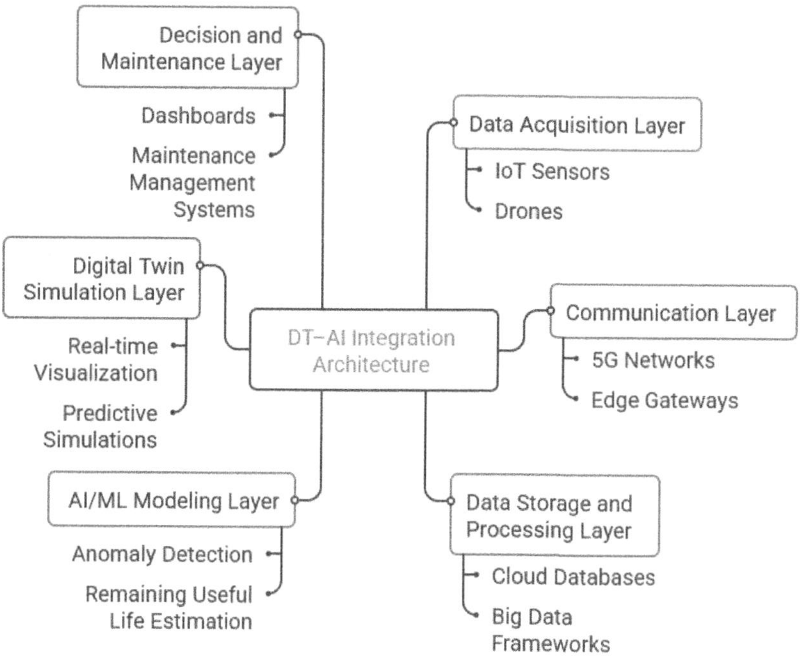

Figure 8.3. *DT–AI integration architecture for predictive maintenance. For a color version of this figure, see www.iste.co.uk/ulhaq/artificial1.zip*

As shown in Figure 8.3, the DT-AI framework brings together the process of acquisition, communication, storage, simulation and AI modeling to make it feasible to facilitate end-to-end predictive maintenance.

8.3.1. *Data acquisition layer*

The architecture is based on the IoT-enabled sensors installed in the assets of renewable energy (Suci et al. 2025). The sensors are able to detect the operation parameters, including the vibration, temperature, current and voltage, as well as the environmental conditions (Ul Haq et al. 2025b). Those insights may be enhanced with the help of drones and thermal imaging (Ejiyi et al. 2025; Ul Haq et al. 2025b).

8.3.2. *Communication layer*

The collected information is sent out over secure and low-latency networks commonly utilizing 5G and private LTE technology or edge gateways (Suci et al. 2025). The energy of preprocessing in the edge – of type noise filtering and normalization, etc. – guarantees efficiency prior to the transmission of data to the cloud.

8.3.3. *Data storage and processing layer*

Data will be stored as text files and visualized in tables in exposed spreadsheets (Ul Haq et al. 2025b). When the transmitted data are distributed, they are stored in cloud databases and distributed platforms to enable real-time analysis, as well as historical analysis (Ejiyi et al. 2025). Preprocessing pipelines guarantee the high quality of data, and AI models are provided with large-scale calculations that are delivered with the help of big data structures (Ul Haq 2024).

8.3.4. *AI/ML modeling layer*

AI modeling is the best of predictive maintenance. Detection of anomalies, prediction and estimation of RUL are performed with the help of ML and DL algorithms (Abdessadak et al. 2025; Ul Haq and Khanday 2025). Mathematically, auto-encoder-based anomaly detection is as follows:

$$\boldsymbol{E_{(x)} = ||x - \hat{x}||, if\ E(x) > \theta \rightarrow Anomaly\ detected} \qquad [8.2]$$

These insights feed directly into the DT for validation and simulation (Ul Haq 2024).

8.3.5. *DT simulation layer*

The DT is a virtual entity, which represents the physical asset, and it receives processed data and AI (Van Dinter et al. 2022). The DT is capable of visualizing in real-time, simulating and applying scenarios, which is why they can predict failure before it happens (Costa et al. 2025).

8.3.6. *Decision and maintenance layer*

This is a layer that maintains the choices and decisions regarding each unionized member at every organization. Lastly, the DT–AI system insights are presented in the dashboard and connected to corporate maintenance management plays. This enables optimum timetables, reduced downtime and condition-based intercession in contrast to established maintenance intervals (Van Dinter et al. 2022; Costa et al. 2025).

8.4. Integration of DTs and AI

The ultimate transformative nature of predictive maintenance in renewable energy is not DTs or AI in isolation, but in combination with each other. DTs provides an active and live virtual image of renewable energy resources, and AI provides the analytical intelligence required to process large volumes of data, compute patterns that are not apparent and make predictions (Van Dinter et al. 2022). DTs and AI work in a closed-loop, self-learning system that enables improving the operational performance of a company, making autonomous decisions and improving the accuracy of fault detection (Costa et al. 2025).

8.4.1. *The rationale for integration*

Erring single autonomy statuses, DTs give detailed simulated images of the behavior of assets and permit the operators to picture the outcomes. Nevertheless, as much as they all do well in the reflection of physical processes, they usually need some further analysis to predict failures correctly. Conversely, AI in itself provides robust predictive service by regressing these big datasets identifying trends and foretelling disruptions (Van Dinter et al. 2022; Costa et al. 2025). However, they often do not physically interoperate and could have a hard time generalizing in cases that are different to what they were trained on.

In comparison, the integration model of DTs and AI brings together the advantages of both methodologies: the DTs would be embedded with physical knowledge and system behavior, whereas AI would deliver adaptive intelligence and data-driven insights. This synergy when combined makes sure that not only can predictions be accurately made, but also that they are explainable and profoundly supported by the underlying physical laws of renewable energy systems (Costa et al. 2025).

8.4.2. *Framework of integration*

A typical DT and AI integration framework in renewable energy assets can be broken down into four key stages (Van Dinter et al. 2022; Costa et al. 2025; Rojas et al. 2025):

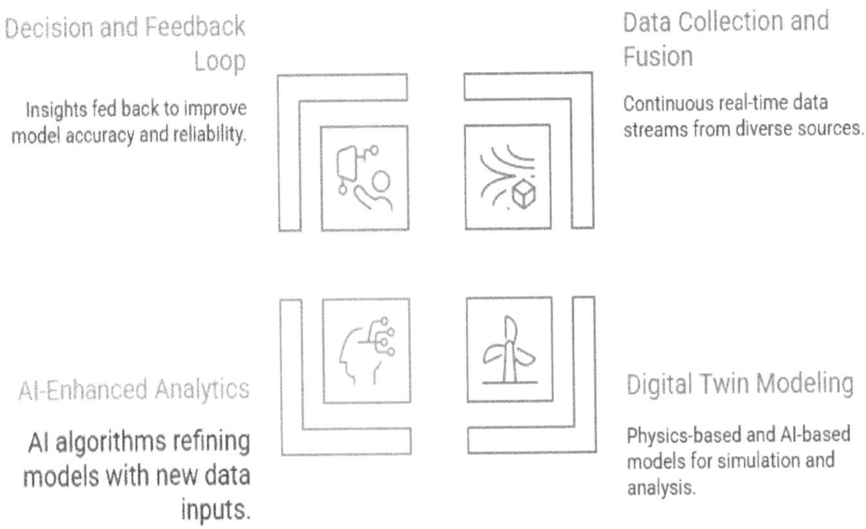

Figure 8.4. *Renewable energy integration framework. For a color version of this figure, see www.iste.co.uk/ulhaq/artificial1.zip*

The integration process of the system in Figure 8.4 is based on data fusion, DT modeling, AI analytics and a feedback loop that enhances the performance of the system continuously.

8.4.2.1. *Data collection and fusion*

Data collection and fusion has IoT sensors, SCADA and the use of drones that feed real-time channels. Environmental factors (wind speed, sun radiance, temperature, humidity and so on) are supplemented by operation parameters (vibration, acoustic emissions and electric currents). This multi-ethnic data provides a platform of accurate and context-sensitive patterns of forecasting (Ejiyi et al. 2025; Ul Haq et al. 2025; Suci et al. 2025).

8.4.2.2. *DT modeling*

The second step is the development of DT modeling. Physics-based models will predict structural behavior, thermal behavior and transport at the material level. AI-based models will analyze historical data and present data to develop deterioration schemes. Hybrid directions, which combine the two directions, are also gaining momentum in order to enjoy a higher accuracy in identifying faults, as well as predicting lifecycles (Van Dinter et al. 2022).

8.4.2.3. *AI-enhanced analytics*

Phase three involves AI-enhanced analytics. New data inputs are continuously fed into AI algorithms in order to improve the DT. DL has been used to identify nonlinear relationships that cannot be readily identified with physics-based models, and to solve the maintenance strategy by experimenting with multiple scenarios in the simulated environment of the twin (Costa et al. 2025).

8.4.2.4. *Decision and feedback loop*

Finally, the process of giving feedback and decision loop becomes a part of the integration loop. The information provided by AI is fed back into the DT to increase the accuracy and reliability of the DT. The new model has some prescriptive suggestions such as modifying the angles of turbine blades, washing the solar panels or switching parts. Over time, the process is a self-corrective and adaptable ecosystem, guaranteeing consistent advancements in renewable energy operations (Costa et al. 2025; Rojas et al. 2025).

8.4.3. *Applications of DT–AI integration in renewable energy*

8.4.3.1. *Wind energy*

Wind turbines are very prone to gearbox vibration, yaw slippage and blade erosion, which results in power losses and unprofitable downtime. DTs reproduce the mechanical–aerodynamic behavior of the turbine, whereas AI models are used to analyze the vibration signals with the aim of detecting anomalies (Ul Haq and Khanday 2025; Ul Haq et al. 2025b).

The vibration RMS for fault detection is given as:

$$RMS = \sqrt{\frac{1}{N}}\left(\sum_{i=1}^{N} x_i^2\right) \quad [8.3]$$

where x_i are vibration samples and RMS indicates fault severity when exceeding a threshold.

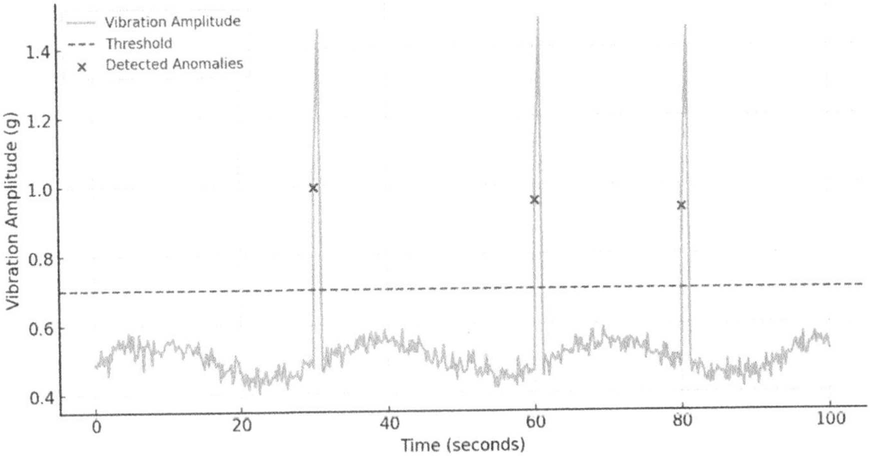

Figure 8.5. *Wind turbine vibration anomaly detection. For a color version of this figure, see www.iste.co.uk/ulhaq/artificial1.zip*

The anomaly detecting actions shown in Figure 8.5 capture the clear surges of vibrations that define the occurrence of the anomalies.

8.4.3.2. *Solar energy*

The system loses its energy to hotspots, soiling, shading and change in temperature, impacting the residence of PV systems.

DTs model the anticipated power output that may be expected in case of certain irradiance, and AI declares the performance deviation between the real and expected outputs (Ul Haq et al. 2025d; Rojas et al. 2025).

The performance ratio (PR) is given as:

$$PR = \frac{E_{actual}}{E_{theoratical}} \times 100\% \qquad [8.4]$$

where E_{actual} is the energy output and $E_{theoratical}$ is the expected output under standard conditions.

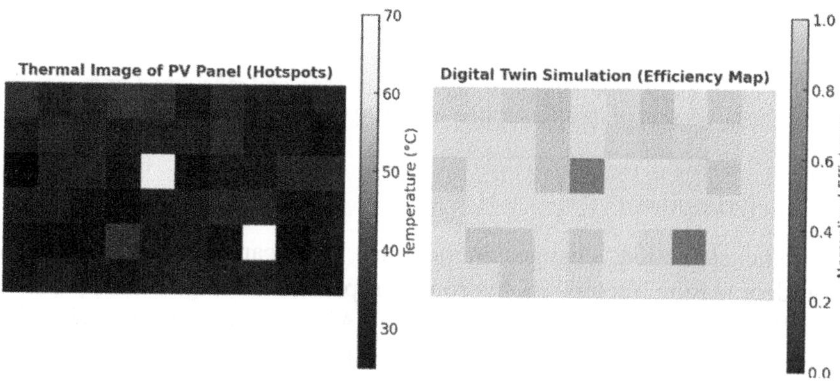

Figure 8.6. *Solar PV panel hotspot detection versus digital twin simulation. For a color version of this figure, see www.iste.co.uk/ulhaq/artificial1.zip*

Figure 8.6 compares thermal hotspot detection of the PV panel against that of the DT efficiency simulation of the device, indicating the effects of local heating.

The blue curve in Figure 8.7 illustrates the slowing down of PR because of dust on the solar panels.

The green dotted line shows that there is a cleaning event at 40 days, after which the efficiency improves.

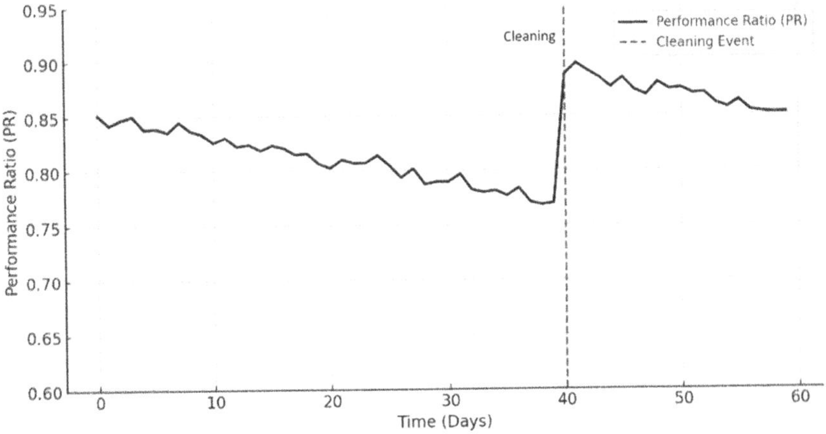

Figure 8.7. *PV performance ratio (PR) decline and recovery. For a color version of this figure, see www.iste.co.uk/ulhaq/artificial1.zip*

8.4.3.3. *Hydropower*

Turbine cavitation, changes in pressure and bearing vibration are the major degradation factors in hydropower plants. Through its apps, DTs model fluid–structure interactions, whereas AI roots pressure and vibration data and detects cavitation (Ejiyi et al. 2025; Rojas et al. 2025).

The cavitation index (σ) is given as:

$$\sigma = \frac{p - p_v}{\frac{1}{2}\rho V^2} \qquad [8.5]$$

where p is local pressure, p_v is vapor pressure, ρ is water density and V is velocity. A low σ indicates higher cavitation risk.

Figure 8.8 illustrates the DT simulation of turbine flow, capturing the pressure distribution across the rotor plane.

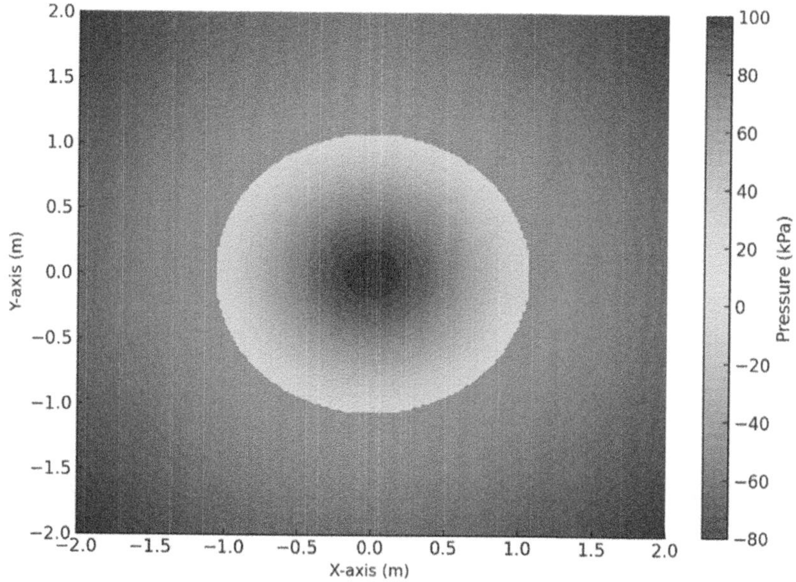

Figure 8.8. *Digital twin simulation of turbine flow. For a color version of this figure, see www.iste.co.uk/ulhaq/artificial1.zip*

8.4.3.4. *Hybrid energy storage systems*

The battery systems (Li-ion, flow batteries) erode because of the charge–discharges cycles and temperature changes. DTs have a fondness for modeling from various electrochemical reactions, whereas AI predicts the State of Charge (SoC) and State of Health (SoH) in real-time (Van Dinter et al. 2022; Ul Haq 2024; Costa et al. 2025; Rojas et al. 2025).

The SoH estimation is given as:

$$SoH(t) = 1 - \frac{Q_{loss}(t)}{Q_{rated}} \quad [8.6]$$

where $Q_{loss}(t)$ is loss capacity and Q_{rated} is nominal rated capacity.

Figure 8.9 shows the SoH degradation curve, indicating how battery health declines with charge–discharge cycles until end-of-life.

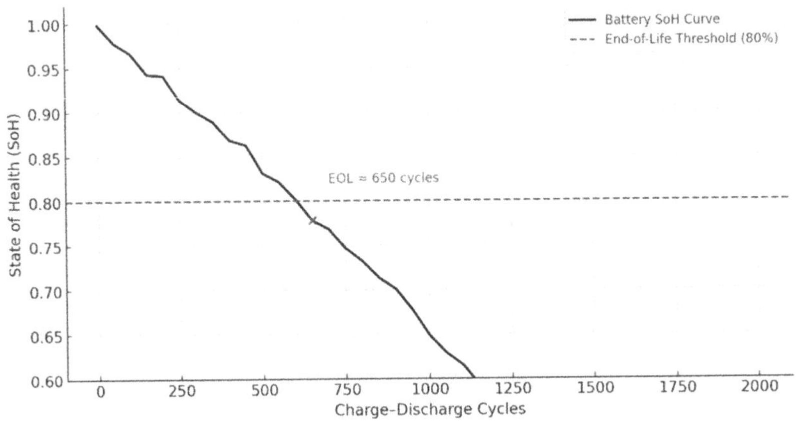

Figure 8.9. *Battery state of health (SoH) degradation curve. For a color version of this figure, see www.iste.co.uk/ulhaq/artificial1.zip*

8.5. Comparative analysis of maintenance strategies

System maintenance methods, as applied in the areas of renewable energy, have moved beyond reactive methods to sophistically intelligent proactive control through DTs and AI (Ul Haq et al. 2024, 2025a; Madaminov et al. 2025; Rahman 2026). When the action is undertaken only after failure in an asset, reactive maintenance is mentioned, which usually takes time and incurs extreme costs. Preventive maintenance enhances reliability as it involves performing unneeded inspections or replacing parts with fixed time frames, but tends to cause more operations and higher operation costs. AI-driven predictive maintenance can be considered as a breakthrough since sensor data, existing patterns and statistical models allow the prediction of failures before they happen. This reduces costs and time wastage, but requires a lot of data availability and integrity (Abdessadak et al. 2025; Al-Shetwi et al. 2025).

The highest level one is DT–AI integrated maintenance that uses virtual assets as real-time asset counterparts to accomplish real-time monitoring and detection of anomalies, as well as ACPE-based simulations. It offers asset-specific information, which is very precise, allows optimization of interventions and reduces the duration of asset life. It also has the disadvantage of requiring substantial up-front investment in sensor infrastructure, data pipelines and simulation models (Van Dinter et al. 2022; Costa et al. 2025).

Parameter	Reactive	Preventive	Predictive (AI based)	DT–AI integrated
Basis of action	After failure occurs	Fixed schedule	Data-driven forecasts	Real-time virtual modeling
Pros	No upfront cost, simple to manage	Reduces sudden failures, easy to plan	Optimized interventions, reduced downtime	High accuracy, asset-specific, scenario testing
Cons	High downtime, costly unplanned repairs	Over-maintenance, not asset specific	Requires reliable sensor data, complex models	High initial setup, complex to implement
Cost impact	Very high (repair + lost energy)	Moderate (labor + parts)	Low to moderate (optimized)	Lowest over lifecycle (saves O&M)
Downtime impact	Very high (long outages)	Moderate (planned shutdowns)	Low (condition-based)	Minimal (real-time monitoring)
Data requirement	None	Low	High (real-time data, ML models)	Very high (IoT simulation, AI)
Scalability	Low	Medium	High	Very high
Example in renewable energy	Gearbox replacement after catastrophic failure	Solar inverter replaced every six months	Wind turbine vibration monitoring with ML	Digital twin of wind farm with AI-driven RUL forecasting

Table 8.1. *Comparison of maintenance strategies for renewable energy assets*

As shown in Table 8.1, DT–AI-integrated maintenance offers the lowest lifecycle impact and highest accuracy compared to traditional approaches.

DT–AI integration thus represents the pinnacle of maintenance intelligence, combining accuracy, adaptability and cost efficiency over the entire asset lifecycle (Van Dinter et al. 2022; Costa et al. 2025).

8.6. Conclusion

Although DT–AI integration could transform prediction in the maintenance of a renewable energy infrastructure, some gaps remain. Vast quantities, of heterogeneous data are needed to conduct high-fidelity modeling but challenges of data scarcity, noise and interoperability between sensor systems usually restrict accuracy. Real-time simulation is computationally expensive and cyber-security issues within the IoT-connected twins also limit the adoption. They reveal the gaps, including the necessity of standardized frameworks, hybrid physics-informed AI models and scalable and safe frameworks. The future prospects lie with blockchain of DTs to achieve data integrity, edge–AI deployment that could be used to create real-time analytics and quantum enhancement optimization that could be applied to inherently complex multi-asset systems. New tendencies also imply the transformation into self-repairing renewable infrastructures, with DT–AI environments automatically sensing, diagnosing and rectifying failures. In summary, despite the existing constraints requiring more thorough research and well-crafted approaches to implementation, DT–AI synergy remains the most promising way to have reliable, cost-efficient and sustainable renewable energy systems, which means that it is an avenue-blocking technology in the global shift toward the net-zero energy prospects.

8.7. References

Abdessadak, A., Ghennioui, H., Thirion-Moreau, N., Elbhiri, B., Abraim, M., Merzouk, S. (2025). Digital twin technology and artificial intelligence in energy transition: A comprehensive systematic review of applications. *Energy Reports*, 13, 5196–5218.

Al-Shetwi, A.Q., Atawi, I.E., El-Hameed, M.A., Abuelrub, A. (2025). Digital twin technology for renewable energy, smart grids, energy storage and vehicle-to-grid integration: Advancements, applications, key players, challenges and future perspectives in modernising sustainable grids. *IET Smart Grid*, 8(1), e70026.

Costa, A., Miranda, J., Dias, D., Dinis, N., Romero, L., Faria, P.M. (2025). Smart maintenance solutions: AR-and VR-enhanced digital twin powered by FIWARE. *Sensors*, 25(3), 845.

Ejiyi, C.J., Cai, D., Thomas, D., Obiora, S., Osei-Mensah, E., Acen, C., Eze, F.O., Sam, F., Zhang, Q., Bamisile, O.O. (2025). Comprehensive review of artificial intelligence applications in renewable energy systems: Current implementations and emerging trends. *Journal of Big Data*, 12(1), 169.

Kavousi-Fard, A., Dabbaghjamanesh, M., Sheikh, M., Jin, T. (2025). A novel deep learning based digital twin model for mitigating wake effects in wind farms. *Renewable Energy Focus*, 53, 100686.

Madaminov, B., Saidmurodov, S., Saitov, E., Jumanazarov, D., Alsayah, A.M., Zhetkenbay, L. (2025). Multi-objective optimization framework for energy efficiency and production scheduling in smart manufacturing using reinforcement learning and digital twin technology integration. *International Journal of Industrial Engineering and Management*, 16(3), 283–295.

Rahman, F. (2026). Scalable safety-constrained learning pipelines for distributed digital-twin-based energy optimization in large-scale electric mobility systems. *SECITS Journal of Scalable Distributed Computing and Pipeline Automation*, 3(1), 1–8.

Rana, S. (2025). AI-driven fault detection and predictive maintenance in electrical power systems: A systematic review of data-driven approaches, digital twins, and self-healing grids. *American Journal of Advanced Technology and Engineering Solutions*, 1(01), 258–289.

Rojas, L., Peña, Á., Garcia, J. (2025). AI-driven predictive maintenance in mining: A systematic literature review on fault detection, digital twins, and intelligent asset management. *Applied Sciences*, 15(6), 3337.

Sghiri, A., Gallab, M., Merzouk, S., Assoul, S. (2025). Leveraging digital twins for enhancing building energy efficiency: A literature review of applications, technologies, and challenges. *Buildings*, 15(3), 498.

Suci, A. M., Amini, R., Asri, A. K., Martin, N. (2025). Artificial intelligence in renewable energy: A review of predictive maintenance and energy optimization. *Journal of Clean Technology*, 2(1), 29–44.

Ul Haq, I. (2024). Diagnosis of neurological disease using bioinspired algorithms. In *Bio-Inspired Optimization for Medical Data Mining*, Srivastava, S., Anand, A., Kumar, A. et al. (eds). John Wiley & Sons, Hoboken, NJ.

Ul Haq, I. and Khanday, A.M.U.D. (2025). Exploring the role of explainable AI in women's health: Challenges and solutions. In *Explainable Artificial Intelligence in the Healthcare Industry*, Kumar, A., Kumar, T.A., Das, P. et al. (eds). John Wiley & Sons, Hoboken, NJ.

Ul Haq, I., Kaur, G., Rather, A.H. (2024). Fruit leaf classification using transfer learning for automation and industrial applications. In *Deep Learning Techniques for Automation and Industrial Applications*, Rathore, P.S., Ahuja, S., Burri, S.R. et al. (eds). John Wiley & Sons, Hoboken, NJ.

Ul Haq, I., Kumar, A., Rathore, P.S. (2025a). Machine learning approaches for wind power forecasting: A comprehensive review. *Discover Applied Sciences*, 7(10), 1139.

Ul Haq, I., Malhotra, J., Rawat, V., Kumari, J., Kaur, G. (2025b). Machine learning approaches for early detection of cervical cancer: A comparative study of classification models. In *Targeted Chemotherapy with Personalized Immunotherapy: An AI Approach*, Kumar, A., Das, P., Rathore, P.S. et al. (eds). John Wiley & Sons, Hoboken, NJ.

Ul Haq, I., Nandal, V., Uppal, H. (2025c). Blockchain applications in aviation securing transactions, streamlining operations, and improving passenger experience. In *Blockchain in the Tourism Industry: A New Era of Secure and Transparent Travel Solutions*, Kumar, A., Abreu, A., Batta, P. et al. (eds). Springer, Cham.

Ul Haq, I., Shah, H.A., Rufai, S.Z. (2025d). Enhancing water security through automation: Case studies and technical advancements in water quality management. In *Computational Automation for Water Security*, Dubey, A.K., Srivastav, A.L., Kumar, A. et al. (eds). Elsevier, Amsterdam.

Van Dinter, R., Tekinerdogan, B., Catal, C. (2022). Predictive maintenance using digital twins: A systematic literature review. *Information and Software Technology*, 151, 107008. doi: 10.1016/j.infsof.2022.107008.

Zaman, S., Vudugula, S., Chebrolu, S.K., Saha, R. (2025). AI and quantum computing for carbon-neutral supply chains: A systematic review of innovations. *American Journal of Interdisciplinary Studies*, 6(1), 40–75. doi: 10.63125/nrdx7d32.

9

Digitally Enhanced Fire Alarm System Using Sensor Driven Arduino Implementation for Smart Energy Management

The primary objective of this chapter is to implement a reliable fire alarm system using Arduino and GSM interfacing in compliance with the Institute of Electrical and Electronics Engineers (IEEE) standards. Enhancing advanced technology, this system preferably aims to alert people about fire hazards. This chapter's goal is to provide a healthy environment for people through smart energy management. The brain of such a proposed system is Arduino Uno microcontroller (ATMEGA328P), which interfaces with other electronic devices including the Global System for Mobile Communications (GSM) module. By using this module, Arduino Uno will be able to send and receive signals through Short Message Service (SMS), connect to the Internet and generate voice calls using a GSM library.

The key components of such a proposed model are the Arduino Uno, Light Emitting Diode (LED) indicator, GSM module, buzzer, metal oxide (MQ2) gas sensor, breadboard, temperature sensors, display resistors and jumping connecting wires. Basically, this proposed model enhances safety aspects through the integration of various components, especially in large applications like residential buildings and big factories. After integrating the components by implanting the program, it is easy to detect fire or smoke issues. It alerts and sends a warning signal. The proposed fire alarm system is an indispensable instrument for ensuring public safety and provides a secure environment for the public by using modern technology. This chapter will provide suitable insights into Arduino implementation with emerging technology to protect the environment, leading toward smart energy management.

Chapter written by Ranjit Kumar BINDAL and Akhil NIGAM.

9.1. Introduction

Although fire has always been extremely helpful to humans, if it is not controlled, it can also be rather dangerous. There is always a chance that a fire may break out in our daily life. Fire is still a major problem, even with the enormous advancements in fire prevention and suppression technologies since the late 20th century, such as the widespread use of sprinkler systems, smoke detectors and emergency evacuation procedures. Fire exacts a heavy price every year, amounting to around 1% of the world gross domestic product (GDP) and creates thousands of fatalities. Recent tragedies highlight how difficult fire safety continues to be. According to data supplied by the Delhi Fire Services (DFS), the capital city saw five fire-related fatalities on average each month in 2023. Even while this is less than the average of seven deaths per month from the prior year, the threat is still present. Notably, there were more fire-related fatalities in 2023 than in 2021, highlighting the necessity of ongoing watchfulness and preventative actions to adequately manage fire risks. Fire alarms are used to identify and alert people to the possibility of fire or smoke in a building or other enclosed area. The numerous problems with fire contribute to the myriad issues with false alarm compatibility.

9.2. Literature review

This chapter proposes a fire detection strategy based on video processing and RGB representation, emphasizing its effectiveness in achieving high accuracy, low false alarm rates, and adaptability across diverse environments. It highlights chromatic investigation of the blazes, energetic investigation of the outlines, smoke location and early fire discovery calculation (Aryanti 2021). In the same year, another study investigated the utilization of controller area network (CAN) for fire location in a savvy domestic environment, highlighting its focal points over conventional frameworks and other conventions. The emphasis is on low cost, ease of implementation, and the potential for more efficient integration into home automation systems. The assessment of the proposed framework is sponsored by tests and is based on engineering on an arrange fire-detection framework. After a few tests, it can be said that the framework fulfills the National Fire Protection Association (NFPA) prerequisites in that the fire caution reaction time is exceptionally brief. Also, as the collector gets fire location information straight from the fire locators, it can be said that the framework is more precise than the customary fire discovery systems (Ul Haq 2024). This chapter presents a strategy for early fire location through video preparation, centering on distinguishing smoke pixels. The approach includes two choice rules: an inactive run of the show based on the grayish color of the smoke and an energetic run of the show depending on the spreading characteristics of the smoke. Test discoveries illustrate that the proposed strategy can issue early warnings with a lower frequency of false warnings, making it exceedingly engaging for basic applications in the military, social security, commercial settings and past (Khan et al. 2022). After that, another proposed real-time fire alert framework is planned to instantly distinguish smoke nearness due to a fire and capture room pictures utilizing an inserted camera. Raspberry Pi and Arduino Uno serve as the inserted frameworks driving this arrangement. Outstandingly, the framework empowers inaccessible alarms upon fire location. When smoke is distinguished, the framework produces a webpage showing a room picture, requiring client affirmation to send an alarm to the firefighter through Brief Message Benefit SMS. This approach limits the probability of false alarms coming to the firefighter. Besides, the system's proficiency is underscored by the camera exclusively capturing pictures, coming about in negligible capacity utilization and control utilization. Generally, this framework gives a viable and dependable fire discovery strategy with inaccessible alarming capabilities, reducing the chance of wrong alerts (Ul Haq et al. 2025b).

Another system component focuses on the implementation of a controlled robot for fire detection and suppression in enclosed areas using an Arduino-based platform. They center on a fire-extinguishing robot used to combat fires and address encased range fires, shielding faculty in fire concealment exercises from the risks of combustion and introduction to poisonous gases. The essential concept of this robot rotates around identifying fires utilizing a remote camera and a fire sensor. Hence, the robot smothers the fire by getting commands from a portable phone using a Bluetooth association, actuating the water pump to quench the fire. They are utilized in ventures like Arduino, remote control frameworks, fire-extinguishing robots, fire sensors, remote cameras and Bluetooth. One unused thing they included was a fire-quenching robot for the assurance of houses. They utilized highlights like wheeled portable robots, maneuverability, Arduino, direct current (DC) engine for car models, L298 engine driver, Bluetooth HC-06, fire sensors and numerous other required components. After that, they got the final result – a fire-detection and quenching robot, fueled by an Arduino-based microcontroller, using a remote camera and fire sensor. The versatile robot communicates with a portable phone through the serial harbor, handling analogue information from the fire sensor to distinguish and quench indoor fires that are challenging to get to effortlessly (Gianluca et al. 2017). Guaranteeing the rights and security of clothing specialists is a pressing concern in current times, with fire dangers being a noteworthy challenge confronted by laborers in industrial clothing facilities. This chapter presents a framework to identify fires and pinpoint their location, tending to the industry's security issues. It includes Raspberry Pi 3, controlling different Arduinos prepared with different sensors and a camera. A 360° hand-off engine is coordinated with the camera to capture pictures from any point where a fire is identified. To avoid false alarms, an affirmation component is consolidated into the fire-detection framework. Upon recognizing a fire, the framework instantly sends a message, including a picture of the affected zone and the Arduino's location. A chairman has the specialist affirm or reject the fire alert. If affirmed, the framework triggers a caution and naturally informs the adjacent fire brigade. This imaginative framework aims to upgrade the security of clothing laborers and moderate the challenges confronted by the industry (Ul Haq and Khanday 2025). To anticipate woodland fires, which are the most common these days, 80% of fire-related misfortunes have to be moderated with inciting fire identification. A hub MCU-based IoT-enabled fire location and observing framework is proposed. The framework incorporates a temperature sensor, a smoke sensor and a buzzer interface with Hub MCU. The temperature sensor recognizes warmth and the smoke sensor recognizes any smoke emanating from a fire. The buzzer acts as an alarm when a fire is detected. The framework follows these five steps: utilizing sensors to procure information, gathering data using the IC introduced in the Arduino of the transmitter circuit, transmitting the data using the transmitter, accepting the data using the Getting station, and showing the temperature and CO_2 levels on the location page accessible through the secretly made framework. Quick fire location is significant to anticipate major misfortunes and ensure a social legacy. Knowing where the fire started helps with speedy control, permitting firefighters to effectively oversee and stifle the fire (Bahrudin et al. 2013). The progression in fire caution frameworks has highlighted their upgraded modernity and accentuation on shielding life and property. The project's objective is to create an IoT-based fire caution route framework, joining GPS, fire and smoke sensors, buzzers, LEDs and a GSM module. The essential point is to offer early alerts, encouraging clearing and fire control to limit casualties and property harm. An overview conducted in a sports generation company in Sialkot, Pakistan, includes comparing reaction times amid fire episodes with (and without) the proposed IoT fire alert framework at the Protect 1122 fire head station (Ul Haq et al. 2025d). Gas leakage detection for home use is detailed, where a microcontroller, GSM and liquefied petroleum gas (LPG) sensors are employed to showcase gas values on LCD. The microcontroller issues a signal upon detecting a gas leak, displaying a warning message on the LCD and sending an informative SMS to the user (Anthony et al. 2024).

The authors introduced an uncomplicated approach to globally monitor weather changes, utilizing sensors and a Bluetooth microcontroller unit. An Android phone is connected to DHT 11 and wind speed sensors to collect data, which is then transmitted to an Arduino via Bluetooth. Nevertheless, these systems are specifically configured to transmit "fire alert" messages and trigger an alarm sound exclusively through short message service (SMS), accompanied by information regarding the fire's location. In addition to factors such as cost, efficiency and responsiveness, there are still unresolved issues. This research project seeks to address these challenges by developing a system that utilizes IoT technology to detect heat and smoke within a fire alarm system, aiming to enhance both reliability and effectiveness (Zhao 2024). In recent years, IoT has been applied in different fields including smart agriculture, smart healthcare and smart homes, which we are using for the alarms to make them more advanced, easy and reliable to use. It also helps in the agricultural sector where fires are automatically produced and cause so much loss (Chen et al. 2004; Ul Haq et al. 2025c). Although fire detection has been the subject of greater research, the precision of such systems is insufficient, since more photos are required to train algorithms that are trained by photographs (Chen et al. 2006). Other techniques have downsides, such as limited accuracy and slow response times. This chapter introduces an innovative IoT approach, moving away from a predominant dependence on Node-RED, aiming to decrease false alarms and offer swifter response times. Furthermore, apart from enhancing device efficiency, the utilization of IoT can lead to financial advantages (Ul Haq et al. 2022).

9.3. Problem formulation

Catastrophic disasters can result from fires, which can have a devastating effect on economies, ecosystems and populations. From destroying wildfires that engulf vast stretches of land, destroying homes, wildlife habitats and natural resources, to infernos within urban environments that claim lives and livelihoods, the impact of fires is profound and far-reaching. Apart from the direct devastation of assets and facilities, fires cause secondary consequences such as soil erosion, air pollution and water contamination, worsening environmental deterioration and endangering the long-term health of the population.

Approximately two children die from burns every two weeks, according to research conducted by the Fire and Rescue Department (FRD). In order to address this problem, we have created a fire detection system that integrates Arduino and IoT. Accurately sensing variations in temperature or smoke content allows the system to take the necessary action to protect people and property.

9.4. Constraints

9.4.1. *Detection accuracy*

Attaining precise and accurate fire detection is a challenging issue. The system is required to be sensitive to small flames to alert households. However, calibrating sensors like temperature sensors and heat sensors to differentiate between nominal activities or abnormal incidents poses a significant limitation.

9.4.2. *Hardware compatibility*

Another seamless issue is integrating with electronic devices in-built with proposed programming. Any irregular connectivity may destroy the program and could impact sensing any smoke. Ensuring flawless functionality is a major concern in detecting smoke or fire issues.

9.4.3. *Data logging functionality*

Reliable data recording and storage play a vital role for effective analysis. Proposed data logger modules must keep all of the data in an appropriate manner and can help in some abnormal conditions. Sometimes, maintaining uninterrupted data may become another challenge.

9.4.4. *Power consumption*

Power consumption may be a problem in installed IoT devices. Due to this, a backup is essential when there is a power cut. There must be continuity and the balancing of power supply is important for various electronic devices, which play a role with IoT modeled devices.

9.4.5. *Response time*

Title	Year	Technology	Remarks
Fire notification and extinguisher system (Ehsan et al. 2022)	2022	IoT-based GSM module	Advantage: fast fire detection. Purpose: designated to occupants and activates water drops. Disadvantage: less effective for heavy fire.
A basic prototype of a forest fire detection system (Negi et al. 2024)	2019	IoT/Node MCU ESP 8266	Advantage: more effective for early fire detection. Purpose: provides smart alerts with 99% accuracy. Disadvantages: limited to only smoke sensors.
Detection of fire and notification system using Raspberry Pi (Anna Devi et al. 2024)	2023	Using wireless sensor networks/IoT	Advantage: high accuracy. Purpose: provides early detection. Disadvantage: relatively expensive.
Fire extinguishing through robots (Ul Haq et al. 2024)	2021	Driver motors and water ejectors	Advantage: features on automated fire extinguishers. Purpose: detects and extinguishes fire. Disadvantage: suitable for small applications.
Fire detection and notification system for visually impaired people (Lee and Lee 2004)	2020	Using image processing/fire prediction	Advantage: improved accuracy up to 80%. Purpose: fire detection for visually impaired people. Disadvantage: requires further improvement in image processing.
Arduino-based fire-detection and alarm (Bhavani et al. 2023)	2017	GSM	Advantage: provides essential assistance. Purpose: configured for tracking purposes. Disadvantage: not suitable for GPS

Table 9.1. *Existing gap in literature review*

Minimizing response time is another constraint for fire alarm systems. The programming must be kept with its consideration. The system must detect smoke and send alerts rapidly to mitigate potential damage. Any delay in detection may harm the whole management system. Table 9.1 shows the existing literature gap in the field of smart technologies.

Figure 9.1 shows a flowchart of a fire alarm system that passes through various stages, and through proper functioning it operates as per user requirement.

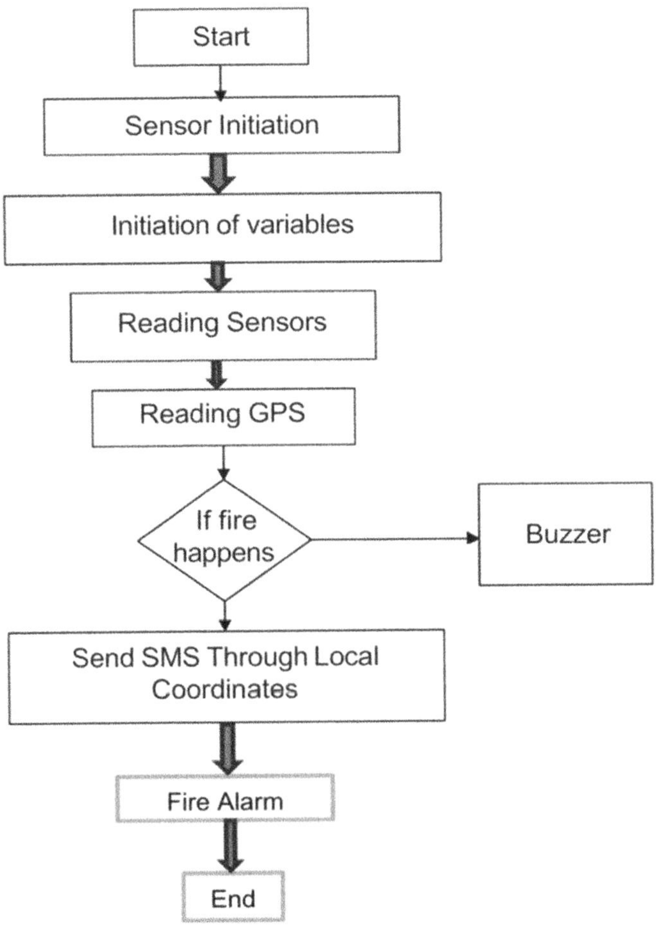

Figure 9.1. *Flowchart of fire alarm system. For a color version of this figure, see www.iste.co.uk/ulhaq/artificial1.zip*

The above flowchart describes how fire alarm systems work along with different types of sensors and GSM modules, which detect smoke or fire issues.

Authors have also preferred firefighting robot systems using fuzzy logic and GSM modules to enhance low cost systems (Khalid et al. 2022). To predict the best location system, a global positioning system (GPS) system is required, so authors have designed a GPS-based detection system that can alert the user (Hopkins and Kibbe 2014). IoT has played a vital role in designing a water monitoring system, hence researchers have identified such as an emerging module (Hanafi et al. 2020). In fire alarm systems, an advanced module can be utilized for the protection of fire (Mahile et al. 2021).

The use of emerging techniques can enhance the efficiency of working systems in various ways, for example, an Arduino, which is an open-source hardware with software enterprise that communicates through the person or user. Such development boards are called Arduino modules, which may be the next version of Arduino microcontrollers. Sometimes, Arduino boards may become moderately expensive as they become popular. The use of such interfacing is increasing day by day. Through proper programming, it provides flexibility and reliability into proposed working models. It is enhancing Arduino kits, which are helpful in building devices. An Arduino employs a microcontroller as ATMEGA328P, which controls the entire operation. It is able to regulate input voltage and provide efficient modeling. It is compatible with C, C++ programming language among students and learners. Arduino Uno is a conglomeration of microcontroller and other essential parts like input–output pins, grounding pins and power supply pins. An Arduino Uno suggests for the user to make an innovative product that may be helpful and may be able to provide sustainability. Physically, an Arduino Uno has to be connected with a Universal Serial Bus (USB) cable with personal PCs, and by transmitting and receiving signals, it provides optimized results. Researchers have designed smart car parking systems using IoT modules, which can provide suitable locations for car parking. From the point of safety operation in mining systems, researchers have suggested IoT systems that can send safety signals to the users (Reguera et al. 2015). In today's era, Arduino has played a vital role in health monitoring systems, which can reduce operating time and cost (Srividyadevi et al. 2013). Similarly, in various universities, they have adapted Arduino environments to provide quality education to students (Vasanthkumar et al.

2021). In addition to this, an open-source model using Arduino has been enhanced, which can provide the best response to users and students (Raju et al. 2017). Learning open-source models just like Arduino has provided 3D printing technologies to researchers, by which they can generate a high-quality response (Ul Haq et al. 2025a). In rainfall harvesting systems, Arduino has provided suitable models to the users and researchers, which can be inbuilt with piezoelectric material for the best measurement of rainfall harvesting systems (Visalatchi and Sandeep 2017). Figure 9.2 shows the working model of a fire alarm detection system that uses a smart interfacing module like Arduino, which controls its operation.

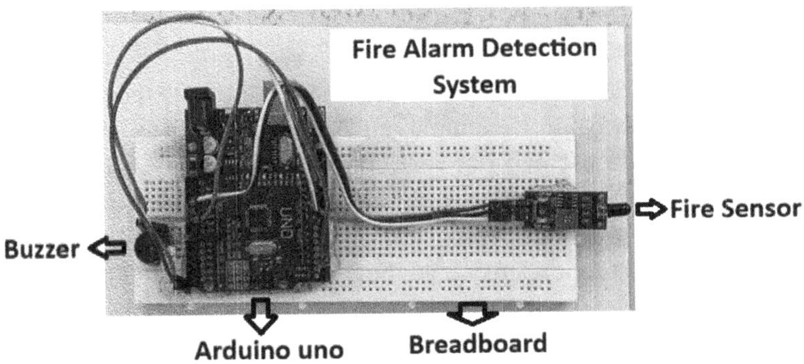

Figure 9.2. *Fire alarm detection system using Arduino. For a color version of this figure, see www.iste.co.uk/ulhaq/artificial1.zip*

There are various versions of Arduino present such as Arduino IDE, Arduino Mega, Arduino Due and Arduino Leonardo. Depending on the application, a user can select any version of Arduino. There are some steps that a user has to follow like communication, designing, modeling and deployment. Out of these versions of Arduino, Arduino Uno has to be kept in consideration for design. An Arduino Uno contains a ATMEGA328P processor with a frequency of 16 MHz. It consists of program memory (32 kB), Erasable Programmable Read-Only Memory (EEPROM) (1 kB) and RANDOM Access Memory (RAM) (2 kB). Arduino Uno has two power supply voltages such as 5 V and 3.3 V. It comprises a pin header arrangement, which is quickly becoming important among users. From the point of power supply, it comes in two modes, power jacks and USB cables. Mostly, it uses USB cables which communicate with personal computers

(PC) and can be preferred for fire detection (Chaudhari et al. 2017). With Bluetooth integration, users can detect and provide suitable signals to sensors from fire (Mangayarkarasi et al. 2021).

After the installation of Arduino software in PCs, its compatibility must be checked during modeling. The board and port must be of the order of Arduino Uno type. If it is not properly selected, then the program cannot run. The suitable length and width of Arduino Uno is suggested to be taken as 69 mm × 54 mm. Then, during interfacing with Arduino Uno, software prototyping is another important aspect.

In this modeling, normally C and C++ programming language has been used. Sometimes, IoT may be preferred in terms of advanced techniques. It aims to use the Internet to connect all PCs to communicate among themselves and collect data.

9.5. Advantages of Arduino Uno over other types of Arduino modules

9.5.1. *Lower cost*

It is available at a lower cost than other types of Arduino and Raspberry Pi. Many users purchase the basic model of Arduino as it is easy to model and provides flexibility with working models.

9.5.2. *Energy efficient*

Arduino Uno must allow lower cost energy consumption. It must be able to work with the suggested power supply mode and other components connected with its interfacing must respond quickly.

9.5.3. *Open-source interfacing*

Arduino with accompanying software must be in an open-source environment. It makes it easier for users and programmers, and must be able to add extensions whenever required. Similarly, from the point of hardware, it must respond quickly, integrating with other electronic devices.

9.5.4. *Providing awareness of more innovative approaches*

Arduino Uno comes with microcontroller interfacing, but there are already existing models that can introduce users to an innovative approach, so existing models can give better responses.

Similarly, when using an advanced and emerging approach, there are some limitations and challenges, such as those listed below.

9.5.5. *Hardware complexity*

Sometimes, with the connection of different electronic devices, the working model may become complex for users. So, they must remember the proper connections and power supply management.

9.5.6. *Compatibility with programming*

To provide better solutions in terms of coding or programming, the working system can only work in a suitable manner. Through improper programming, there may be less chance of receiving a true response.

9.5.7. *Limited executing power*

In an interfacing of Arduino, a power supply must be kept in mind because some electronic devices are only applicable to low power supply operating voltages. High power supply voltages may damage the equipment.

9.5.8. *Small storage*

Small storage capacity is a key limitation in Arduino-based systems, as these microcontrollers have restricted memory resources (both RAM and flash). This constraint affects the ability to store large datasets, complex algorithms, or high-resolution sensor data. Therefore, efficient memory management techniques and optimized programming practices are essential to ensure reliable system performance in embedded applications.

9.5.9. *Automated system*

A home can be automated through the use of Arduino Uno and some suggestive microcontrollers. We can control the lighting operation system through the connection of Arduino with relays. Similarly, Arduino can help to manage water level management systems as it can be installed with timers and buzzers. On completing management of the water level, it sends a signal and provides a fast response. For security systems, Arduino plays a vital role for users.

9.5.10. *Robotics operation*

In recent times, users and programmers have been interested in the modeling of drones and robotic cars. When installing electronic devices, there is also a need to control motors and wind blades as required. So, through enhancing with Arduino, we can provide suitable solutions. Through this, a communication system can also be in-built with wi-fi and Bluetooth. By using these platforms, we can control the operation of any proposed model.

9.5.11. *Industry applications*

Arduino Uno has found many applications in the industrial field. It is able to monitor and regulate temperature, humidity, pressure and flow in the manufacturing field. For protection from any abnormal conditions, sensors activate and send signals to remove that faulty section.

9.5.12. *Renewable energy sources*

This era is for the use of renewable energy sources, as such energy sources are free to use and no cost is required. Hence, Arduino is playing an important role. For example, a solar PV cell is able to extract maximum power during the day time, so for this operation, Arduino Uno provides the best position for the sensor to extract maximum sunlight and is able to provide more power to users. It is also helpful in monitoring and regulating the battery level.

9.5.13. *Integration with IoT*

An IoT is an advanced emerging technique as it can collect and monitor data to provide optimal solutions. In the case of smart energy meters, Arduino can monitor and transmit energy consumption data to the cloud for real-time operation. Similarly, with different types of sensors for the collection of environment data like humidity and temperature, the user can make suggestive models.

9.5.14. *Healthcare and medical operation*

Automated machines are used in the field of healthcare. These have reduced manpower operation and can provide emerging solutions. Through the use of Arduino, it is possible to make automated machines to operate on patients and regularly monitor them. Such mobility provides the best solution of life for each individual. Arduino has played an important role in the protection of smart energy meters from theft. Smart meters using Arduino can generate automated energy bills and send them to users (Taha and Marhoon 2018). Similarly, Arduino has been used in the measurement of energy and power. Arduino can measure the total energy and power used by users and send predicted energy usage for the next month to users (Chen et al. 2021).

9.6. Concluding remarks

In conclusion, the objective of this chapter on fire alarms is to explore trends, challenges and solutions for fire detection and prevention in both the present and future through the use of various sensors, technologies and techniques. In this chapter, a literature survey was mentioned in order to further utilize smart interfacing. Many authors have proposed different interfacing topologies due to which the operation of proposed models can be controlled. The basic key findings have been studied in terms of wireless networks, IoT devices, GSM modules, etc. In preference of these smart devices, authors have proposed different models. In smart city environments, the deployment of such topologies is essential to meet increasing system demands, and security measures must be implemented effectively to ensure reliable protection. In addition, a smart energy management system is also required because there may be some faults from internal or external activities, which can impact the performance of the proposed model. So, in order to attain more accurate results, researchers may utilize heuristic and meta-heuristic optimization techniques. Some advanced sensors, along with optimization techniques, may be preferred for the enhancement of optimal solutions. Similarly, in the future, users can build AI proposed real-time models, which can predict fires early and send signals to users. Users can control the operation of such enhanced models in terms of humidity, gas, smoke, etc. Researchers can integrate with renewable energy sources to provide an uninterrupted power supply. Through such modules, researchers can monitor continuously using smart applications. At the end, users can combine data from multiple types of sensors and improve the efficiency of the proposed system.

9.7. References

Anna Devi, E., Therase, L.M., Joany, R.M., Saravanan, A.S. (2024). Fire alarm based obstacle avoiding and bluetooth controlled robot. In *2024 10th International Conference on Communication and Signal Processing (ICCSP)*, Melmaruvathur.

Anthony, B., Esteva Miguel, A., Anthea, L., Rizki, R., Achmad, R., Wangkun, X., Daphne, T. (2024). Assessing the efficacy of IoT-based forest fire detection: A practical use case networking and Internet architecture. *arXiv*. doi: 10.48550/arXiv.2407.09117.

Aryanti, A., Mekongga, I., Dewi, R.S. (2021). GPS-based fire detection system (global positioning system) and SMS gateway. *IOP Conference Series: Materials Science and Engineering*, 1108, 012023.

Bahrudin, M.S.B., Kassim, R.A., Buniyamin, N. (2013). Development of a fire alarm system using Raspberry Pi and Arduino Uno. *In 2013 International Conference on Electrical, Electronics and System Engineering (ICEESE)*. IEEE.

Bhavani, M., Koushika Sai, K., Bhavana, K., Gayathri, P., Anitha, P. (2023). Fire detection and alerting system using Raspberry Pi. *YMER Journal*, 22(4), 1–9.

Chaudhari, S., Rathod, P., Shaikh, A., Vora, D., Ahir, J. (2017). Smart energy meter using Arduino and GSM. In *2017 International Conference on Trends in Electronics and Informatics (ICEI)*, IEEE, Tirunelveli.

Chen, T.H., Wu, P.H., Chiou, Y.C. (2004). An early fire-detection method based on image processing. In *2004 International Conference on Image Processing*. IEEE, Singapore.

Chen, T.H., Yin, Y.H., Huang, S.F., Ye, Y.T. (2006). The smoke detection for early fire-alarming system based on video processing. In *2006 International Conference on Intelligent Information Hiding and Multimedia*. IEEE, Pasadena, CA.

Chen, W., Hao, X., Lu, J., Yan, K., Liu, J., He, C, Xu, X. (2021). Research and design of distributed IoT water environment monitoring system based on LoRa. *Wireless Communications and Mobile Computing*, 9403963, 1–13. doi: 10.1155/2021/9403963.

Ehsan, I., Irfan Khalid, M., Ricci, L., Iqbal, J., Alabrah, A., Sajid Ullah, S., Alfakih, T.M. (2022). A conceptual model for blockchain-based agriculture food supply chain system. *Scientific Programming*, 2022(1), 7358354.

Gianluca, A., Caruso, M., Miceli, R., Riggi, L., Romano, P., Schettino, G., Viola, F.. (2017). Piezoelectric rainfall energy harvester performance by an advanced Arduino-based measuring system. *IEEE Trans. Ind. Appl.*, 54(1), 458–468.

Hanafi, N., Hidayat, T., Purwanto, A., Al Ayyubi, M.C., Rachmadi, R.R. (2020). Fi-ona: Fire warning alarm system using internet of things based on fuzzy logic. In *Proceedings of the Int. Symp. Wirel. Pers. Multimed. Commun (WPMC)*. IEEE, Okayama.

Hopkins, M.A. and Kibbe, A.M. (2014). Open-source hardware in controls education. *Computers in Education Journal*, 5(4), 62–70.

Khalid, M.I., Iqbal, J., Alturki, A., Hussain, S., Alabrah, A., Ullah, S.S. (2022). Blockchain-based land registration system: A conceptual framework. *Applied Bionics and Biomechanics*, 1–21.

Khan, Z., Almazah, M.M., Hamood Odhah, O., Alshanbari, H.M. (2022). Generalized pareto model: Properties and applications in neutrosophic data modeling. *Mathematical Problems in Engineering*, 2022(1), 3686968.

Lee, K.C. and Lee, H.H. (2004). Network-based fire-detection system via controller area network for smart home automation. *IEEE Transactions on Consumer Electronics*, 50(4), 1093–1100.

Mahile, N., Chakole, D., Kotangale, N., Charde, M., Pendam, T., Sawwashere, S. (2021). Review on existing fire monitoring and extinguishing systems in various domain verticals. *Journal of University of Shanghai for Science and Technology*, 23(3), 143–148.

Mangayarkarasi, T., Umapathy, K., Sivagami, A., Subitha, D. (2021). An IoT based safe assembly point Alert system. *Proceedings of the J. Phys. Conf. Ser*, 1964(7), 1–4.

Negi, P., Pathani, A., Bhatt, B.C., Swami, S., Singh, R., Gehlot, A., Thakur, A.K., Gupta, L.R., Priyadarshi, N., Twala, B. et al. (2024). Integration of Industry 4.0 technologies in fire and safety management. *Fire*, 7(10), 1–30.

Raju, J., Mohammed, S.S., Paul, J.V., John, G.A., Nair, D.S. (2017). Development and implementation of arduino microcontroller based dual mode fire extinguishing robot. In *2017 IEEE International Conference on Intelligent Techniques in Control, Optimization and Signal Processing (INCOS)*, Krishnankoil.

Reguera, P., García, D., Domínguez, M., Prada, M.A., Alonso, S. (2015). A low-cost open source hardware in control education. Case study: Arduino-feedback Ms-150. *IFAC-PapersOnLine*, 48(29), 117–122.

Srividyadevi, P., Pusphalatha, D.V., Sharma, P.M. (2013). Measurement of power and energy using Arduino. *Research Journal of Engineering Sciences*, 2(10), 10–15.

Taha, I.A. and Marhoon, H.M. (2018). Implementation of controlled robots for fire detection and extinguishing to closed areas based on Arduino. *TELKOMNIKA (Telecommunication Computing Electronics and Control)*, 16(2), 654–664.

Ul Haq, I. (2024). Diagnosis of neurological disease using bioinspired algorithms. In *Bio-Inspired Optimization for Medical Data Mining*, Srivastava, S., Anand, A., Kumar, A. et al. (eds). John Wiley & Sons, Hoboken, NJ.

Ul Haq, I. and Khanday, A.M.U.D. (2025). Exploring the role of explainable AI in women's health: Challenges and solutions. In *Explainable Artificial Intelligence in the Healthcare Industry*, Kumar, A. Kumar, T.A., Das, P. et al. (eds). John Wiley & Sons, Hoboken, NJ.

Ul Haq, I., Kumar, N., Koul, N., Verma, C., Eneacu, F.M., Raboaca, M.S. (2022). Machine learning techniques for result prediction of one day international (ODI) cricket match. In *The International Conference on Recent Innovations in Computing*. Springer, Singapore.

Ul Haq, I., Kaur, G., Rather, A.H. (2024). Fruit leaf classification using transfer learning for automation and industrial applications. In *Deep Learning Techniques for Automation and Industrial Applications*, Rathore, P.S., Ahuja, S., Burri, S.R. et al. (eds). John Wiley & Sons, Hoboken, NJ, 151–178.

Ul Haq, I., Kumar, A., Rathore, P.S. (2025a). Machine learning approaches for wind power forecasting: A comprehensive review. *Discover Applied Sciences*, 7(10), 1139.

Ul Haq, I., Malhotra, J., Rawat, V., Kumari, J., Kaur, G. (2025b). Machine learning approaches for early detection of cervical cancer: A comparative study of classification models. In *Targeted Chemotherapy with Personalized Immunotherapy: An AI Approach*, Kumar, A., Das, P., Rathore, P.S. et al. (eds). John Wiley & Sons, Hoboken, NJ.

Ul Haq, I., Nandal, V., Uppal, H. (2025c). Blockchain applications in aviation securing transactions, streamlining operations, and improving passenger experience. In *Blockchain in the Tourism Industry: A New Era of Secure and Transparent Travel Solutions*, Kumar, A., Abreu, A., Batta, P. et al. (eds). Springer, Cham.

Ul Haq, I., Shah, H.A., Rufai, S.Z. (2025d). Enhancing water security through automation: Case studies and technical advancements in water quality management. In *Computational Automation for Water Security*, Dubey, A.K., Srivastav, A.L., Kumar, A. et al. (eds). Elsevier, Amsterdam.

Vasanthkumar, P., Arunraj, P.V., Khan, N.M.B., Akash, A.V., Mukunthan, R., Babu, R.H. (2021). Fuzzy logic algorithm and GSM IoT based fire fighting robot. *J. Phys. Conf. Ser*, 2040(1), 1–8.

Visalatchi, S. and Sandeep, K.K. (2017). Smart energy metering and power theft control using Arduino & GSM automated smart metering. In *2017 2nd International Conference for Convergence in Technology (I2CT)*. Pune, Maharashtra.

Zhao, X. (2024). Design and implementation of intelligent fire detection and alarm system in electrical safety system. In *2024 International Conference on Telecommunications and Power Electronics (TELEPE)*, Frankfurt.

10

AI and Blockchain for Renewable Energy Trading

By establishing intelligent, decentralized and transparent energy ecosystems, the convergence of blockchain technology and artificial intelligence (AI) is completely changing the landscape of renewable energy. The limitations of traditional energy markets – centralized control, grid instability, high transaction costs and lack of transparency – are examined in this chapter, along with how these technologies work together. While AI helps with demand forecasting, smart grid optimization, predictive analytics and operational efficiency, blockchain ensures immutability, trust and decentralized peer-to-peer (P2P) energy trading through smart contracts. When combined, they allow for verifiable energy provenance, automated contract execution and real-time energy management. The chapter further discusses the emergence of decentralized autonomous organizations (DAOs) for energy. The progressive transformation in the direction of developing renewable energy markets that are hyper-local, equitable and self-regulating is a complicated set of challenges and opportunities. In that respect, predictive energy trading, automated certification and improved cybersecurity are determined as essential applications. The limitation analysis highlights scalability, interoperability and regulatory challenges, while identifying future research directions for achieving a fully decentralized, optimized and sustainable green energy ecosystem. This synergy of AI and blockchain accelerates the decarbonization and democratization of the global energy future.

10.1. Introduction

The need to obtain sustainable and renewable energy sources has acquired a new sense of urgency at this stage of global history due to the drastic change of the global energy situation.

Chapter written by Hitendra SINGH, Pradeep Kumar SHARMA, Deepti GUPTA, Fardeen Ahmad KHAN, Bandana KUMARI, Shivani SHARMA, Prashant KUMAR and Sanny KUMAR.

In order to ensure the longevity of future generations of the world, renewable energy modalities in the form of photovoltaic (PV), wind, hydroelectric, geothermal and bioenergy should be given priority when building a sustainable future.

Furthermore, in the 21st century, the owners of the fossil-based energy regime need to find safer energy sources, as traditional sources not only pose risks to environmental sustainability, but also compromise energy security, public health, and geopolitical stability (Elavarasan et al. 2020).

10.1.1. *The climate crisis and emissions reduction imperative*

The spirit of the importance of renewable energy is based on its inevitability in mitigating the climate crisis, which is the most significant environmental issue facing humanity.

Approximately 75% of global greenhouse gas emissions and nearly 90% of all carbon dioxide emissions come from fossil fuels, such as coal, oil and natural gas. These fuels continue to be the main causes of climate change. Massive amounts of carbon dioxide and other greenhouse gases are released into the atmosphere when fossil fuels are burned, trapping heat and accelerating global warming.

In 2018 alone, 89% of global CO_2 emissions originated from fossil fuels and industry, with coal being identified as the single dirtiest fossil fuel, responsible for over 0.3°C of the 1°C increase in global average temperatures (Ul Haq et al. 2022).

Recent data also suggest that fossil-fuel usage is not decreasing at all. In 2023, 36.8 billion metric tons of carbon dioxide was released into the atmosphere by fossil fuels alone, a staggering 1.1% increase from the previous year.

This is a distressing situation, as outlined by the Intergovernmental Panel on Climate Change, who said that if they are not halved within 11 years, the emissions from fossil fuels will have catastrophic climate consequences. All efforts to minimize global warming to 1.5°C above pre-industrial levels, as stated in the Paris Agreement, will never be sufficient if fossil-fuel emissions are not curbed.

Renewable energy offers a clean and sustainable source of energy by producing power, emitting minimal greenhouse gases and not releasing any harmful pollutants in the atmosphere. Sources like solar, wind, hydro and biomass stand as a stark contrast to fossil-fuel combustion, and provide clean operation with no environmental hazards. The International Renewable Energy Agency (IREA) stated that we need 2x the amount of renewable energy to reduce greenhouse gas emissions by up to 70% by 2050, and that its adoption can decrease emissions from conventional sources by 80% by 2050. It is estimated that coal power plants produce almost 2.2 pounds of carbon dioxide for every kilowatt-hour of electricity produced, while solar and wind turbines create virtually no emissions during the course of energy production (Ali et al. 2025).

10.1.2. *Global energy transition progress and momentum*

The transition to a renewable source of energy has been extraordinary in current years, and the deployment metrics have surpassed far beyond the initial speculations. The 2025 Global Carbon Budget analysis states that since 2010, the world has successfully managed to avoid 1,372 exajoules of fossil fuels and prevented the emission of 110 gigatons of greenhouse gases, replacing them with renewable and nuclear energy sources, which is a remarkable feat. Countries like China have shown astonishing potential in deploying renewable energy systems for nearly 60% of renewable power supply additions in 2024 and approximately two-thirds of all new global capacity of solar and wind power since 2022. In the first quarter of this year, the metric increased to three-quarters of global additions, enabling China to account for nearly one-quarter of the low-emissions power required to meet its 2050 deployment targets – almost double the global average. Globally, India alone has added 20 gigawatts of renewable energy, which exceeded the United States' contribution during the same period. Fueled by the Chinese market, the solar export to emerging economies doubled from 2022–2024, overtaking many developed countries. Countries such as Brazil, India, Pakistan and even Saudi Arabia have emerged as leading importers of solar energy; Africa has shown promising growth as well.

The need to adopt renewable energy is more urgent than ever. Climate change is impacting the world globally, and the adoption of renewable energy resources has shown the potential to reduce greenhouse gases emissions, provide a clean source of energy, and even boost employment, job opportunities and GDP growth. Public health gains from reduced air pollution translate into saved lives and reduced healthcare costs, whereas environmental benefits preserve ecosystems and biodiversity for future generations. The world now approaches the 2030 milestone of the Paris Agreement, so we must accelerate our efforts to achieve the necessary benchmark of limiting global warming to 1.5°C, ensuring a sustainable tomorrow for everyone (Ul Haq et al. 2025b).

10.2. AI in renewable energy

AI has emerged as a transformative technology in the renewable energy sector, enhancing forecasting accuracy, optimizing grid performance, predicting equipment failures and improving consumer engagement through intelligent applications. This chapter explores how AI is reshaping energy systems across four major domains – predictive modeling of energy production and consumption, smart grid optimization, predictive infrastructure maintenance and consumer-focused innovations in electric vehicles (EVs) and smart homes (Şerban and Lytras 2020). Through the integration of data-driven algorithms, machine learning (ML) models and intelligent control systems, AI enables more efficient, sustainable and resilient energy management, thereby accelerating the transition toward a decarbonized global energy economy.

10.2.1. *Predicting energy production and consumption*

Forecasting is one of the most critical challenges in renewable energy management due to the inherent variability of sources like solar and wind. AI enhances forecasting accuracy through the use of ML and deep learning (DL) algorithms that can analyze large volumes of weather, environmental and historical energy data. AI-based forecasting models, such as artificial neural networks (ANNs) and recurrent neural networks (RNNs), identify nonlinear relationships between meteorological variables and power generation output (Ul Haq et al. 2024). On the demand side, AI supports energy consumption forecasting by analyzing patterns in residential, commercial and industrial data, helping utilities to balance generation with consumption and reduce grid stress.

10.2.2. *Smart grid optimization*

The smart grid represents an intelligent, adaptive and data-driven evolution of the traditional electrical grid. AI serves as its decision-making core, enabling self-learning and automated control for improved reliability and efficiency. AI-driven optimization manages distributed energy resources (DERs), detects anomalies and dynamically adjusts power flow. Reinforcement learning and multi-agent systems allow grid operators to respond autonomously to fluctuations, voltage instability or faults (Kumar et al. 2021). AI supports demand-side management by predicting energy demand and coordinating distributed storage, microgrids and EVs to ensure minimal load imbalance.

10.2.3. *Predictive renewable infrastructure maintenance*

Maintenance of renewable infrastructure – such as wind turbines, solar PV panels and hydropower systems – is essential for continuous operation. AI-powered predictive maintenance analyzes real-time sensor data to identify potential failures before they occur. In wind farms, AI evaluates vibration, torque and acoustic data to detect gearbox faults. In solar plants, AI image analysis detects cracks or degradation (Ul Haq et al. 2025d). This condition-based maintenance reduces downtime and operational costs, and extends equipment lifespan.

10.2.4. *Consumer-focused applications (EVs and smart homes)*

AI technologies have significantly influenced the consumer end of renewable energy systems, particularly in EVs and smart homes. In EVs, AI optimizes battery management, charging infrastructure and route planning. Smart charging systems leverage AI to predict grid demand and schedule charging during off-peak hours. In smart homes, AI systems regulate energy through smart thermostats and Home Energy Management Systems (HEMS). Blockchain-integrated AI platforms also enable P2P energy trading (Yang and Wang 2021).

10.2.5. *Future prospects and challenges*

Despite its potential, AI integration faces challenges such as data privacy, high computational costs and cybersecurity risks. Future advancements in edge computing, federated learning and explainable AI are expected to address these challenges and enhance scalability. Collaboration among energy providers, AI researchers and policymakers is vital for ethical and efficient AI adoption.

AI is redefining renewable energy by enabling data-driven intelligence, predictive capabilities and operational optimization. From forecasting and smart grids to predictive maintenance and consumer-focused applications, AI enhances efficiency and sustainability, playing a crucial role in achieving carbon neutrality and global energy security (Ul Haq et al. 2025a).

10.3. Renewable energy with blockchain

Blockchain is an ever-growing, secure, shared record keeping system in which each user of the data holds a copy of the records, which can only be updated if all parties involved in a transaction agree to update. This means that there is no central controller in the network, and all participants talk to each other directly. This property allows for cash transactions to be exchanged directly among the peers without third-party involvement, such as by a bank (Boumaiza 2024).

Figure 10.1 shows an architectural diagram of a layered structure of a blockchain system, with its base being the physical infrastructure reaching up to the interaction with the user. The internet is the first base, which facilitates the P2P network to carry out communication among the nodes. Thc corc blockchain protocol is above the networking layer and it handles transactions (data of actions), packages them into blocks and uses consensus mechanisms to guarantee that there is an agreement on the validity of the chain. This is used to update the persistent data that are controlled by the state machine. Blockchain applications (smart contracts) are applications at the application layer that establish the programmable logic of a complex operation. Lastly, users/nodes are on the top spot that symbolizes the people who make transactions, as well as computers that host, validate and maintain the whole decentralized system. This design provides transparent, secure and decentralized operation on all levels.

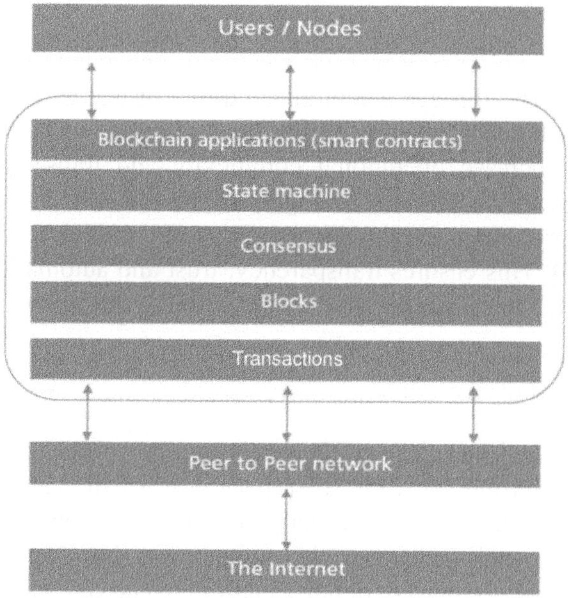

Figure 10.1. *Architecture of blockchain*

On the one hand, renewable energy (solar, wind, hydro, etc.) is naturally decentralized – energy is generated in many small areas. Blockchain offers a secure, transparent and decentralized method of recording, verifying and trading energy data (Okwuibe et al. 2023). They facilitate reliable transactions of energy together with the encouragement of P2P energy trading.

10.3.1. *P2P energy trading*

Smart meters capture production and consumption data as blockchain allows electricity to be traded directly between consumers and producers without any middlemen. Smart contracts automatically carry out transactions in case of fulfilling conditions (such as price and demand). Digital tokens or stablecoins are processed in real-time and payments are made and received. In the Brooklyn Microgrid Project (LO3 Energy, USA), people sell excess solar energy to their neighbors with the help of blockchain (Zhang et al. 2022). Blockchain-based trading has a number of advantages to its use.

Eliminates middlemen and transaction costs

In a conventional energy market, electricity generated by solar or wind producers must pass through a centralized utility or energy exchange, which records transactions, manages billing and charges service fees. These intermediaries increase operational complexity and transaction costs. By using blockchain's decentralized ledger, all transactions are automatically verified, recorded and executed through smart contracts (Ul Haq and Khanday 2025). This ensures transparency, trust and automation – allowing prosumers to sell excess renewable energy directly to nearby consumers in real-time.

Promotes local energy markets and grid resilience

With the aid of blockchain, P2P energy trading solutions and prosumers (households or businesses with solar panels or small wind turbines) can directly sell surplus energy directly to their neighbors in localized microgrids. This will minimize the reliance on big, centralized power stations and the long-range energy distribution, which can be quite expensive and likely to cause losses or failures. This makes blockchain promote the development of more self-reliant and sustainable communities by promoting local energy markets. Additionally, grid resilience is increased since local-level energy production and distribution systems would remain operational even when the central grid is being affected by failures or outages. The transparency and automation of blockchain transactions enable real-time balancing of energy supply and demand, thereby supporting a more stable and adaptable energy infrastructure (Aggarwal et al. 2021).

Encourages renewable energy production at the community level

Historically, large utility companies dominated the production of renewable energy due to high entry and control. Nevertheless, blockchain technology makes the energy market more democratic and democratized by the means of P2P trading, allowing the domestic producers, also referred to as prosumers, to sell the surplus of the energy straight to the local residents or consumers near them. This creates economic motivations for communities to invest in clean energy systems like rooftop solar panels, miniature wind turbines or on-site storage facilities. There is fair price, trust and accountability, as transactions are transparent and automated in the blockchain, and the trading of energy is profitable and efficient at the local level. With a higher number of people utilizing renewable energy technologies, communities will be self-reliant and environmentally conscious, which will serve larger plans of decarbonization, energy independence and social empowerment (Ul Haq et al. 2025c).

10.3.2. *Renewable energy certificates (RECs) and carbon credits*

Blockchain can increase the authenticity, traceable and transparency of environmental features such as RECs and carbon credits. Conventional RECs systems are susceptible to fraud and duplication, as well as sluggish authentication. Blockchain gives a simplified answer to this issue.

Every MWh of renewable energy generated is tokenized in the form of a unique digital certificate. In the production of renewable energy, say, by a solar farm or wind turbine, its production information (including time, location and source) is sent to the blockchain. The system then generates a special digital certificate commonly referred to as an REC or energy token that is equivalent to the precise quantity of energy produced. Such tokens may be purchased, sold or exchanged between producers, consumers and regulation bodies, and form a transparent and efficient way of checking claims of renewable energy and attaining sustainability targets. The tokenization also helps to avoid duplication and fraud since each certificate is stored safely and cannot be copied or modified (Ge et al. 2023).

Renewable energy trading involves the encryption, time-stamping and validation of every transaction, including the sale of a renewable energy token, ownership transfer and energy origin verification, which is verified by participants in the network. These entries are not subject to any alteration, deletion or tampering once they are recorded, hence all stakeholders are assured of full transparency and trust.

Such immutability prevents chances of fraud, duplicating money or manipulating records on an energy supply, which are also typical issues in conventional centralized systems. It also offers an auditable record of energy production, ownership and use of the generated energy, allowing regulators, producers and consumers to track all units of renewable energy to their source.

The process of ensuring that the renewable energy is authentic and sourced in a traditional system may be cumbersome as it requires lengthy paperwork, agents/intermediaries and manual inspections, and is subject to errors or even fraud. Under blockchain, though, every certificate of varying quantity of renewable energy is mathematically verified and has rich metadata, namely, the identity of the producer, time of generation, place and source of energy (solar, wind or hydro). Since every ledger is secured on an immutable and distributed registry, buyers like companies with an interest in meeting sustainability requirements or governments monitoring renewable energy adherence can immediately trace and confirm the authenticity and source of each certificate without using intermediaries. This openness does not only decrease administrative load, but also ensures improved trust, accountability and efficiency in the market, making renewable energy trading more credible and interoperative at an international scale. This structure on energy trading systems offers different benefits for the smooth and transparent operation of every activity. It helps to eliminate the possibility of certificate duplication and fraud, facilitates open trading of green assets in the world and expedites carbon offset and sustainability reporting (Yan et al. 2021).

10.3.3. *Decentralized microgrids*

A microgrid is a localized collection of sources and users of energy that may act either independently or in conjunction with the main grid. The combination of AI and blockchain with decentralized microgrids essentially reinvents the electric utility model on the basis of its hierarchy to a distributed system of local energy marketplaces. The physical basis of this change is microgrids, self-sufficient energy clusters that include the local generation and storage of renewable energy. This localized design will provide the advantage of increased energy resilience, enabling local communities to island or disconnect to the main grid in the case of a widespread power outage, providing them with sustained power (Boumaiza and Sanfilippo 2024). The main problem of dealing with intermittent sources of renewables, such as solar and wind, is addressed with the assistance of the digital intelligence overlay, a secure and transparent transaction layer and blockchain to provide some form of autonomy and trust to these systems. All this is the synergy between AI and blockchain, as well as a dynamic token economy that encourages grid stability and the adoption of renewables. One of the energy nodes (solar panel, wind turbine or battery) is added to the blockchain. It automates the power distribution, and pricing in the microgrid, data generation, usage and payments are safely stored in smart contracts as shown in Figure 10.2. As an example, microgrids based on blockchain have been introduced by Power Ledger (Australia) and Sun Exchange (South Africa). These installations empower remote communities to be energy independent. It is also strengthening grid resilience in case of grid failure and supporting localized energy economies that are sustainable (Shibu et al. 2024).

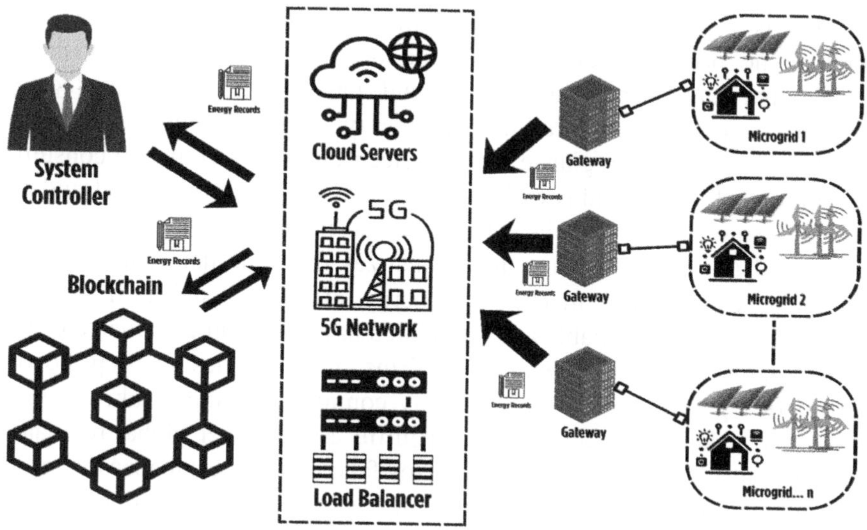

Figure 10.2. *Blockchain framework for distributed energy system network. For a color version of this figure, see www.iste.co.uk/ulhaq/artificial1.zip*

10.3.4. *Supply chain visibility and equipment monitoring*

The blockchain will make the renewable energy supply chain, both in the manufacturing and maintenance process, more transparent and accountable. It assists in tracking the source of solar panels, wind turbines and batteries in order to have ethical sourcing. It offer information on verification of performance, maintenance and lifecycle information of renewable equipment. This openness of supply chain processes incorporates Internet of Things (IoT) gadgets that supply operational information in real-time to blockchain for predictive maintenance. Another benefit is that: it enhances the adherence to the ESG (Environmental, Social, and Governance) standards. This is a great point to make! The union of the microgrids, which are decentralized, with the blockchain and AI makes the process of compliance with the Environmental, Social, and Governance (ESG) norms much higher because of the verifiability and transparency, which were never as high as they are now. The combination of AI and blockchain, in decentralized microgrids is an effective driver toward enhancing ESG compliance, especially on the environmental (E) aspect. The imperative characteristics of blockchain such as immutability and transparency, will remove the principles of greenwashing because they have established a ledger that cannot be manipulated and has carefully documented the provenance and the path of all units of energy. This will allow investors and regulators to check at a glance that the electricity that a company consumes was produced locally and is really a renewable source, eliminating fraud and the duplication of RECs. The AI aspect also improves the governance (G) and social (S) pillars because it automatizes real-time data collection and reporting, offers clear metrics of energy efficiency and utilizes smart contracts to ensure equitable and automated pay to prosumers. Such a degree of verifiable granular data enables firms and societies to step beyond self-reporting to prove the sustainability commitments they make, gain the necessary stakeholder confidence and fulfill ever-tougher global regulatory requirements. This model also minimizes fake materials, enhances warranty control and builds trust among the suppliers, regulators and consumers (Akkaoui et al. 2025).

10.4. AI–blockchain synergy

AI combined with blockchain is a synergy that will increase the management, distribution and optimization of renewable energy. Although blockchain is transparent, traceable and decentralized, AI is predictive, automated and adaptive. When they are combined, they constitute the basis of the next generation of smart energy systems. Figure 10.3 indicates the various elements of AI-blockchain synergy (Ul Haq 2024).

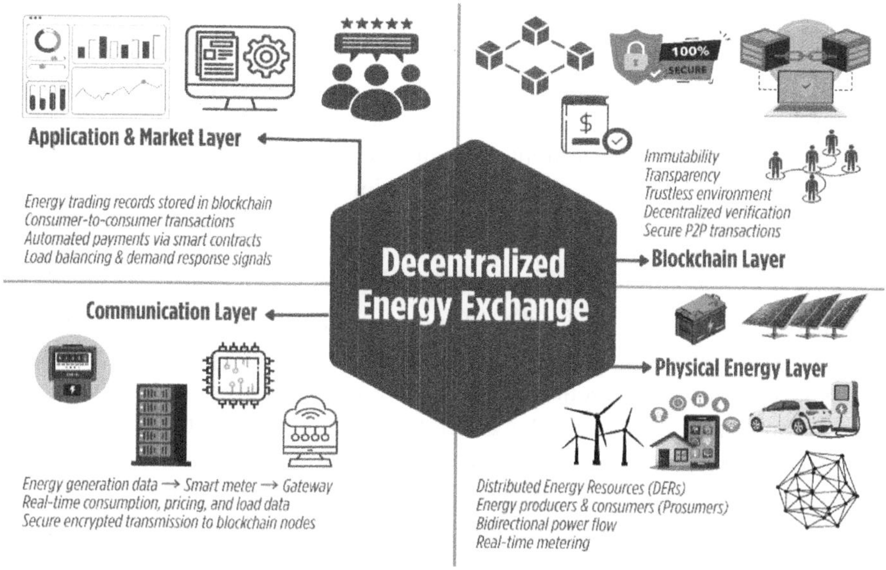

Figure 10.3. *Intelligent decentralized energy system. For a color version of this figure, see www.iste.co.uk/ulhaq/artificial1.zip*

10.4.1. *Intelligent decentralized energy systems*

Energy supply and demand are automatically balanced by smart contracts. This system increases efficiency, decreases waste, automates operations without central control and optimizes the use of renewable resources. Imagine a smart microgrid where AI forecasts solar output and blockchain safely logs every transaction, enabling smooth local energy trading. The entire transaction is instantiated through a smart contract on the microgrid's blockchain ledger when a demand-side user (such as a neighbor who needs to charge their EV) accepts the AI-determined price. The terms of this contract are automatically defined, including the quantity of energy to be transferred, the fixed price and the terms of payment. The physical transfer of energy from the solar-producing "prosumer" to the "consumer" is recorded by the blockchain in an unchangeable block, guaranteeing an accurate and auditable record (Lo et al. 2023). The smart contract self-executes after the contracted energy volume is transferred, instantly transferring payment (typically in the form of digital tokens) from the buyer to the seller, enabling smooth local energy trading without the need for an intermediary.

10.4.2. *Stable grids and secure transactions*

AI and blockchain ensure the stability of the grid and secure transparent financial settlements. The primary challenge when injecting a high penetration level of intermittent renewables, such as solar and wind, is to maintain grid stability – that means maintaining steady frequency and voltage. In such a decentralized microgrid, AI takes up this responsibility (Patel et al. 2022).

Real-time load balancing: the AI monitors data from every aspect of the microgrid (generation, storage and consumption) with IoT sensors input constantly. It allows prediction about fluctuations not only minutes ahead, but also seconds ahead. In case solar generation goes down due to cloud cover, it will immediately command localized battery storage within the building to discharge power or initiate a transaction to draw power from the main utility grid by making sure that no frequency and voltage deviations occur.

Predictive dispatch: the AI manages them as a single unit. It can incentivize or command specific DERs, such as home batteries to discharge, or industrial loads that are capable of being ramped up or down to consume or release power. In this way, predictive and fast dispatch prevents grid congestion from ever building up and cascading failures from occurring, operating the microgrid in its own safe parameters (Shamsi and Cuffe 2022).

10.4.3. *Prosumers and community energy markets*

In the developing renewable energy setup, prosumers – those individuals or entities that produce and consume energy simultaneously – hold a major place in community energy markets. In stark contrast to traditional consumers who depend solely on centralized utilities for their needs, prosumers use renewable sources of energy such as solar panels, wind turbines or biogas units to generate electricity. The surplus energy they create can be sold or traded locally within their own communities. This will merge blockchain technology with a model for community-driven energy, so that the evolution changes the consumer into an active stakeholder within the clean energy transformation, making the systems more democratic, sustainable and resilient (Cui et al. 2020).

Figure 10.4 shows that the AI–blockchain duo empowers prosumers (producers + consumers) to actively participate in community-based energy ecosystems. AI analyzes usage patterns to recommend when to sell or store excess energy. Blockchain enables secure P2P energy transactions and fair pricing through smart contracts. Together, they create dynamic local energy economies driven by data and trust. This system provides fair energy pricing, and transparent and automated market operations with the encouragement of renewable adoption at the household level (Hussain et al. 2024). For example, AI can recommend a prosumer to sell solar power in the peak afternoon hours; blockchain instantly executes the trade and records it for community transparency (Hussain et al. 2024).

Several pioneering initiatives worldwide demonstrate the powerful synergy between AI and blockchain in renewable energy. For example, the Energy Web Foundation (EWF) uses blockchain and AI to create digital identities for energy assets and optimize grid operations, while Power Ledger in Australia integrates AI analytics for energy trading with blockchain for transaction verification. The IBM and TenneT project in Germany employs AI for energy demand forecasting and blockchain for balancing grid operations. In the United States, Brooklyn Microgrid by LO3 Energy applies AI to forecast local demand and blockchain to securely handle P2P energy transactions. In Europe, WePower utilizes AI to optimize renewable generation data alongside blockchain-based green energy certificates. AI contributes essential capabilities such as predictive analytics, optimization and control, fault detection and demand forecasting. Meanwhile, blockchain ensures immutable energy records, a decentralized transaction system, transparent auditing and secure P2P settlements. Together, these technologies enable smarter, trusted energy trading, autonomous smart grids, improved system resilience and more efficient energy distribution, fostering the integration and adoption of renewable energy at a community and grid scale.

The combination of blockchain and AI is reshaping how renewable energy is produced, traded and consumed. Together, they promise transparency, automation and efficiency in energy markets. However, like all emerging technologies, their adoption faces a range of challenges and limitations. These issues are not only technical, but also economic, regulatory and ethical in nature. This chapter explores these challenges in detail, drawing insights from recent studies and industry reports.

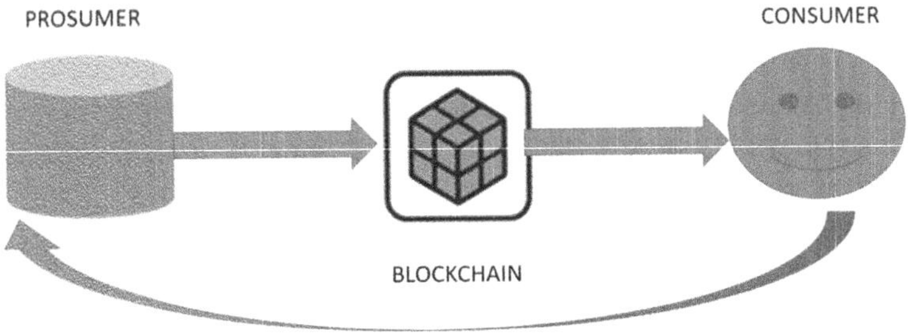

Figure 10.4. *Prosumers and community energy market*

10.5. Challenges and limitations in blockchain and AI-based renewable energy trading

10.5.1. *Technical barriers: scalability and integration*

One of the most pressing challenges in using blockchain for renewable energy trading is scalability. As pointed out by Ul Haq et al. (2024), blockchain systems can struggle to process large numbers of transactions quickly. In real-world energy markets, where countless micro-transactions occur between producers and consumers every second, limited transaction capacity can lead to slow processing and higher costs.

AI integration can further complicate this issue. Since AI models require significant computing power for real-time forecasting and decision-making, running these models alongside blockchain transactions can create performance bottlenecks.

Beyond scalability, integration with existing energy systems remains difficult. Most traditional grids and energy management systems were not designed to communicate with decentralized platforms. Elavarasan et al. (2020) highlight that differences in data standards, communication protocols and device compatibility make it hard to link smart meters, IoT devices and blockchain ledgers into one seamless system.

To overcome these barriers, researchers and engineers are focusing on interoperability standards, lightweight blockchain protocols and hybrid architectures that combine centralized efficiency with decentralized transparency.

10.5.2. *Economic and financial limitations*

While blockchain and AI can make energy trading more transparent and efficient, their economic feasibility is still uncertain.

Haq et al. (2022) argue that high implementation costs are still one of the major barriers. Small manufacturers or local energy communities tend not to have the financial resources needed to implement the extreme investments necessary to create a blockchain network, educate AI models and place Internet of Things enabled smart meters.

Another concern is return on investment (ROI). As Ul Haq et al. (2025b) explain, it can take years for investors to recover the initial setup costs, especially in pilot projects or local markets. Moreover, energy prices fluctuate, and cryptocurrency-based transactions can add financial uncertainty.

Additionally, operational costs are not insignificant. Large amounts of energy are used in consensus processes like Proof of Work, and ongoing technical expertise is needed to maintain the infrastructure. Small-scale producers or developing regions find it challenging to engage in blockchain-enabled trading systems due to these operational and financial obstacles.

Governments and business associations must develop shared infrastructure frameworks, incentive models and subsidies that lower financial risk and promote wider adoption in order to advance.

10.5.3. *Data privacy and security issues*

Complex data privacy and cybersecurity issues are brought about by the use of blockchain and AI in energy trading. While blockchain's transparency fosters trust, it may also reveal private information about users' energy consumption, financial transactions and trading habits.

As noted by Şerban and Lytras (2020), ensuring privacy in a transparent system is a delicate balance. Once data is recorded on the blockchain, it cannot easily be modified or deleted – a feature that conflicts with privacy regulations like the General Data Protection Regulation (GDPR).

AI systems also add another layer of risk. These models depend on large volumes of training data, and any compromise in data integrity can lead to inaccurate forecasts or even malicious manipulation. Ul Haq et al. (2024) caution that AI models can be vulnerable to "adversarial attacks" or data poisoning, where small data changes cause large prediction errors.

To safeguard data, energy systems must employ robust encryption, multi-layer authentication, regular audits and privacy-preserving techniques such as federated learning or zero-knowledge proofs. These approaches can help ensure that transparency does not come at the cost of security.

10.5.4. *Regulatory and policy issues*

The major obstacle to the adoption of blockchain and AI in renewable-energy trading is regulatory uncertainty. Lack of internationally established regulative norms governing the functioning of the decentralized energy markets is an indication of the infantile phase of the two technologies.

Ul Haq et al. (2022) states that many jurisdictions are yet to implement articulate regulations related to P2P trading, data owning and smart contracts. Therefore, without a standard legal regulation, investors and businesses hesitate to put their money in blockchain-based systems.

Additionally, there are problems with accountability. It becomes difficult to assign blame in the event of mistakes or system failures when AI algorithms make autonomous trading decisions. Furthermore, laws like privacy acts that mandate data modification or deletion may clash with blockchain's immutable nature.

To overcome such challenges, regulators have to develop flexible policies that will create a balance between innovation and compliance. To protect the consumers, ensure markets are stable and create environmental sustainability, governments should consider encouraging experimentation by forming regulatory sandboxes without denying them protective measures.

10.5.5. *Conclusion*

Blockchain technologies and AI technologies have the potential to radically change how renewable energy is traded by allowing a decentralized, transparent and intelligent system to be used. However, this change is not direct. Technical scalability, prohibiting high costs, privacy and uncertainty on regulations limit large-scale deployment.

The studies of Ul Haq et al. (2024), Elavarasan et al. (2020), and Lytras (2020) and others state that to overcome these difficulties, cooperation among technologists, legislators, investors and energy suppliers will be required. It is only when there are effective governance and innovation through collaboration that the blockchain and AI will be able to achieve their full potential in creating a sustainable and fairer energy future.

10.6. Future prospects

The integration of AI, blockchain, IoT and 5G technologies is transforming global energy systems into decentralized, intelligent and sustainable ecosystems. These technologies collectively represent the foundation for the future of renewable energy management and urban development. In this chapter, the authors consider how AI-driven decentralized energy markets, IoT-5G-based smart cities and ways to implement net-zero carbon operations affect the sustainable energy revolution.

10.6.1. *Decentralized autonomous energy markets powered by AI*

A transformative paradigm in energy systems, decentralized autonomous energy markets (DAEMs) allow autonomous agents driven by blockchain and AI to dynamically trade, distribute and optimize energy flow. Utilities make top-down decisions in conventional centralized grids, which frequently leads to inefficiencies and slow reactions to changes in energy demand or the availability of renewable energy sources. DAEMs, on the other hand, enable individual entities, such as households, businesses and microgrids, to act as prosumers, producing and consuming energy and participating in P2P trading.

The key driver of such transformation is AI. The reinforcement learning algorithms are used to predict the best trading actions using live market indicators, weather patterns and energy demand forecasts.

Machine-learning models allow the products of renewable energy to be predicted, including solar and wind, as it is possible to examine long-term historical data on energy use.

To illustrate, deep neural networks can be used to optimize the charging and discharging of batteries through prediction of PV output using the temperature and irradiance readings.

Blockchain acts as the trust layer in DAEMs, facilitating transparent, tamper-proof and automated transactions. Smart contracts ensure that energy trades and settlements are executed automatically when conditions – such as price thresholds or available energy – are met. This eliminates intermediaries and reduces administrative costs while maintaining security and transparency. The advantages of such systems are multi-fold: autonomy, resilience, transparency and inclusivity. Future DAEMs are envisioned as self-regulating ecosystems, where federated learning allows AI models to be trained across nodes without sharing sensitive local data. Tokenized incentive mechanisms will further encourage sustainable behavior, creating energy democracies that reward clean energy generation and efficient usage.

10.6.2. *IoT, 5G and smart cities integration – 5G smart cities*

The evolution of smart cities is intrinsically linked to the synergy between IoT, 5G and AI technologies. IoT provides the sensory network of interconnected devices, collecting continuous streams of environmental, energy and transportation data. 5G communication ensures these data are transmitted instantaneously with ultra-low latency and high reliability – critical for real-time decision-making. Together, they enable a hyper-connected urban ecosystem that can optimize energy consumption, reduce congestion and improve quality of life of citizens.

In energy management, 5G-enabled IoT networks connect millions of smart meters, sensors and renewable assets. AI algorithms process this big data to dynamically balance supply and demand across neighborhoods and industries. For instance, during peak hours, intelligent systems can defer non-critical loads such as EV charging or HVAC operation, thereby stabilizing grid frequency and avoiding power outages.

The applications are numerous: smart grids that autonomously reroute power around faults, smart mobility solutions that integrate electric vehicles with renewable charging infrastructure, smart buildings that use real-time occupancy data to regulate temperature and lighting and environmental monitoring systems that ensure air and water quality compliance. Collectively, these applications contribute to energy efficiency, emission reduction and overall sustainability.

Security remains a critical challenge in large-scale IoT ecosystems. Blockchain technology, combined with AI-based anomaly detection, provides a robust solution. Blockchain ensures decentralized authentication and integrity of transmitted data, while AI identifies potential cyber threats through pattern recognition and predictive analytics. This combination ensures a secure and resilient digital infrastructure for future smart cities.

Cities that use these technologies will develop into self-sufficient, energy-positive settings by 2035. In order to move closer to the goal of sustainable, livable and carbon-neutral communities, they will display characteristics of circular economies, where waste heat, data and materials are continuously reused.

10.6.3. *Paths to net-zero and carbon neutrality*

The most important front in the fight against climate change is the route toward net-zero and carbon neutrality. More than two-thirds of the world's greenhouse gas emissions come from energy systems, and changing them is essential in order to reach the objectives of the Paris Agreement. The technological foundation for quickening this transition is made up of blockchain and AI.

AI assists in multiple dimensions of decarbonization. By predicting renewable energy availability and load patterns, predictive models optimize energy dispatch and lessen dependency on fossil fuel-based generation. By spotting process bottlenecks, anticipating equipment failures and reducing waste, AI also improves industrial efficiency. Deep reinforcement learning algorithms are used in grid management to optimize the utilization of renewable energy sources by dynamically reconfiguring energy flows.

The responsibility and visibility of carbon accounting are achieved through blockchain innovation, thus improving AI abilities. DLL technologies will make it possible to catalogue carbon credits, emission data and RECs without editing them. Smart contracts can guarantee that compliance with sustainability is automated, and this is why the businesses and individuals are able to participate actively in the carbon markets with the help of tokenized carbon assets. This plan will make the concept of sustainability democratic, and every stakeholder would be able to play a role in achieving the target of reducing emissions.

AI-assisted carbon capture and storage optimization, digital twin simulations of energy systems for emission prediction and AI-guided hydrogen economy management are some of the technological routes to net-zero. Green hydrogen, produced through renewable electrolysis, is a promising alternative for hard-to-abate sectors, and AI algorithms can optimize production schedules based on renewable availability and market demand.

The achievement of net-zero also depends on behavioral change, economic incentives and government regulations. Policies that support renewable integration, electric mobility and decentralized energy systems are critical. AI can further aid policymakers by simulating the long-term impacts of carbon taxation and renewable subsidies on energy economics. By 2050, the combined application of AI, blockchain, IoT and 5G will lead to intelligent carbon-neutral ecosystems. Every aspect of energy generation, distribution and consumption will be optimized for sustainability. These developments will support economic growth through green innovation and sustainable jobs, in addition to assisting countries in meeting global emission targets.

10.7. Summary

The fusion of AI, blockchain, IoT and 5G technologies represents the cornerstone of future sustainable development. Through decentralized autonomous energy markets, intelligent smart cities and carbon-neutral pathways, humanity can redefine its relationship with energy. Renewable resources alone will not power the future; intelligent systems that can coordinate them effectively, openly and fairly will. These innovations will give the world a more intelligent, green and inclusive world as we move to the year 2050. Table 10.1 outlines the description of major attributes.

Key theme	Summary description
Integration of emerging technologies	The combined use of artificial intelligence, blockchain, Internet of Things (IoT) and 5G forms the foundation of future sustainable development.
Decentralized energy markets	These technologies support the creation of autonomous and transparent energy markets that operate efficiently and equitably.
Intelligent smart cities	Advanced digital systems help design smart cities that are cleaner, more efficient and highly responsive to citizens' needs.
Carbon-neutral development	Innovation enables societies to transition toward carbon-neutral pathways, reducing environmental impact on a global scale.
Transformation of human–energy relationship	Intelligent energy systems redefine how humans generate, manage and use energy resources.
Role of intelligent resource management	Renewable energy in the future will be managed by intelligent systems capable of optimizing distribution and usage.
Vision for 2050	By 2050, the fusion of these technologies aims to create a greener, smarter and more inclusive global society.

Table 10.1. *Summary of technological integration for sustainable development*

10.8. References

Aggarwal, S., Kumar, N., Tanwar, S., Alazab, M. (2021). A survey on energy trading in the smart grid: Taxonomy, research challenges and solutions. *IEEE Access*, 9, 116231–116253. doi: 10.1109/ACCESS.2021.3104354.

Akkaoui, R., Palensky, P., Epema, D.H.J., Ştefanov, A. (2025). A cyber secure and scalable blockchain-based framework for monitoring and controlling distributed energy resources. *IEEE Access*, 13, 138460–138474. doi: 10.1109/ACCESS.2025.3595944.

Ali, A., Yousif, M., Numan, M., Ali Abbas Kazmi, S.A. (2025). Coordinated generation and transmission expansion planning with energy storage systems to facilitate high penetration of renewable energy. *IEEE Access*, 13, 176801–176812. doi: 10.1109/ACCESS.2025.3617374.

Boumaiza, A. (2024). Design and implementation of a blockchain-enabled transactive energy market. *IEEE Access*, 12, 143118–143130. doi: 10.1109/ACCESS.2024.3440180.

Boumaiza, A. and Sanfilippo, A. (2024). A testing framework for blockchain-based energy trade microgrids applications. *IEEE Access*, 12, 27465–27483. doi: 10.1109/ACCESS.2024.3367999.

Cui, S., Wang, Y.W., Li, C., Xiao, J.W. (2020). Prosumer community: A risk aversion energy sharing model. *IEEE Transactions on Sustainable Energy*, 11, 828–838. doi: 10.1109/TSTE.2019.2909301.

Elavarasan, R.M., Shafiullah, G.M., Padmanaban, S., Kumar, N.M., Annam, A., Vetrichelvan, A.M., Mihet-Popa, L. Holm-Nielsen, J.B. (2020). A comprehensive review on renewable energy development, challenges, and policies of leading Indian states with an international perspective. *IEEE Access*, 8, 74432–74457. doi: 10.1109/ACCESS.2020.2988011.

Ge, X., Yang, D., Lv, Y., Wang, F., Yu, J., Lu, J., Yang, Z., Tian, Y., Ren, H. (2023). Blockchain and green certificates based market structure and transaction mechanism of direct power-purchase for industrial users. *IEEE Transactions on Industry Applications*, 59, 2892–2903. doi: 10.1109/TIA.2023.3246966.

Hussain, I., Hussain, H.A., Ullah, N., Misak, S. (2024). A novel prosumer-centric smart contract based approach for blockchain-enabled energy scheduling using electric vehicles. *IEEE Access*, 12, 120747–120760. doi: 10.1109/ACCESS.2024.3451186.

Kumar, A., Alaraj, M., Rizwan, M., Nangia, U. (2021). Novel AI based energy management system for smart grid with RES integration. *IEEE Access*, 9, 162530–162542. doi: 10.1109/ACCESS.2021.3131502.

Lo, S.K., Liu, Y., Lu, Q., Wang, C., Xu, X., Paik, H.Y., Zhu, L. (2023). Toward trustworthy AI: Blockchain-based architecture design for accountability and fairness of federated learning systems. *IEEE Internet of Things Journal*, 10(4), 3276–3284. doi: 10.1109/JIOT.2022.3144450.

Okwuibe, G.C., Brenner, T., Tzscheutschler, P., Hamacher, T. (2023). Survey and analysis of local energy markets based on distributed ledger technologies. *IEEE Access*, 11, 23771–23791. doi: 10.1109/ACCESS.2023.3254508.

Patel, R.K., Kumari, A., Tanwar, S., Hong, W.C., Sharma, R. (2022). AI-empowered recommender system for renewable energy harvesting in smart grid system. *IEEE Access*, 10, 24316–24326. doi: 10.1109/ACCESS.2022.3152528.

Şerban, A.C. and Lytras, M.D. (2020). Artificial intelligence for smart renewable energy sector in Europe – Smart energy infrastructures for next generation smart cities. *IEEE Access*, 8, 77364–77377. doi: 10.1109/ACCESS.2020.2990123.

Shamsi, M. and Cuffe, P. (2022). Prediction markets for probabilistic forecasting of renewable energy sources. *IEEE Transactions on Sustainable Energy*, 13(2), 1244–1253. doi: 10.1109/TSTE.2021.3112916.

Shibu, N.B.S., Devidas, A.R., Balamurugan, S., Ponnekanti, S., Ramesh, M.V. (2024). Optimizing microgrid resilience: Integrating IoT, blockchain, and smart contracts for power outage management. *IEEE Access*, 12, 18782–18803. doi: 10.1109/ACCESS.2024.3360696.

Ul Haq, I. (2024). Diagnosis of neurological disease using bioinspired algorithms. In *Bio-Inspired Optimization for Medical Data Mining*, Srivastava, S., Anand, A., Kumar, A. et al. (eds). John Wiley & Sons, Hoboken, NJ.

Ul Haq, I. and Khanday, A.M.U.D. (2025). Exploring the role of explainable AI in women's health: Challenges and solutions. In *Explainable Artificial Intelligence in the Healthcare Industry*, Kumar, A. Kumar, T.A., Das, P. et al. (eds). John Wiley & Sons, Hoboken, NJ.

Ul Haq, I., Kumar, N., Koul, N., Verma, C., Eneacu, F.M., Raboaca, M.S. (2022). Machine learning techniques for result prediction of one day international (ODI) cricket match. In *The International Conference on Recent Innovations in Computing*. Springer, Singapore.

Ul Haq, I., Kaur, G., Rather, A.H. (2024). Fruit leaf classification using transfer learning for automation and industrial applications. In *Deep Learning Techniques for Automation and Industrial Applications*, Rathore, P.S., Ahuja, S., Burri, S.R. et al. (eds). John Wiley & Sons, Hoboken, NJ, 151–178.

Ul Haq, I., Khanday, A.M.D., Shah, H.A., Rufai, S.Z. (2025a). Enhancing water security through automation: Case studies and technical advancements in water quality management. In *Computational Automation for Water Security*, Dubey, A.K., Srivastav, A.L., Kumar, A. et al. (eds). Elsevier, Amsterdam.

Ul Haq, I., Kumar, A., Rathore, P.S. (2025b). Machine learning approaches for wind power forecasting: A comprehensive review. *Discover Applied Sciences*, 7(10), 1139.

Ul Haq, I., Malhotra, J., Rawat, V., Kumari, J., Kaur, G. (2025c). Machine learning approaches for early detection of cervical cancer: A comparative study of classification models. In *Targeted Chemotherapy with Personalized Immunotherapy: An AI Approach*, Kumar, A., Das, P., Rathore, P.S. et al. (eds). John Wiley & Sons, Hoboken, NJ.

Ul Haq, I., Nandal, V., Uppal, H. (2025d). Blockchain applications in aviation securing transactions, streamlining operations, and improving passenger experience. In *Blockchain in the Tourism Industry: A New Era of Secure and Transparent Travel Solutions*, Kumar, A., Abreu, A., Batta, P. et al. (eds). Springer, Cham.

Yan, M., Shahidehpour, M., Alabdulwahab, A., Abusorrah, A., Gurung, N., Zheng, H., Ogunnubi, O., Vukojevic, A., Paaso, E.A. (2021). Blockchain for transacting energy and carbon allowance in networked microgrids. *IEEE Transactions on Smart Grid*, 12(6), 4702–4714. doi: 10.1109/TSG.2021.3109103.

Yang, Q. and Wang, H. (2021). Privacy-preserving transactive energy management for IoT-aided smart homes via blockchain. *IEEE Internet of Things Journal*, 8(14), 11463–11475. doi: 10.1109/JIOT.2021.3051323.

Zhang, M., Eliassen, F., Taherkordi, A., Jacobsen, H.A., Chung, H.M., Zhang, Y. (2022). Demand–response games for peer-to-peer energy trading with the hyperledger blockchain. *IEEE Transactions on Systems, Man, and Cybernetics: Systems*, 52(1), 19–31. doi: 10.1109/TSMC.2021.3111135.

11

Smart Energy Grids: Architecture, Security and Emerging Technologies

The architecture of an Internet of Things (IoT)-enabled smart energy grid is organized into multiple interoperable layers that collectively support intelligent energy monitoring, control and optimization. At the foundation, the device layer comprises smart meters, sensors, actuators and other field devices that continuously capture operational parameters such as voltage, current, load demand and environmental conditions. The collected data are transmitted through the network layer using reliable wired and wireless technologies, including 5G and LPWAN, to ensure seamless, secure and low-latency communication across geographically distributed assets. The data processing layer integrates cloud and edge computing platforms to perform real-time analytics, storage and decision support, enabling responsive control actions and efficient energy management. At the top, the application layer delivers user-centric services such as demand forecasting, billing automation, grid reliability assessment and interactive consumer dashboards. Together, these layers establish a scalable, resilient and intelligent smart grid ecosystem that enhances operational efficiency, reliability and sustainability through data-driven automation.

11.1. Introduction

The integration of digital technologies with traditional infrastructures represents a paradigm shift in the existing energy system. The most stirring developments of this shift are the IoT, which allows devices associated with the electrical system to collect, communicate and process data rapidly and in real-time across a large heterogeneous network. A smart energy grid is replacing the traditional power system, typically a reactive, centralized and static system. The smart energy grid is an intelligent, data-driven and

Chapter written by Dhruv GOEL, Pratham KUMAR, Mamta NARWARIA and Md Jauhar IMAM.

self-adaptive system that can optimize the processes of generation, transmission and consumption. A constellation of technologies, some examples being sensor technologies, communication protocols, cloud computing, edge computing and artificial intelligence (AI), has come together to form the IoT-enabled smart grid. Together, these enable the grid to be developed in a self-healing mode, physically adaptable to changes in the environment, and able to optimize energy efficiency and sustainability. The International Energy Agency (IEA) estimates that smart grids will improve efficiency of renewable integration from 25% to more than 25% and reduce transmission losses globally up to 15% (International Energy Agency 2023).

The IoT is essential to this transition by linking together millions of smart meters, transformers, substations and end-user appliances to centralized or distributed data systems. These data systems aggregate and analyze data to improve demand-side management (DSM), locate faults and trigger automation. Unfortunately, despite the many benefits associated with how IoT will contribute to the energy transition, deploying IoT networks may introduce vulnerabilities that put confidentiality, availability and integrity of critical pieces of energy infrastructure at risk. Cyberattacks have been documented in various IoT deployments, including Distributed Denial of Service (DDoS), data spoofing and unauthorized access (Mehmood et al. 2021).

This chapter significantly investigates a comprehensive overview of the interrelations between complex digital infrastructure and re-imagining the energy paradigm for IoT and smart grids by providing a renewable sustainability framework. This shows co-relationship between the IoT and smart grids through a wide-ranging perspective of linkages between advanced technical systems and reconceptualization of the energy paradigm into a new and sustainable ecosystem.

11.1. Literature review/background

11.2.1. *Evolution of smart grids*

Smart grids were proposed in the early 2000s to solve the most common problems of the traditional distribution systems, including high transmission loss, outages and limited access to renewable energy. Early on, the grid was a one-way sort of event: electricity flowed from generation plants to consumers with little or no monitoring or feedback. The introduction of SCADA Systems and AMI was the very early steps in this early digitalization of the grid (Gellings 2020).

IoT took it a notch further with the introduction of context awareness and data-driven intelligence to energy networks. IoT sensor technology now makes voltage, temperature and energy demand measurements possible on a real-time basis. Analytics driven by the cloud will enhance decision-making in areas such as load balancing, predictive maintenance and energy forecasting.

As per the U.S. Department of Energy (DOE), IoT technologies–smart grids poses 40% improved system reliability and 30% reduced downtime in tested regions (U.S. Department of Energy 2022).

11.2.2. *IoT in energy systems*

The energy sector's IoT consists of three primary levels, which are described in detail:

1) Perception layer: this perception layer deals with data acquisition through hardware, such as the use of RFID, smart meters and temperature sensors.

2) Network layer: communication takes place in this layer, and different possible protocols include ZigBee, LoRaWAN, 5G and Wi-Fi.

3) Application layer: in this layer, there are energy management systems, data analysis systems and consumer interfaces.

The IoT-enabled power grid can serve several purposes, such as demand response, fault detection, theft identification and predictive maintenance, among others. It generally helps to ensure that distribution and demand are in sync through real-time data analytics and are dynamic.

11.2.3. *Related work*

The amalgamation of IoT and smart grid applications is explored by the different literature:

– Gharavi and Ghafurian (2011): tested a distributed sensing model to monitor renewable energy sources and facilitate improved scalability and reliability.

– Fang et al. (2012): explored interoperability challenges within IoT-based smart grid applications, as well as developed an open communication standard.

– Bedi et al. (2018): provided a mountain review of cyber-efficiency threats and suggested potential solutions to mitigate against IoT-enabled energy systems.

While several methods have been proposed, issues remain with respect to security, interoperability and scalability requirements in IoT-based solutions, especially when coupled with heterogeneous devices and limited resources.

11.2.4. *Key standards and protocols*

The two primary standards used in IoT smart grid communication are IEEE 802.15.4 and ZigBee. Table 11.1 provides a summary of some of the main IoT communication standards that have application in smart grid technology.

Standard	Description/use case
IEEE 802.15.4	It utilizes short-range, wireless and low-power communication for sensor network systems
ZigBee	Widely used in coordination with IEEE 802.15.4 for home automation functionality and for integration within advanced metering infrastructure
LoRaWAN	Supports wireless, long-range low-power communications for remote monitoring in grid installations
5G/LTE	High-speed, low-latency communication suitable for real-time control
MQTT CoAP	Lightweight communication protocol standards based entirely on constrained IoT devices

Table 11.1. *Overview of IoT communication standards in smart energy applications*

These standards aid in the communication between distributed devices and centralized energy management platform, and the form of communication protocol chosen will be relative to the range requirements, amount of data required and efficiency attributes of the other subsystem being supported.

11.3. IoT-enabled smart energy grid framework (methodology)

11.3.1. *Overview*

The smart grid, utilizing IoT, is structured in a layered architecture that brings together the underlying functionality of sensors, the communication technology and the applications. The different layers and specific technologies are discussed in the next subsections.

11.3.2. *System architecture*

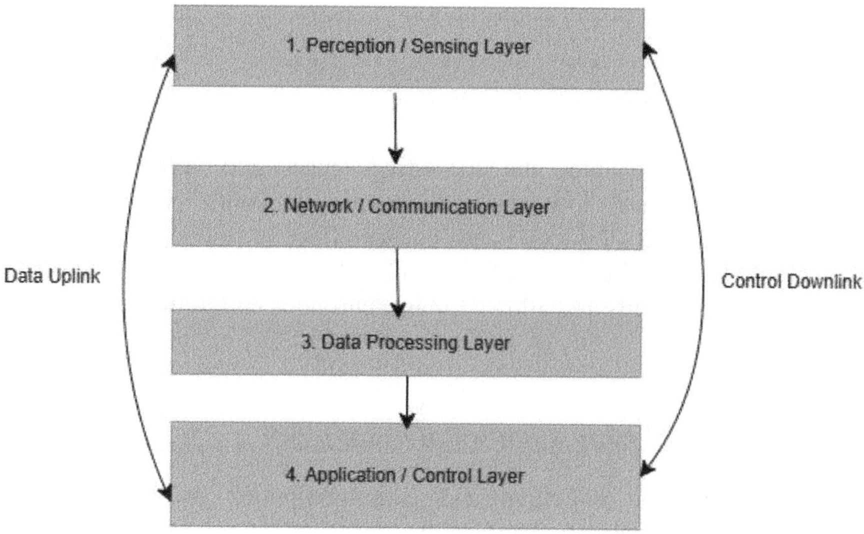

Figure 11.1. *The IoT-based smart energy grid architecture (skills the journey of data from sensors through gateways and cloud analytics toward the control room and end-user interface)*

A typical architecture of an IoT-based smart grid (shown in Figure 11.1) is made up of the following layers:

– *Device layer*: it includes physical devices (sensors, actuators and smart meters) that collect information on physical domain parameters.

– *Network layer*: it ensures reliable communications utilizing 5G, LPWAN or satellite networks.

– *Data processing layer*: it utilizes cloud computing and edge computing to enable real-time processing and analytics.

– *Application layer*: it enables application-level functionality (e.g. demand forecasting, auto-cycling bills and consumer dashboards).

11.3.3. *Sensing and data acquisition technologies*

Sensors are an essential element of the IoT-enabled grid. Smart meters measure voltage, current and power factor, while phasor measurement units (PMUs) allow for monitoring of transmission networks in real-time. Micro-electro-mechanical system (MEMS) sensors also offer increased accuracy and reduced power consumption.

11.3.4. *Communication technologies*

Communication enables the IoT-based smart grid. Wireless sensor networks (WSN) and low-power wide-area networks (LPWAN) can send/receive data at low-cost and energy-effective mode. The MQTT protocol is chosen because of its pub-sub model, which minimizes bandwidth requirements and allows for asynchronous communication in data exchanges.

11.3.5. *Cloud and edge computing integration*

The incorporation of cloud and edge computing creates a hybrid architecture that efficiently handles the massive data generated by IoT devices. Edge computing processes latency-sensitive data near the source, reducing response time and network congestion, while cloud computing provides scalable resources for storage, advanced analytics and long-term data management. This collaborative model improves system performance, scalability and reliability, enabling real-time decision-making alongside centralized intelligence. As a result, the cloud edge hybrid approach is well suited for data-intensive IoT applications such as smart cities, healthcare systems and industrial automation.

Edge computing minimizes latency by performing the computation at the location of data generation. Cloud computing extends a long-term storage solution for offloading local data, provides machine learning (ML) capabilities and scales to support large-scale analytics capabilities (Yi et al. 2015). This hybrid model will promote rapid response characteristics of the system and provide computing capabilities for real-time operations with reliable decisions.

11.3.6. *Security framework*

IoT-based smart grids face a range of security issues including data tampering, insider attacks and denial-of-service (DoS) attacks. There are several strong defenses, including blockchain-based identity management, public-key infrastructure (PKI) and anomaly detection using ML models (Mehmood et al. 2021).

Figure 11.2 illustrates the cloud-based integration for IoT-based smart energy grid architecture.

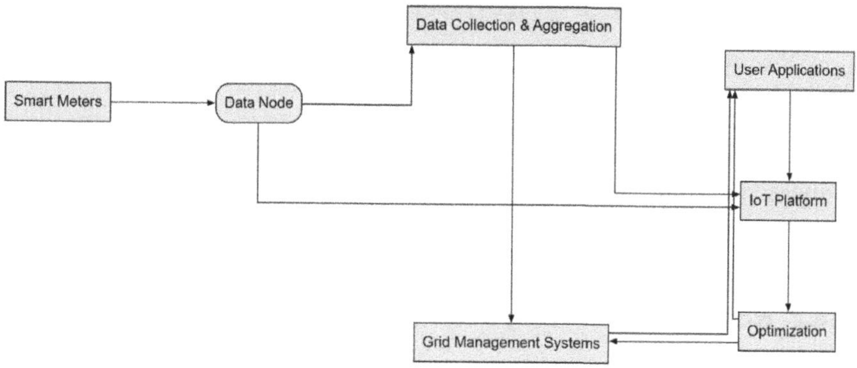

Figure 11.2. *Cloud-edge integration in the IoT smart grid (illustrates how IoT sensors send data to edge gateways, which preprocess it, and send the pre-processed data for cloud analytics for global optimization)*

Smart grids that make use of IoT technologies have enhanced operational efficiency, load balancing and consumer engagement. There are many simulation and pilot programs that show actual performance improvement benefits from implementing IoT devices into grid systems.

Feature	Traditional grid
Communication	One-way (generation to consumer)
Monitoring	Manual or periodic
Fault detection	Reactive (after occurrence)
Control	Centralized
Integration of renewables	Limited

Table 11.2. *Threat and attack models in IoT-based smart grids*

11.4. Results and discussion

11.4.1. *Performance evaluation of IoT in smart grids*

The Indian Smart Grid Forum (ISGF) recently completed a pilot Smart Grid project with IoT-based sensors and AMI that produced the following performance metrics:

– 20% reduction in power theft;

– 30% improvement in outage response times;

– 15% improved accuracy for load forecasting (Walawalkar and Sen 2024).

The two-way data exchange of IoT-based systems ensures that decisions are more "real-time" instead of using static schedules as baselines. This has reduced operational generation costs (and carbon emissions).

11.4.2. *Real-time data analytics*

The utilization of ML algorithms enables the application of predictive analytics to predict anomalies, failures, etc. For example, neural networks and regression models could be used to generate short-term load forecasting, with reinforcement learning applied to optimize decisions on energy dispatch.

Edge analytics enhances responsiveness by analyzing data at the edge and only sending a summary of the analysis to the cloud. This allows for a distributed approach to data analysis, reducing traffic on the network and improving scalability, especially for extensive grids encompassing large areas.

11.4.3. *Demand-side management*

The IoT enables smart DSM, where the demand is dynamically adjusted based on supply availability, grid conditions and price. Smart meters and connected devices offer consumers the opportunity to engage in the grid ecosystem in a meaningful way through remote monitoring, scheduling and even automated load shifting. This results in improved energy sustainability through reduced peak demand and enhances the integration of renewable energy resources.

11.5. Security vulnerabilities and threat models

Smart grids that incorporate IoT are highly beneficial but increase the attack surface area of the energy network. Normally, IoT-enabled devices communicate with one another and use underresource hardware that communicates across multiple, disparate protocols, demonstrating many interconnected security weaknesses. This section will help to define common threat models and attack types seen, and then present some applicable mitigation measures for IoT-enabled smart grids.

11.5.1. *Threat landscape*

Grids that are enabled with IoT are subject to threats at the physical layer, communication layer and application layer. As shown in Figure 11.3, multiple threat domains surround the IoT-based smart energy ecosystem.

11.5.1.1. *Physical layer threats*

Physical attacks are attack types that target IoT devices directly, such as tampering with smart meters to alter usage readings or disabling sensors at substations.

Countermeasures include the following:

– employ tamper detection and use physical tamper seals;

– utilize cryptographic signatures upon device authentication.

11.5.1.2. *Communication layer threats*

This layer may be targeted by eavesdropping, replay attacks and DoS attacks. Transfer of data in plaintext in protocols (e.g. MQTT and CoAP) is the most vulnerable.

Mitigations include the following:

– apply transport layer security (TLS) or Datagram TLS (DTLS) for secured communications;

– use multi-channel routing and frequency hopping approaches to reduce risk of interception or lessen exposure.

11.5.1.3. *Application layer threats*

Application layer threats include malware injection, data modification and unauthorized access to dashboards.

Mitigations include the following:

– use blockchain-based access control for data integrity;

– use role-based access control (RBAC) and multifactor authentication (MFA) for user accounts.

11.5.2. *Attack models*

Attack type	Description/impact
Man-in-the-middle	Attacker intercepts communication between IoT devices to alter data
Denial of service (DoS/DDoS)	Overwhelms the system with fake requests, causing service disruption
Replay attack	Captures valid data packets and replays them to gain unauthorized access
Data injection	False data injected into sensors leads to incorrect analytics and control actions
Firmware exploit	Malware embedded in device firmware to gain persistent unauthorized control

Table 11.3. *Common cyberattack models in IoT-enabled smart grids*

11.5.3. *Security mitigation frameworks*

Researchers have created several frameworks to address these types of threats:

– Blockchain based-authentication: decentralized ledgers eliminate the author genomic and therefore single points of failure. All transactions or updates to data are verified cryptographically, preventing unauthorized access (Christidis and Devetsikiotis 2016).

– AI for anomaly detection: ML models such as autoencoders and LSTM (long short-term memory) networks are able to detect shifts from baseline behavior in streams of sensor data.

– Zero trust architecture (ZTA): every device and user is always checked and verified before getting access. This reduces the chances of an attacker using compromised credentials to get access.

– End-to-end encryption (E2EE): this ensures that intercepted data are kept encrypted as it travels from the device to the cloud.

11.5.3.1. *Security evaluation metrics*

Metric	Description
Authentication late	Time required to verify device identity
Data integrity rate	Percentage of transmitted data verified as untampered
Detection accuracy	Effectiveness of AI models in identifying anomalies
System uptime	Availability of services during cyberattacks

Table 11.4. *Key metrics for evaluating IoT smart grid security*

11.5.4. *U.S. Department of Energy Smart Grid Investment Grant (SGIG)*

In the United States, the SGIG program had advanced IoT metering technology and predictive maintenance systems in different states. Utilities reported greater fault tolerance, reduced maintenance costs and improved accuracy in load forecasting (Ganta et al. 2025).

11.6. Challenges and future scope

11.6.1. *Significant challenges*

Despite recent advancements, IoT-enabled smart grids will continue to face numerous challenges:

1) *Scalability*:

Scaling to millions of IoT nodes will necessitate reliance on distributed architectures to manage the future exponential growth of data.

2) *Interoperability*:

Different vendors utilize standards that are not integrated and compatible.

3) *Security and privacy*:

Ensuring data confidentiality and integrity of the system within the multi-layered ecosystem is still a major concern.

4) *Energy efficiency of IoT devices*:

IoT sensors are usually battery operated, and for long-term sustainability, ensuring low energy usage is not trivial.

5) *Regulatory and compliance issues*:

In the realm of cross-border energy data sharing, privacy and data sovereignty regulations must be taken into consideration and must be enforced.

11.6.2. *Role of advanced technologies*

11.6.2.1. *Blockchain*

Blockchain ensures decentralized trust, immutability and traceability for energy transactions. Smart contracts automate billing and peer-to-peer energy trading between consumers and producers (Aggarwal et al. 2018).

11.6.2.2. *AI*

AI algorithms can probe a large volume of data for predictive maintenance, anomaly detection and energy forecasting. AI will also enable self-healing grids able to reconfigure themselves automatically when failures occur (Habbak et al. 2023).

11.6.2.3. *ML*

ML allows load profiles to be classified and clustered on a real-time basis and utilities to dynamically adjust tariffs. Reinforcement learning will enable autonomous decisions in dispatching to distributed energy resources.

11.6.2.4. *Edge and fog computing*

These paradigms offer added privacy of data and latency reduction through information processing close to the source and diminished reliance on the cloud.

11.6.3. *Future scope*

1) AI-driven autonomous energy systems: future grids will be self-optimizing based on demand changes and be able to dynamically reconfigure with digital twins and reinforcement learning models.

2) Quantum-enhanced security: quantum cryptography may enable unbreakable encryption, even with the weakness of existing classical cryptography algorithms.

3) Integration with 6G networks: the communication technology of ultra-low latency will support real-time control of distributed resources.

4) Squarable IoT hardware: the communication technology of ultra-low latency will support real-time control of distributed resources.

5) Policy harmony: global coordination efforts will be required in order to have common standards with regard to security and data transfer associated with the various energy systems.

11.7. Conclusion

The smart energy grid is a major paradigm shift in that it marks a radical change in energy generation, transmission, distribution and consumption, all of which are made possible by IoT solutions. It is also a major technological leap as it provides a two-way communication system as opposed to one way flow of power in a traditional energy grid. The smart energy grid also facilitates a major technological leap in that it provides a dynamic system that has a sense and respond mechanism within a shorter time. Additionally, it provides a complete sensing system of all generation stations, etc., and provides a complete monitoring process as it provisions all information concerning load, voltage, frequency, etc. Lastly, the smart energy grid uses an automated system that provides a complete communication network of all devices connected to the grid. By using sensors that are connected all over, such as in generation stations, substations and even in consumer premises, a complete monitoring system of all energy parameters is provided. Further, the smart energy grid provides a complete sensing and communication system that enables utility companies to get all details of all processes in the grid. Relying on data gained from sensors positioned in generation stations, smart grids are fully protected against overload. For example, smart grids are able to detect any malfunctioning in transformers. Also, they can facilitate complete forecasting mechanism as they enable a balance between demand and level of energy accordingly, and provide an automated system that enables fast monitoring in that any fault or overload in any place of the grid is quickly and automatically isolated by central control stations. On the consumption front, smart meters and smart home/building management systems offer complete usage data and control of all household and building devices. Customers and businesses can engage in demand response, which helps in managing consumption by changing it according to prices, thereby enhancing the effectiveness of energy and reducing costs.

Thus, the combination of connectivity, sensing, communication and analytics helps to redefine the power system in a smart way and supports future innovations such as microgrids, peer-to-peer energy trading and greater use of renewables.

11.8. References

Agarwal, S., Pradish, M., Kapoor, S., Shivakumar, V., Jain, A., Sawale, B.A. (2022). AMI system evaluation of service providers with prepaid features. In *Metering India 2022 Resilient Utilities and Empowered Consumers*, New Delhi.

Aggarwal, S., Chaudhary, R., Aujla, G. S., Jindal, A., Dua, A., Kumar, N. (2018). Energy chain: Enabling energy trading for smart homes using blockchains in smart grid ecosystem. In *Proceedings of the 1st ACM MobiHoc Workshop on Networking and Cybersecurity for Smart Cities*. Association for Computing Machinery, New York.

Amin, R. and Kazmi, A.A. (2024). Smart grids: A comprehensive review of technologies, challenges, and future directions. *Journal of Engineering and Computational Intelligence Review*, 2(2), 45–70.

Bangalore Electricity Supply Company (BESCOM) (2022). Smart grid pilot project. Report.

Bedi, G., Venayagamoorthy, G.K., Singh, R., Brooks, R.R., Wang, K.C. (2018). Review of Internet of Things (IoT) in electric power and energy systems. *IEEE Internet of Things Journal*, 5(2), 847–870.

Christidis, K. and Devetsikiotis, M. (2016). Blockchains and smart contracts for the Internet of Things. *IEEE Access*, 4, 2292–2303.

Fang, X., Misra, S., Xue, G., Yang, D. (2012). Smart grid – The new and improved power grid: A survey. *IEEE Communications Surveys & Tutorials*, 14(4), 944–980.

Ganta, B.G., Golla, H.P., Yemula, P.K. (2025). The role of distribution utilities in enabling electric vehicle ecosystems: A multi-perspective analysis with case studies. In *2025 IEEE Transportation Electrification Conference and Expo, Asia-Pacific (ITEC Asia-Pacific)*, Singapore.

Gellings, C.W. (2020). *The Smart Grid: Enabling Energy Efficiency and Demand Response*. River Publishers, New York.

Gharavi, H. and Ghafurian, R. (eds) (2011). Smart grid: The electric energy system of the future. *Proceedings of the IEEE*, 99(6), 917–921.

Habbak, H., Mahmoud, M., Metwally, K., Fouda, M.M., Ibrahem, M.I. (2023). Load forecasting techniques and their applications in smart grids. *Energies*, 16(3), 1480.

International Energy Agency (IEA) (2023). Digitalization and energy. Report.

Mehmood, M.Y., Oad, A., Abrar, M., Munir, H.M., Hasan, S.F., Muqeet, H.A.U., Golilarz, N.A. (2021). Edge computing for IoT-enabled smart grid. *Security and Communication Networks*, 2021(1), 5524025.

U.S. Department of Energy (2022). Smart grid system. Report.

Walawalkar, R. and Sen, D. (2024). Energy storage: Enabling a greener grid. In *India's Energy Revolution*, Styczynski, A.B. (ed.). Routledge India, London.

Yi, S., Li, C., Li, Q. (2015). A survey of fog computing: Concepts, applications and issues. In *Proceedings of the 2015 Workshop on Mobile Big Data*, Hangzhou.

Zanella, A., Bui, N., Castellani, A., Vangelista, L., Zorzi, M. (2014). Internet of things for smart cities. *IEEE Internet of Things Journal*, 1(1), 22–32.

List of Authors

Abdul Malik ANSARI
Lovely Professional University
Phagwara
India

Anzah BASHIR
Department of CSE
Lovely Professional University
Phagwara
India

Ranjit Kumar BINDAL
Department of Electrical Engineering
Chandigarh University
Mohali
India

Biswajit DAS
School of Computer Science in Emerging Technologies
Noida Institute of Engineering and Technology (NIET)
Greater Noida
India

Dhruv GOEL
Department of Computer Science and Engineering
Sharda University
Greater Noida
India

Monika GOYAL
Manav Rachna University
Faridabad
Haryana
India

Anand Kumar GUPTA
CSE (AI)
Noida Institute of Engineering and Technology (NIET)
Greater Noida
India

Deepti GUPTA
Noida Institute of Engineering and Technology (NIET)
Greater Noida
India

Vidhi GUPTA
Apex Institute of Technology
Chandigarh University
Mohali
India

Md Jauhar IMAM
Department of Computer Science and Engineering
Sharda University
Greater Noida
India

Sanna Mehraj KAK
Noida Institute of Engineering and Technology (NIET)
Greater Noida
India

Inderdeep KAUR
Department of Computer Science and Engineering
Chandigarh University
Mohali
India

Jagdeep KAUR
Department of Physics
Chandigarh University
Mohali
India

Fardeen Ahmad KHAN
Shri Ram Murti Smarak College of Engineering and Technology
Bareilly
India

Prashant KUMAR
Noida Institute of Engineering and Technology (NIET)
Greater Noida
India

Pratham KUMAR
Department of Computer Science and Engineering
Sharda University
Greater Noida
India

Sanny KUMAR
School of Computer Science in Emerging Technologies
Noida Institute of Engineering and Technology (NIET)
Greater Noida
India

Bandana KUMARI
Noida Institute of Engineering and Technology (NIET)
Greater Noida
India

Hema MAHAWAR
Computer Science and Engineering
Bansal Institute of Research and Technology
Bhopal
India

Monika MEHRA
School of Computer Science in Emerging Technologies
Noida Institute of Engineering and Technology (NIET)
Greater Noida
India

Khalid Hafiz MIR
Department of CSE
Lovely Professional University
Phagwara
India

Mamta NARWARIA
Department of Computer Science and Engineering
Sharda University
Greater Noida
India

Akhil NIGAM
Department of Electrical Engineering
Chandigarh University
Mohali
India

Himanshu PABBI
School of Computer Science in Emerging Technologies
Noida Institute of Engineering and Technology (NIET)
Greater Noida
India

Ashish PANDEY
Computer Science and Engineering
Babu Banarasi Das University
Lucknow
India

Mrinal PANDEY
Manav Rachna University
Faridabad
Haryana
India

Priya PANDEY
School of Computing Science & Engineering
Galgotias University
Greater Noida
India

Aditi RAJ
Apex Institute of Technology
Chandigarh University
Mohali
India

Muhammad Sher RAMZAN
Faculty of Computing and Information Technology (FCIT)
King Abdulaziz University
Jeddah
Saudi Arabia

Pradeep Kumar SHARMA
Shri Ram Murti Smarak College of Engineering and Technology
Bareilly
India

Shivani SHARMA
Noida Institute of Engineering and Technology (NIET)
Greater Noida
India

Hitendra SINGH
Noida Institute of Engineering and Technology (NIET)
Greater Noida
India

Shweta SINGH
School of Computer Science in Emerging Technologies
Noida Institute of Engineering and Technology (NIET)
Greater Noida
India

Inam UL HAQ
School of Engineering and Technology (SET)
CGC University Mohali
Punjab
India

Index

E, F

G, H

I, L, M

N, P

R, S, T

Other titles from

ISTE

in

Computer Engineering

2026

BHAMBRI Pankaj, DUTTA Pushan Kumar, KHAN Mudassir, STAROSTKA-PATYK Marta
Next-Gen Supply Chains: AI, Automation, and Sustainability in a Disrupted World

DARCHE Philippe
Computer Memories 1: Core Concepts
Computer Memories 2: Static Random-Access Memory

KUMAR Abhishek, BATTA Priya, AHUJA Sachin, RATHORE Pramod Singh
AI-driven Innovations in Physiotherapy and Oncology 3

KUMAR Abhishek, BATTA Priya, ANANTH J.P.
AI-driven Healthcare Innovations: Applications in Neurology and Medicine

MACHADO Carolina, DAVIM J. Paulo
Artificial Intelligence Technologies in Management and Engineering

MAHOUT Vincent, ROCACHER Thierry, AURIOL Guillaume
Programming of Embedded Systems: Applications to SM32F10x µControllers

2025

CHIKH Azeddine
Systemic Approach to Categorizing and Modeling Requirements

KUMAR Abhishek, BATTA Priya, AHUJA Sachin,
RATHORE Pramod Singh
AI-driven Innovations in Physiotherapy and Oncology 1
AI-driven Innovations in Physiotherapy and Oncology 2

TANEJA Ashu, KUMAR Abhishek, LIMKAR Suresh Vishnudas,
OUAISSA Mariya, OUAISSA Mariyam
Driving Innovation through AI and Digital Twin for 6G Powered Sustainable Ultra Smart Cities

TANEJA Ashu, KUMAR Abhishek, LIMKAR Suresh Vishnudas,
OUAISSA Mariya, OUAISSA Mariyam
6G Urban Innovation: AI and Digital Twin for Next-Gen Sustainable Cities

2024

CHAKRABORTY Rajdeep, GHOSH Anupam, KUMAR MANDAL Jyotsna,
CHOUDHURY Tanupriya, CHATTERJEE Prasenjit
Smart Edge Computing: An Operation Research Perspective
(International Perspectives in Decision Analytics and Operations Research Set – Volume 2)

HOMÈS Bernard
Fundamentals of Software Testing (2nd edition, revised and updated)

JERBI Abdessalem
Discrete-Event Simulation: Concepts and Production in Arena

PRADHAN Devasis, KUMAR SAHU Prasanna, MYO TUN Hla,
CHATTERJEE Prasenjit
Artificial and Cognitive Computing for Sustainable Healthcare Systems in Smart Cities
(International Perspectives in Decision Analytics and Operations Research Set – Volume 3)

2023

CHOUDHURY Tanupriya, KHANNA Abhirup, CHATTERJEE Prasenjit, UM Jung-Sup, BHATTACHARYA Abhishek
Blockchain Applications in Healthcare: Innovations and Practices (International Perspectives in Decision Analytics and Operations Research Set – Volume 1)

PAI G A Vijayalakshmi
A Textbook of Data Structures and Algorithms 1: Mastering Linear Data Structures
A Textbook of Data Structures and Algorithms 2: Mastering Nonlinear Data Structures
A Textbook of Data Structures and Algorithms 3: Mastering Advanced Data Structures and Algorithm Design Strategies

2022

HOMÈS Bernard
Advanced Testing of Systems-of-Systems 1: Theoretical Aspects
Advanced Testing of Systems-of-Systems 2: Practical Aspects

MEHTA Shikha, TIWARI Sanju, SIARRY Patrick, JABBAR M.A.
Tools, Languages, Methodologies for Representing Semantics on the Web of Things

SIDHOM Sahbi, KADDOUR Amira
Systems and Uses of Digital Sciences for Knowledge Organization (Digital Tools and Uses Set – Volume 9)

ZAIDOUN Ameur Salem
Computer Science Security: Concepts and Tools

2021

DARCHE Philippe
Microprocessor 4: Core Concepts – Software Aspects
Microprocessor 5: Software and Hardware Aspects of Development, Debugging and Testing – The Microcomputer

DELHAYE Jean-Loïc
Inside the World of Computing: Technologies, Uses, Challenges

HARDIN Thérèse, JAUME Mathieu, PESSAUX François,
VIGUIÉ DONZEAU-GOUGE Véronique
Concepts and Semantics of Programming Languages 1: A Semantical Approach with OCaml and Python
Concepts and Semantics of Programming Languages 2: Modular and Object-oriented Constructs with OCaml, Python, C++, Ada and Java

MKADMI Abderrazak
Archives in The Digital Age: Preservation and the Right to be Forgotten (Digital Tools and Uses Set – Volume 8)

TOKLU Yusuf Cengiz, BEKDAŞ Gebrail, NIGDELI Sinan Melih
Metaheuristics for Structural Design and Analysis (Optimization Heuristics Set – Volume 3)

2020

DARCHE Philippe
Microprocessor 1: Prolegomenes – Calculation and Storage Functions – Models of Computation and Computer Architecture
Microprocessor 2: Core Concepts – Communication in a Digital System
Microprocessor 3: Core Concepts – Hardware Aspects

DUVAUT Patrick, DALLOZ Xavier, MENGA David, KOEHL François,
CHRIQUI Vidal, BRILL Joerg
Internet of Augmented Me, I.AM: Empowering Innovation for a New Sustainable Future

LAFFLY Dominique
TORUS 1 – Toward an Open Resource Using Services: Cloud Computing for Environmental Data
TORUS 2 – Toward an Open Resource Using Services: Cloud Computing for Environmental Data
TORUS 3 – Toward an Open Resource Using Services: Cloud Computing for Environmental Data

LAURENT Anne, LAURENT Dominique, MADERA Cédrine
Data Lakes
(Databases and Big Data Set – Volume 2)

OULHADJ Hamouche, DAACHI Boubaker, MENASRI Riad
Metaheuristics for Robotics
(Optimization Heuristics Set – Volume 2)

SADIQUI Ali
Computer Network Security

VENTRE Daniel
Artificial Intelligence, Cybersecurity and Cyber Defense

2019

BESBES Walid, DHOUIB Diala, WASSAN Niaz, MARREKCHI Emna
Solving Transport Problems: Towards Green Logistics

CLERC Maurice
Iterative Optimizers: Difficulty Measures and Benchmarks

GHLALA Riadh
Analytic SQL in SQL Server 2014/2016

TOUNSI Wiem
Cyber-Vigilance and Digital Trust: Cyber Security in the Era of Cloud Computing and IoT

2018

ANDRO Mathieu
Digital Libraries and Crowdsourcing
(Digital Tools and Uses Set – Volume 5)

ARNALDI Bruno, GUITTON Pascal, MOREAU Guillaume
Virtual Reality and Augmented Reality: Myths and Realities

CARDON Alain
Beyond Artificial Intelligence: From Human Consciousness to Artificial Consciousness

HOMAYOUNI S. Mahdi, FONTES Dalila B.M.M.
Metaheuristics for Maritime Operations
(Optimization Heuristics Set – Volume 1)

JEANSOULIN Robert
JavaScript and Open Data

PIVERT Olivier
NoSQL Data Models: Trends and Challenges
(Databases and Big Data Set – Volume 1)

SEDKAOUI Soraya
Data Analytics and Big Data

SALEH Imad, AMMI Mehdi, SZONIECKY Samuel
Challenges of the Internet of Things: Technology, Use, Ethics
(Digital Tools and Uses Set – Volume 7)

SZONIECKY Samuel
Ecosystems Knowledge: Modeling and Analysis Method for Information and Communication
(Digital Tools and Uses Set – Volume 6)

2017

BENMAMMAR Badr
Concurrent, Real-Time and Distributed Programming in Java: Threads, RTSJ and RMI

BOUHAÏ Nasreddine, SALEH Imad
Internet of Things: Evolutions and Innovations
(Digital Tools and Uses Set – Volume 4)

HÉLIODORE Frédéric, NAKIB Amir, ISMAIL Boussaad, OUCHRAA Salma, SCHMITT Laurent
Metaheuristics for Intelligent Electrical Networks
(Metaheuristics Set – Volume 10)

MA Haiping, SIMON Dan
Evolutionary Computation with Biogeography-based Optimization
(Metaheuristics Set – Volume 8)

PÉTROWSKI Alain, BEN-HAMIDA Sana
Evolutionary Algorithms
(Metaheuristics Set – Volume 9)

PAI G A Vijayalakshmi
Metaheuristics for Portfolio Optimization: An Introduction using MATLAB®
(Metaheuristics Set – Volume 11)

REYES-GARCIA Everardo
The Image-Interface: Graphical Supports for Visual Information
(Digital Tools and Uses Set – Volume 3)

REYES-GARCIA Everardo, BOUHAÏ Nasreddine
Designing Interactive Hypermedia Systems
(Digital Tools and Uses Set – Volume 2)

SZONIECKY Samuel, BOUHAÏ Nasreddine
Collective Intelligence and Digital Archives: Towards Knowledge Ecosystems
(Digital Tools and Uses Set – Volume 1)

2016

BLUM Christian, FESTA Paola
Metaheuristics for String Problems in Bio-informatics
(Metaheuristics Set – Volume 6)

DEROUSSI Laurent
Metaheuristics for Logistics
(Metaheuristics Set – Volume 4)

DHAENENS Clarisse, JOURDAN Laetitia
Metaheuristics for Big Data
(Metaheuristics Set – Volume 5)

LABADIE Nacima, PRINS Christian, PRODHON Caroline
Metaheuristics for Vehicle Routing Problems
(Metaheuristics Set – Volume 3)

LEROY Laure
Eyestrain Reduction in Stereoscopy

LUTTON Evelyne, PERROT Nathalie, TONDA Alberto
Evolutionary Algorithms for Food Science and Technology
(Metaheuristics Set – Volume 7)

MAGOULÈS Frédéric, ZHAO Hai-Xiang
Data Mining and Machine Learning in Building Energy Analysis

RIGO Michel
Advanced Graph Theory and Combinatorics

ZELM Martin, DOUMEINGTS Guy, MENDONÇA Joao Pedro
Enterprise Interoperability: in the Digitized and Networked Factory of the Future

2015

BARBIER Franck, RECOUSSINE Jean-Luc
COBOL Software Modernization: From Principles to Implementation with the BLU AGE® Method

CHEN Ken
Performance Evaluation by Simulation and Analysis with Applications to Computer Networks

CLERC Maurice
Guided Randomness in Optimization
(Metaheuristics Set – Volume 1)

DURAND Nicolas, GIANAZZA David, GOTTELAND Jean-Baptiste, ALLIOT Jean-Marc
Metaheuristics for Air Traffic Management
(Metaheuristics Set – Volume 2)

MAGOULÈS Frédéric, ROUX François-Xavier, HOUZEAUX Guillaume
Parallel Scientific Computing

MUNEESAWANG Paisarn, YAMMEN Suchart
Visual Inspection Technology in the Hard Disk Drive Industry

2014

BOULANGER Jean-Louis
Formal Methods Applied to Industrial Complex Systems
Formal Methods Applied to Complex Systems: Implementation of the B Method

EXPOSITO Ernesto, DIOP Codé
Smart SOA Platforms in Cloud Computing Architectures

GARDI Frédéric, BENOIST Thierry, DARLAY Julien, ESTELLON Bertrand, MEGEL Romain
Mathematical Programming Solver based on Local Search

KRICHEN Saoussen, CHAOUACHI Jouhaina
Graph-related Optimization and Decision Support Systems

LARRIEU Nicolas, VARET Antoine
Rapid Prototyping of Software for Avionics Systems: Model-oriented Approaches for Complex Systems Certification

LAURAS Matthieu, ZELM Martin, ARCHIMÈDE Bernard, BÉNABEN Frédérick, DOUMEINGTS Guy
Enterprise Interoperability: Interoperability for Agility, Resilience and Plasticity of Collaborations

OUSSALAH Mourad Chabane
Software Architecture 1
Software Architecture 2

QUESNEL Flavien
Scheduling of Large-scale Virtualized Infrastructures: Toward Cooperative Management

RIGO Michel
Formal Languages, Automata and Numeration Systems 1: Introduction to Combinatorics on Words
Formal Languages, Automata and Numeration Systems 2: Applications to Recognizability and Decidability

SAINT-DIZIER Patrick
Musical Rhetoric: Foundations and Annotation Schemes

TOUATI Sid, DUPONT DE DINECHIN Benoit
Advanced Backend Code Optimization

2013

ANDRÉ Étienne, SOULAT Romain
The Inverse Method: Parametric Verification of Real-time Embedded Systems

BOULANGER Jean-Louis
Safety Management for Software-based Equipment

DELAHAYE Daniel, PUECHMOREL Stéphane
Modeling and Optimization of Air Traffic

FRANCOPOULO Gil
LMF — Lexical Markup Framework

GHEDIRA Khaled
Constraint Satisfaction Problems: CSP Formalisms and Techniques

GOVAERT Gérard, NADIF Mohamed
Co-Clustering: Models, Algorithms and Applications

LANDRAGIN Frédérick
Man–Machine Dialogue: Design and Challenges

LUCAS Laurent, LOSCOS Céline, REMION Yannick
3D Video: Models, From Capture to Diffusion

ROCHANGE Christine, UHRIG Sascha, SAINRAT Pascal
Time-Predictable Architectures

WAHBI Mohamed
Algorithms and Ordering Heuristics for Distributed Constraint Satisfaction Problems

ZELM Martin, VAN SINDEREN Marten, FERRAIRA PIRES Luis, DOUMEINGTS Guy
Enterprise Interoperability: Research and Applications in the Service-oriented Ecosystem

2012

ARBOLEDA Hugo, ROYER Jean-Claude
Model-Driven and Software Product Line Engineering

BLANCHET Gérard, DUPOUY Bertrand
Computer Architecture

BOULANGER Jean-Louis
Industrial Use of Formal Methods: Formal Verification
Formal Methods: Industrial Use from Model to the Code

CALVARY Gaëlle, DELOT Thierry, SÈDES Florence, TIGLI Jean-Yves
Computer Science and Ambient Intelligence

MAHOUT Vincent
Assembly Language Programming: ARM Cortex-M3 2.0: Organization, Innovation and Territory

MARLET Renaud
Program Specialization

SOTO Maria, SEVAUX Marc, ROSSI André, LAURENT Johann
Memory Allocation Problems in Embedded Systems: Optimization Methods

2011

BICHOT Charles-Edmond, SIARRY Patrick
Graph Partitioning

BOULANGER Jean-Louis
Static Analysis of Software: The Abstract Interpretation

CAFERRA Ricardo
Logic for Computer Science and Artificial Intelligence

KORDON Fabrice, HADDAD Serge, PAUTET Laurent, PETRUCCI Laure
Distributed Systems: Design and Algorithms
Models and Analysis in Distributed Systems

LORCA Xavier
Tree-based Graph Partitioning Constraint

RIDHA MAHJOUB A.
Progress in Combinatorial Optimization: ISCO2010

TRUCHET Charlotte, ASSAYAG Gerard
Constraint Programming in Music

VICAT-BLANC Pascale, GOGLIN Brice, GUILLIER Romaric,
SOUDAN Sébastien
Computing Networks: From Cluster to Cloud Computing

2010

AUBRUN Christophe, SIMON Daniel, SONG Ye-Qiong
Co-design Approaches for Dependable Networked Control Systems

AUDIBERT Pierre
Mathematics for Informatics and Computer Science

BABAU Jean-Philippe, BLAY-FORNARINO Mireille, CHAMPEAU Joël,
ROBERT Sylvain, SABETTA Antonino
Model Driven Engineering for Distributed Real-Time Systems: MARTE Modeling, Model Transformations and their Usages

BOULANGER Jean-Louis
Safety of Computer Architectures

SIGAUD Olivier, BUFFET Olivier
Markov Decision Processes in Artificial Intelligence

MONMARCHÉ Nicolas, GUINAND Frédérick, SIARRY Patrick
Artificial Ants

SOLNON Christine
Ant Colony Optimization and Constraint Programming

2009

FOURNIER Jean-Claude
Graph Theory and Applications: with exercises and problems

GUÉDON Jeanpierre
The Mojette Transform: theory and applications

JARD Claude, ROUX Olivier H.
Communicating Embedded Systems: Software and Design

LECOUTRE Christophe
Constraint Networks: Techniques and Algorithms

2008

BANÂTRE Michel, MARRON Pedro Jose, OLLERO Anibal, WOLITZ Adam
Cooperating Embedded Systems and Wireless Sensor Networks

MERZ Stephan, NAVET Nicolas
Modeling and Verification of Real-time Systems: Formalisms and Software Tools

PASCHOS Vangelis Th.
Combinatorial Optimization and Theoretical Computer Science: Interfaces and Perspectives

WALDNER Jean-Baptiste
Nanocomputers and Swarm Intelligence

2007

BENHAMOU Frédéric, JUSSIEN Narendra, O'SULLIVAN Barry
Trends in Constraint Programming

JUSSIEN Narendra
A to Z of Sudoku

2006

BABAU Jean-Philippe, CHAMPEAU Joël, GÉRARD Sébastien
From MDD Concepts to Experiments and Illustrations – DRES 2006

HABRIAS Henri, FRAPPIER Marc
Software Specification Methods: An Overview Using a Case Study

MURAT Cécile, PASCHOS Vangelis Th.
Probabilistic Combinatorial Optimization on Graphs

PANETTO Hervé, BOUDJLIDA Nacer
Interoperability for Enterprise Software and Applications: Proceedings of the Workshops and the Doctorial Symposium of the Second IFAC/IFIP I-ESA International Conference: EI2N, WSI, IS-TSPQ 2006

2005

GÉRARD Sébastien, BABAU Jean-Philippe, CHAMPEAU Joël
Model Driven Engineering for Distributed Real Time Embedded Systems

PANETTO Hervé
Interoperability of Enterprise Software and Applications: Workshops of the INTEROP-ESA 2005 International Conference (EI2N, WSI, ISIDI and IEHENA 2005)

Printed and bound by CPI Group (UK) Ltd, Croydon, CR0 4YY

13/09/2026

14960986-0002